Finding Funding

Grantwriting for the Financially Challenged Educator

Ernest W. Brewer
Charles M. Achilles
Jay R. Fuhriman

CORWIN PRESS, INC.
A Sage Publications Company
Thousand Oaks, California

For information address:

Corwin Press, Inc.
A Sage Publications Company
2455 Teller Road
Newbury Park, California 91320

SAGE Publications Ltd.
6 Bonhill Street
London EC2A 4PU
United Kingdom

SAGE Publications India Pvt. Ltd.
M-32 Market
Greater Kailash I
New Delhi 110 048 India

Printed in the United States of America

Library of Congress Cataloging-in-Publication Data

Brewer, Ernest W.
    Finding funding : grant writing for the financially challenged
educator / Ernest W. Brewer, Charles M. Achilles, Jay R. Fuhriman.
        p.   cm.
    Includes bibliographical references (p.   ).
    ISBN 0-8039-6093-X
    1. Proposal writing in education—United States—Handbooks,
manuals, etc.   2. Federal aid to education—United States—
Handbooks, manuals, etc.   3. State aid to education—United States—
Handbooks, manuals, etc.   4. Education—United States—Finance—
Handbooks, manuals, etc.   I. Achilles, Charles M.   II. Fuhriman, Jay R.
III Title.
LB2342.4.U6B74   1993   93-8395
379.1'2'0973—dc20

93 94 95 96 97 10 9 8 7 6 5 4 3 2 1

Corwin Press Production Editor: Marie Louise Penchoen

Contents

Acknowledgments

We wish to express appreciation to the many persons who have helped us by providing ideas, encouragement, and information. We have regularly attended and have given seminars, workshops, and briefing sessions related to grant proposal development and project implementation and have attended more proposal-preparation sessions and seminars in the past ten years than we can recall during our collective 54 years of proposal preparation and project administration. We also have served as readers (evaluating grant applications submitted for funding). We have carefully read newsletters, articles, "Dear Colleague" letters, government publications and circulars, application packets, the *Federal Register (FR),* the *Catalog of Federal Domestic Assistance (CFDA),* the *Code of Federal Regulations (CFR),* and other books about funding. In preparing this book we have cited sources whenever possible. As collectors of useful and potentially useful items, we have files full of examples, samples, worksheets, and the like. If we have included examples obtained at a workshop or seminar, we have given credit if the materials were identified by any citation.

If the materials did not include information about sources, and if we could not reconstruct the workshop or session where we obtained the materials, we still included them if we felt they would help this collection. We did not omit any source on purpose. If anyone using this book recognizes materials and sources, please send us the information so we can make appropriate amends in any revision.

We have developed numerous grant and contract proposals. Each proposal-development process is a learning experience—we have learned much from those who have cooperated, collaborated, or co-authored in the process. We have also learned from various funding-source administrators and personnel who have helped us over difficult times. Given the extent of the help we have received, it is not possible to list all who have contributed to our collective ideas about proposal development. Perhaps some of the people will be partially rewarded by seeing that the authors have incorporated into this volume ideas that they have acquired from these many interactions. Within the book we have provided direct credits whenever we could remember exact sources.

We also relied on many other sources of ideas, such as publications from The Grantsmanship Center, from the Education Funding Research Council, and from other grant-service groups. We have benefited from federal circulars and publications relating to proposal development. We have improved because of comments of other proposal writers, friends in various offices and agencies, and review panels who evaluated our proposals.

We thank our students and seminar participants who have worked through portions of this material and who have made helpful comments.

We thank Ms. Sue Carey, Bureau of Educational Research and Service, The University of Tennessee, Knoxville, for a thorough initial editing; Ms. Deetra Thompson, University of North Carolina, Greensboro, for some initial typing; Mr. Terry Hoskins at Ohio State University for some computer and technical layout assistance; Ms. Connie Hollingsworth and Mr. Joel Coates, Associate Directors of funded projects at The University of Tennessee, Knoxville, for their reveiw and use of our rough draft and their input for suggested modifications.

Our thanks also goes to our family members who encouraged and supported us to complete this book.

We thank personnel at Corwin Press for helpful tips in manuscript preparation and for final editing.

Finally, we have synthesized information from others, from experience, and from "doing proposals." In the final analysis, any deficiencies in the text are the authors' own.

Ernest W. Brewer
Charles M. Achilles
Jay R. Fuhriman

About the Authors

Ernest W. Brewer is Associate Professor and Principal Investigator/Project Director in the Department of Technological and Adult Education, College of Education, The University of Tennessee, Knoxville. He is currently serving as the Principal Investigator/Project Director of seven federally funded grants. Prior to joining the university in 1976, he earned his doctorate degree from The University of Tennessee in Vocational-Technical Education and served as the Executive Director of the Institute of Human Resources.

Over the years he has acquired external funds for a variety of research, service, and developmental activities. During this time he has served as both editor and editorial board member of professional journals and he has authored a variety of grant proposals, professional articles, and annual performance reports. His grants have ranged from five thousand to over a million dollars with more than $25,000,000 in grant support to date. As time permits, he serves as a "field reader" of proposals submitted to Washington, D.C.

In addition to administering funded projects, Brewer has taught graduate courses, given seminars, and participated in a variety of grantwriting, project design, and program implementation workshops. A favorite graduate course that he has repeatedly taught is his "Grantwriting and Program Implementation" course. He also teaches a noncredit course entitled "Grantwriting and Project Administration: Foundations to Federal" that is available to community agency personnel and nonprofit organizations.

Charles M. Achilles is Professor of Educational Leadership, School of Education, University of North Carolina at Greensboro. He received his doctorate degree in Educational Administration from the University of Rochester and worked briefly at the (former) U.S. Office of Education and for 21 years at the Bureau of Educational Research and Service, The University of Tennessee, Knoxville.

Since March 1968, Achilles has had continuous grant support for research, development, service, education, or training activities. He has served as author, co-author, member of a proposal-development team, or advisor for more than 400 proposals. Not counting all multiple-year continuations, this work has resulted in more than 230 funded projects for more than $37,000,000 in support of education and education-related agencies.

He has taught graduate classes, seminars, and short workshops on application and proposal development for grants and contracts. He has also reviewed proposals for the federal government.

Jay R. Fuhriman is Professor of Education and Director of Bilingual Education at Boise State University, Idaho. He earned his doctorate degree from Texas A&I University in Curriculum and Instruction and worked as a consultant and teacher prior to joining the university in 1977.

His grantwriting experience dates back to 1982, resulting in more than $10,000,000 worth of grant support. During this period he has provided grant application consulting services to approximately 20 universities in the United States. He has also taught a grantwriting course and provided a variety of workshops on the topic.

He has served both as editor and on the board of editors of professional journals and has published articles in the field of grant writing.

Introduction

$\mathbf{F}$or some people writing a grant proposal is a chore or burden. For others putting ideas down clearly so people can read, understand, and appreciate them is exciting; if the ideas are funded, it may be a near-religious experience that elicits the urge to compete for yet another chance to finance needed activities or projects.

Historical Development

History shows that the Lewis and Clark expedition was funded by the federal government in 1803. However, the actual grant-making process dates back to 1842 when the 27th Congress made a grant award of $30,000 to Professor Samuel F.B. Morse. The funds allowed expense money and personal reimbursement to field test the electromagnetic telegraph system and explore the feasibility of the system for public use. The grant award was significant in that it represented the first time Congress fully participated in the grant-making process. Later in the 19th century congressional interest in research was manifested by the enactment of the Hatch Act, Smith-Hughes Act, Bankhead-Jones Act, and the Morrill Act all of which established land-grant colleges throughout the United States.

In the beginning there *was* federal support for education, but the Northwest Ordinances were not the grantwriter's dream. The opportunity to develop proposals to the federal government for support of an individual's or a group's ideas did not really blossom until the 1950s with the Cooperative Research Act (1956) and the National Defense Education Act (1958). The 1960s began the grantwriter's utopia with the Civil Rights Act, the Vocational Education Act, the Higher Education Act, the Elementary and Secondary Education Act, and the many reauthorizations of these and other acts serving special "categories," such as bilingual education or handicapped children.

The increase in opportunities to secure external funds brought a new grants business—newsletters, seminars, grantwriters, and offices of proposal development. Consulting firms, grants offices, and specialized grantwriters became the supermarkets of the trade, severely challenging individuals and small agencies who were the "Mom and Pop" grocery stores serving the needs of local areas.

Increased Competition for Grant Monies

Still, new individuals enter the arena each year, both as aspiring grantwriters and as new project directors; there are seminars or workshops on proposal development and graduate courses in "Grants and Contracts" or "State and Federal Relations" at some universities. The materials collected, developed, and compiled in this volume are mostly related to grant proposal development for education, but the push for uniformity in grants among the various federal agencies (begun in 1977 with the uniform requirements) means that the materials have wider application. Some of the ideas and tips—especially in Part II, "Writing Grant Proposals"—may be of general interest and value to a grantwriter; some ideas about "project management" in Part III should benefit anyone operating a project.

Organization of Book

This book is divided into three major *parts* and several additional supporting sections, such as this Introduction, References, and Appendixes. Part I, "Exploring in the Grants World," includes Chapters 1-4 and discusses the planning and some of the major "tools of the trade" needed to get started in the grant/project field. Part II, "Writing Grant Proposals," includes Chapters 5-9 and covers some important steps in developing a successful grant application. Part III, "Implementing, Operating, and Terminating a Project," includes Chapters 10-13 and discusses both closing out a project annually and the often difficult but realistic element of terminating the project at the end of external support. Appendixes include potentially useful information, lists and addresses that seemed inappropriate for the regular text.

Funding Questions: What Are the Federal Levels of Support for Education?

The grantwriter needs to know about the funding potential for grant support. According to the U.S. Office of Management and Budget (OMB) (Budget of the U.S. Government, Fiscal Years 1967-1990), total federal support for education was about $58 billion in Fiscal Year (FY) 1989. This was an increase since 1980 of about 48 percent, but a moderate loss (.7 percent) when corrected for inflation. *Total* support includes on-budget items such as research, Chapter 1, higher education, and off-budget items such as student loans (that are projected to be repaid later). Off-budget items may fluctuate because of changes in tuition and fees or in formulas for computing them. Off-budget funds are not really available for grantwriters; funds for programs that work through the grants process are on-budget and have remained fairly constant or have decreased (1980-1990) when adjusted for inflation. Most increase in total education funding is due to off-budget increases.

As an example, the federal budget for the U.S. Department of Education is outlined in Table I.1. It lists the 1992 appropriations and President's fiscal request for 1993. The last column shows the House's proposed fiscal 1993 spending plan for the Education Department.

Table I.1. Budget Appropriations for 1992 and 1993 President and House Requests

Major Education Department	1992 Appropriations	1993 President Request	1993 House Request
Compensatory Education for the Disadvantaged Programs	$6,706,254,000	$6,828,207,000	$6,759,924,000
Impact Aid	$771,698,000	$532,130,000	$763,981,000
School Improvement Programs	$1,571,895,000	$1,620,447,000	$1,557,855,000
Bilingual and Immigrant Education	$225,407,000	$233,645,000	$231,308,000
Rehabilitation Services and Disability Research	$2,199,037,000	$2,263,866,000	$2,246,490,000
Vocational and Adult Education	$1,428,460,000	$1,447,260,000	$1,509,016,000
Student Financial Assistance	$9,537,042,000	$10,619,795,000	$11,031,328,000
Higher Education	$827,903,000	$853,481,000	$831,408,000
College Housing Program	$8,095,000	$740,000	$3,730,000
Education Research, Statistics, and Improvement	$270,744,000	$415,396,000	$279,844,000
Libraries	$147,247,000	$35,000,000	$145,774,000
Total — Department of Education	$27,275,434,000	$29,241,217,000	$28,931,697,000

AAA Phenomenon

With the passage of a law or the start of a new federal initiative, there may be considerable hoopla and hype about the amount of money *authorized*. Don't get excited yet! It is a long way from funds authorized to support something and funds actually *allocated* to do the job. Along the way is the *appropriations* process. Familiarily with the three steps—authorization, appropriation, and allocation, or the AAA phenomenon—is vital to the grantwriter, because those steps give clues to the importance of, political impetus behind, and actual funds available for a project. Perhaps the best way to think of the AAA phenomenon is that *authorization* is the *ceiling,* or the most that a program could receive if it, in fact, *receives any funds.* An *authorization* level is built into each Public Law (PL), but an authorization does not guarantee that any funds will ever be appropriated or allocated. An authorization is typically set to provide flexibility in case the law is ever "funded."

Appropriation of funds to support federal activity is a separate step from passing public laws to put activities "on the books." An appropriations bill begins in the House of Representatives and after being finally negotiated and passed, provides the maximum that an agency can use to operate the program for which funds were appropriated. *Allocation* of funds is the administrative activity of disbursement of funds for specific purposes of the authorizing legislation. In a given year this could be less than the appropriation due to impoundments or recisions. The distribution of the allocated funds is the most important step in the whole process for the grantwriter. How many dollars are actually available for the program from which the proposer seeks support; how many projects will be funded, and what will be the expected range of the awards? If this information is not in the *Federal Register* notice or in the grant application package, a call to the agency to find out is a good investment. Once assigned to the agency, the appropriated funds may have many purposes other than support for your project: those other purposes might include program administration, obligations for multi-year funding, earmarked funds to support inter- or intra-agency efforts, etc. *If information on the actual availability of funds is not readily available, seek it out.*

—— **Grant Tip** ——

Find out the distribution of the allocated funds. This is the most important step in the whole process for the grantwriter.

Authorization • Appropriation • Allocation

Should You Seek Federal Support?

Certainly it is an honor and great achievement when an agency evaluates your proposal as worthy of funding, and there are positive benefits to receiving funding support. People usually emphasize the positive. There are, however, some potential negatives that are seldom mentioned. One should try to negate these negatives.

Potential Benefits from External Funding Support

Perhaps the biggest *plus* in getting a grant is that you now have some resources to meet an important need and to work toward a goal that is of interest to your organization. Funds for your project may support new equipment, books, or other resources and may provide some salaries. The activity may expand your capability, as well as that of your organization and others associated with the project, through training and professional growth; in fact, the project may even create new areas of expert skill/knowledge (expertise) among personnel. Persons who work assiduously on the project may be able to conduct financed research (or evaluation) that could provide material for a professional paper or published article. "Soft money" jobs often pay slightly more than regular positions because of the job insecurity. However, while they also have a predetermined length, they may allow you to demonstrate skills that will support your move to a regular position. Having control over funds may provide some autonomy, some opportunity to secure support personnel, and expanded options for professional travel and for meeting new professional experts. Not insignificantly, there are the personal benefits of a challenging task and the recognition that can come from operating a successful project that achieves positive results. Figure I.1 summarizes some potential positive outcomes from securing grant support.

Figure I.1. Benefits From Securing External Funds

•Meeting a Need
•Financial Support for Your Organization
•Autonomy/Released Time
•Challenging Opportunities
•Ability to Secure Support Personnel
•Financed Research (perhaps for a professional article)
•New Equipment
•Recognition/Model Program
•Salary Increases
•Expanded Capabilities
•Create New Areas of Expertise
•Advanced Training from Experts in New Fields
•Professional Travel and Presentation(s) at Professional Meetings

Potential Negative Aspects from External Funding

What you need to do for the project may run afoul of the usual policies or operations of your organization (such as your need to travel extensively or to stay in places not covered by regular travel expense policy). The managerial and legal responsibilities of a project carry high levels of paperwork (red tape) and often unrealistically high expectations for "super success." As a grant administrator you will be subjected to site visits, audits, or both, and to an outrageous level of accountability. As the "new kid on the block," you may get limited or second-class space, equipment, furnishings, and priorities—unless the grant is large enough to support autonomous action. Project-related uncertainties, often over deadlines and about continued funding, can add stress to the job. There may be no firm intraorganizational support for the project, and if project personnel appear to have extra benefits (real or perceived), personality conflicts may develop (jealousy over travel, for example). The project may be assigned a subordinate role in the organization, and project activities may suffer if the funding agency has a shift in priorities. Don't forget the probable "hassle" in trying to serve both the funding agency and your own organization. Trying to serve two masters is *never* easy. Some potential negative aspects of receiving external funding support are listed in Figure I.2.

Figure I.2. Negative Factors of Securing External Funding Support

•Managerial/Legal Responsibilities
•Priority Shift May Cause Disharmony
•Lack of Strong Internal Support
•Personalities/Jealousies
•Subordinate Role of Project in Organization's Total Operations
•Skewed Priories at the Institution if Dependent on External Funds
•Uncertainty for Continuity
•Stress Increase Due to Ambiguity and the Success Syndrome
•High Level of Accountability
•Paperwork/Red Tape
•Sometimes Impossible Expectations
•Implementations in a Timely Manner/Time Tensions
•Limited or Second-Class Space, Materials, Equipment, and Support
•Dealing with Policies and Purposes of Two Masters: Funding
   Agency and Your Organization

Grant Tip

Don't forget the probable "hassle" in trying to serve both the funding agency and your own organization. Trying to serve two masters is never easy.

Various Roles the Grant Administrator Must Play

The person who writes the grant typically implements and maintains the project throughout its funding cycle. However, some professionals just write proposals. If one of their proposals is funded, they turn it over to someone else to implement and direct. The individual who implements and maintains the grant often has to wear a variety of hats in performing the work requirements that are associated with external funding support. Figure I.3 lists various roles in which grant administrators might find themselves while operating a funded project.

Figure I.3. Major Activities or Roles of a Grant Administrator in Operating a Funded Project

• Administrator/Supervisor	• Evaluator
• Public Relations Activities	• Planner
• Marketing	• Innovator
• Researcher	• Persuader
• Negotiator	• Devil's Advocate
• Fiscal Officer	• Interpretor
• Entrepreneur	• Personnel Manager
• Strategist	• Visionary

Summary

In reality, if people never write a *formal* proposal for a state or federal grant, at some point they will probably develop at least one proposal to do something of professional interest. That document will include many of the elements discussed in this handbook: analysis of need, goals and objectives, activities, some management details—timelines, personnel, budget, reports—evaluation, and probably dissemination of results.

Prior to the actual writing of the document, there will be a period of exploring the feasibility of what is being proposed: planning, seeking a sponsor (or funding source if appropriate), strategies to sell the idea or project, etc. If the idea (proposal) is accepted, the project developer will be concerned with implementing the project to do what was proposed. At some point the project will be closed down and terminated. That is what this volume is all about—exploring, writing, implementing, and terminating your successful idea as a strong proposal and as an operating project.

PART I

Exploring in the Grants World

In Part I, Chapters 1-4, we present some pre-writing elements that will help you get started in grant proposal development. These include some general, useful information about grants and the funding game, a review of some of the aids to help the grant seeker and proposal writer, and a chapter each on two major tools of the trade.

1

Unraveling the Mystique in Grant Applications

Introduction

External funding is often available to support program development efforts. Getting external funding is not usually easy, but there are procedures and techniques (i.e., rules of the game) that can help you prepare a competent proposal. Persons trained in proposal writing, institutions of higher education personnel, and employees of consulting firms that specialize in proposal development get the majority of external funds. Nevertheless, some tips, guidelines, and ideas will help newcomers and part-time proposal writers develop proposals that are competitive in the funding game. This handbook presents a summary of ideas about proposal development, specific information to help a proposal writer, examples from successful proposals, and some tips to help a person become more successful in proposal writing. The major emphasis in this handbook and the examples are programs funded through the United States Department of Education, but the concepts, techniques, and tips will help a person writing proposals for other agencies. The handbook provides strategies, vocabulary, examples, sources of ideas, and general information to aid both the novice and the experienced proposal writer in improving their proposals for funding support.

——Grant Tip——
Getting external funding is not usually easy, but there are procedures and techniques that will help you prepare a competent proposal.

Proposal Development

Proposal development is hard work, but the result can be rewarding. Contrary to the opinion of some cynics, getting a grant is not entirely the result of politics or chance. Undoubtedly, the successful proposal is a fortuitous blend of certain ingredients, but the serious proposal writer can gain the upper hand by careful attention to ideas and strategies that have been proven to be successful. It seems fair to say that although there is some luck in obtaining funding through the development of a proposal, there are also ways to improve the odds. Development of a successful proposal is not entirely style and technique. First, you need a good idea that connects with the particular interests of some funding source. Through planned approaches, study, and attention to detail, you can dramatically increase your chances of success.

Besides needing a good idea, writing ability, and a general knowledge of proposal processes, you will also need access to information and to "tools of the trade" that help in the writing of a proposal. In developing a proposal for the federal government, you will need access to some primary sources, including the *Federal Register (FR)*, the *Catalog of Federal Domestic Assistance (CFDA)*, and when necessary, the *Code of Federal Regulations (CFR)*. These are covered in detail in Chapter 3, "Using the *Federal Register (FR)* and the *Code of Federal Regulations (CFR)*," and Chapter 4, "Using the *Catalog of Federal Domestic Assistance (CFDA)*." Other primary sources are the program guidelines (or application packet) and some Federal Management Circulars (FMCs). Secondary sources include articles and reference books about grants, newsletters from professional associations, and professional reading that helps explain various programs and grant processes.

What Is a Proposal?

———**Grant Tip**———
The formal proposal, in the required form and format, connects your ideas and interests with the ideas, interests, and programs of a funding source.

A formal proposal for funding, as the term is used here, is a written document developed in accordance with specific rules or guidelines. The document, in the required form and format, connects your (a person's or institution's) ideas and interests with the ideas, interests, and programs of a funding source. Usually, the proposal is the only direct contact with the funding agency during the competition period. A *competition* is initiated by the funding agency inviting institutions, agencies, etc. to submit proposals. Deadlines are established, and all parties submit their proposals to the funding source. The proposals are reviewed and rated. Certain ones are selected to receive funds. (This process, known as a "competition," is explained in detail in Chapter 6.) Therefore, your proposal should be clear, cogent, and concise and should clearly convey your ideas and the relationship of your project to the funding agency's goals. Any project that does not explicitly advance the purposes of the program and/or agency to which it is proposed will not be considered for funding.

In its simplest form a proposal expresses relationships among three important variables: performance, time, and cost. The proposer offers to perform something (the project) in a specified amount of time for a related cost. These three variables—performance, time, and cost—are carefully integrated and interrelated in the proposal.

```
┌─────────────────────────┐
│    PERFORMANCE          │
│          ╱╲             │
│         ╱  ╲            │
│ TIME  ╱____╲  COST      │
└─────────────────────────┘
```

The overall relationships among these variables as expressed in the proposal should remain constant. Therefore, during budget negotiations for a grant that has been accepted (see Chapter 8, "Understanding How Grants are Awarded"), if the Grants/Contracts Officer disallows a specific expenditure, the proposer must realign the time and/or cost variables to maintain the integrity of the relationships among the three variables. For example, assume that your original budget was for $100,000 and the negotiator allows only $85,000. At that time the proposer should adjust the performance and time variables to correlate with the new cost. Having clearly established relationships among the three variables of performance, time, and cost is an important basis for a strong proposal and project. In this handbook a proposal is treated as a rational expression of relationships among performance, time, and cost as expressed in a formal document to a funding agency.

In spite of the seeming complexity of many proposals, you can generally express the relationship among these variables by relying on the guiding questions of successful media reporters: what, why, how, who, when, and how much? In form and structure, a proposal often moves from the very general (why and how) to the very specific (when and how much). A budget, although only an estimate of proposed expenditures, must relate specific costs for particular activities and persons (staff). Figure 1.1 identifies the general flow of the proposal from general to specific. Following sections of the handbook address these concepts in more detail.

———Grant Tip———

A proposal is a rational expression of relationships among performance, time, and cost as expressed in a formal document to a funding agency.

Terminology

A *grant* is awarded based upon an *application* developed in response to a Request for Applications (RFA). A *contract* is awarded based upon a *proposal* developed in response to a Request for Proposal (RFP). In reality, proposal writers speak of writing grants in response to RFPs.

A *program* is the agency's large-scale initiative. The application or proposal is to operate a *project* to meet and carry forth the purposes of the agency's *program*.

Figure 1.1. Proposal Guiding Questions: General to Specific

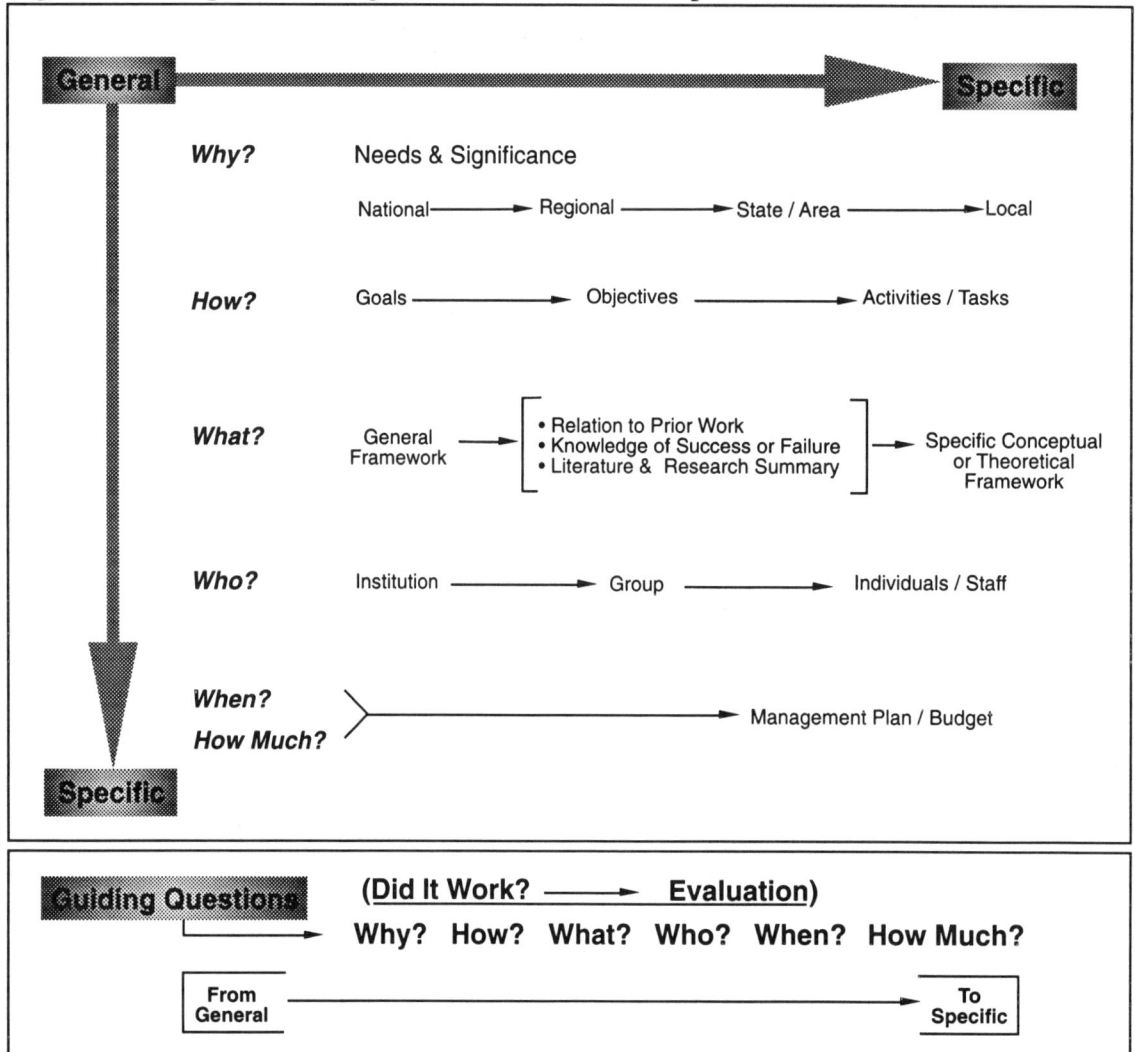

Grants and Other Funding Instruments

There are many ways to think about and to categorize types and sources of external support. This handbook focuses primarily on a source of support known as a grant and specifically a grant from the federal government. Examples are drawn primarily from grants available through the United States Department of Education.

Broadly speaking, the federal government has three categories of instruments for supporting funding. These three categories are the grant, the contract, and the cooperative agreement. There are many differences between and among these categories, but the basic differences are fairly easy to understand.

Grant • Contract • Cooperative Agreement

A *grant* is an award made to advance the purposes of a specific federal program, such as Education of the Handicapped, Chapter 1, Upward Bound, Women's Educational Equity, and so forth. Chapter 7, "Reviewing a Funded Proposal," presents the proposal of the College Assistance Migrant Program (CAMP), which falls in the grant category. Program personnel specify fairly broad and general guidelines describing the program's purpose and announce a competition inviting people to design projects to carry forth the purposes of the program. The proposer has considerable latitude and flexibility in determining what to do within the purposes and general guidelines of the program. Typically there are several successful grant proposals, depending on the amount of funds available to support the program. The government announces the grants competition in the *Federal Register*. The proposal writer obtains a copy of the grant application package, which contains guidelines to help in preparing the grant application (proposal). This handbook is designed primarily to help you develop a successful application or proposal for *grant* funding.

A *contract* is the government's way of soliciting for work that has been clearly specified. The government personnel know what needs to be done, have developed a set of specifications, and are looking for a qualified entity to conduct the work. Typically, there is only one, or at best a few, successful bidders to conduct the work specified for the contract. Solicitation for a contract is made public through a Request for Proposals (RFP). Government personnel announce many RFPs in a daily publication entitled the *Commerce Business Daily.*

A *cooperative agreement* falls between a contract and a grant. In a cooperative agreement the funding agency personnel know in general what needs to be done, and although the funds are awarded to allow considerable discretion in their eventual use, the government works very closely with the recipient agency in defining, clarifying, and conducting the work requested in the cooperative agreement. Cooperative agreements are often used for large-scale projects such as Federal Research and Development (R&D) Centers. Cooperative agreement competitions are announced through the *Federal Register,* which is published every working day. The *Federal Register,* one of

—— **Grant Tip** ——
A grant is made to advance the purposes of a specific federal program. You have considerable latitude and flexibility within the guidelines of the program.

the necessary "tools of the trade" for a grant writer, is explained in detail in Chapter 3, "Using the *Federal Register (FR)* and the *Code of Federal Regulations (CFR)*." In a cooperative agreement competition, there is usually a very limited number of successful competitors. Once grantees have been awarded a cooperative agreement, they will coordinate with government personnel to achieve the cooperative agreement's goals. Figure 1.2 is a summary of some key differences among grants, contracts, and cooperative agreements. (This is a modification of a handout that was gathered from a workshop [source is unknown]).

Figure 1.2. Summary of Differences Among Three Funding Instruments

PROCEDURE	FEDERAL AGENCY	RELATIONSHIP
Grant	Patron	The grantee is responsible for performance with little or no federal or state agency involvement during performance. The agency supports the grantee's well-defined and well-written ideas.
Cooperative Agreement	Partner	The federal or state agency is involved during the performance and shares responsibility for performance. The agency and grantee plan together and maintain a cooperative working arrangement.
Contract	Purchaser	The federal or state agency is procuring for direct or third party use. The successful bidder will conform to pre-determined activities.

The Grant Application Package

The grant application package (guidelines) is a packet of material prepared by personnel at the funding agency. Material in the packet explains the purposes of a particular program and the specific processes for developing a proposal to seek funding support from that program. The guidelines usually consist of a copy of the federal regulations that govern the program, the forms required in the proposal, and supporting or helpful information about the program itself. As soon as the program personnel announce a grant competition in the *Federal Register,* the proposal writer must contact the funding source and obtain the application packet or guidelines. The guidelines will include a closing date for proposals in the competition. The proposer is responsible for seeing that the proposal is mailed or delivered on or before the closing date. The proposal deadline is an extremely important factor in determining whether or not you should even attempt to prepare a proposal. You need enough time to prepare a quality proposal, and the deadline is a fixed target. There is no such thing as a late proposal. *Proposals that do not meet the deadline may be returned unopened.*

Categories of Grants and Sources of Support

There are many sources of support for projects built upon sound ideas.

Although the focus of this handbook is federal funding in the Department of Education, the handbook reader needs to understand the variety of support sources available. A simple categorization of support sources will help you organize and plan a grant-seeking strategy. For purposes of this categorization, consider that there are two sectors that provide funds: the *public sector* (or government), and the *private sector.*

Public ••• Private

Within the *public sector* support may be available through city, county, or other levels of government, but primarily public sector grant support usually comes from the federal and state levels of government. Some federal money for particular programs flows through to state government, which, in turn, distributes the funds in accordance with federal guidelines, often imposing some additional state restrictions as well. These funds, once they flow through to the state level, are thought of as state funds, and state personnel administer grants awarded from that funding source. To manage these funds, the federal government typically requires the state government to prepare a *state plan* (really, a contract) that spells out how the state will administer the funds in accordance with federal program priorities.

Within the *private sector* the primary sources of funding are philanthropic foundations established by major companies or by families wishing to designate gifts to support humanitarian purposes. Some large, local businesses and industries contribute significantly to local improvement ideas. These plant managers' funds may be turned to your benefit.

-----**Grant Tip**-----
There is no such thing as a late proposal. Proposals that do not meet the deadline may be returned unopened.

A third category of sources of support is emerging (although in some cases it would be categorized under either a public or private sector). This additional category is the community foundation, a foundation set up to support specific purposes or community activities. With passage of limiting legislation on funding, community foundations have become fairly popular to support activities of public schools. Quasi-public corporations are generally established for the sole purpose of administering community foundation funds; they typically have boards of directors that represent the community at large.

Essentially, two types of grants are available: *competitive* and *noncompetitive*. A noncompetitive grant is typically awarded based on a formula and it is sometimes called an *entitlement*. The proposer agrees to conduct activities within a restricted range of options to achieve specific purposes of an established program. An entitlement or formula grant is more like a contract than a grant. Funds are available to the requesting agency if that agency develops a proposal in accordance with fairly definitive guidelines. Funding is based upon a formula, such as the number of youths who come from families with a particular income level.

────Grant Tip────

A noncompetitive grant is sometimes called an entitlement and is more like a contract than a grant.

| Competitive ••• Noncompetitive |

Of considerable interest to the grant seeker are *competitive grants.* Support under the *competitive* category is generally open, although certain programs may be limited to applicants in broad ranges of categories, such as public schools, private schools, higher education, and state education agencies. These programs are advertised (in the case of the federal government, in the *Federal Register*), and the proposer must take the initiative in seeking the funds. Unlike entitlements where a designated amount of money is set aside for a specific purpose usually administered by a designated agency, in the competitive grants arena the proposer must specify what will be done in a particular time frame and what the costs (within reason) should be.

Some people categorize the type of funds according to the focus of the funds. Some funds have a very narrow or special purpose called *categorical funding.* Categorical funding is popular with politicians because it targets special-interest groups (thus pleasing lobbyists and the special-purpose groups and giving politicians content for speeches to constituencies). Additionally, if aid is targeted to a particular category, accountability seems easier, and evaluations can show changes relative to the status of that category.

Categorical • • • General

General aid is for general purposes. The logic behind general aid is that those closest to the problems should identify the problems and establish procedures to remediate them. Because the federal government (or funding source) cannot know the problems as well as local personnel do, the responsibility for designating recipient groups should rest with the grant application developers.

Access to Information

Even with a good idea, adequate writing skills, and a supporting organization, you still need access to information about grant programs. But access to information is not sufficient. You also need to know what information is most important and how to use it. Primary sources of information include documents produced by the funding source, such as the *Federal Register,* which is addressed in Chapter 3, the *Catalog of Federal Domestic Assistance (CFDA)*, which is covered in Chapter 4, and the application packets provided by the federal government. Secondary sources include news media, newsletters of professional associations, and even word of mouth. Persons who work in organizations with grant and contract offices may obtain information through those offices. Persons may obtain information by attending meetings or by talking with people who have previously received support for specific programs. The successful proposal writer will take an active interest in seeking information from many different sources.

Judging the importance of information and using it correctly are valuable skills. Following is an example. The proposal developer needs to know the total amount of funding available in a given year for a program, but sometimes finding out the details of available funds requires mathematical ability. It is not enough to know that the legislature has appropriated a particular sum for a program; you also need to know how much of that appropriation is available for new projects. This information may be in an application packet. If not, you should contact the funding agency to determine the amount available for new projects, the agency's estimate of the number of projects to be funded, and the general funding range for the projects. One confusing aspect in determining a funding level is that some programs allow multiple-year projects wherein the proposal writer develops a project for two, three, or more years. The agency may approve the project for a multiple-year time frame. In this case a portion of the agency's budget each year is obligated to support the continuing project's activities. The cumulative total of funding for continuing projects will not be available for new projects.

A continuing project becomes a *noncompeting continuation.* Near the end of each project year, project personnel must show that they have successfully achieved objectives for that year. If the project has been successful and funds continue to be available, the project becomes a noncompeting continuation, and project personnel do not need to develop a full, new competitive proposal. They prepare a much shorter continuation document. Generally, a noncompeting continuation proposal reviews activities from the preceding year and expresses a scope of work—including objectives, major activities, and a proposed budget—for the coming year.

Some programs reserve portions of their annual appropriations for administration and evaluation or for other costs. *Earmarked funds* reduce funding available for new projects. Thus you need to obtain some indication of funds available for new projects and use that information as a guideline in developing the scope of a new project. Next, apply some good common sense. If an agency has only $1,000,000 and hopes to fund 10 or 15 projects, you probably should not develop a proposal requesting $500,000.

A productive source of information about successful grants is the federal government. Successful, funded proposals are in the public domain—they are public information. You can go to government offices and review successful proposals. (Some proposal sections, such as budget, salaries, or personnel, may be excluded from public review.) Grant seekers should notify the agency in advance and identify exactly what they wish to review.

Besides access to and knowing how to use the information available, you need access to tools of the trade. "Tools of the trade" are those documents, books, newsletters, outlines, and other elements that help the proposal writer develop successful proposals. (This handbook could qualify as a "tool of the trade.") A tool might be a network that provides support and information. Special information sessions and grant-writing seminars are part of the communication network that arguably is one of the most important tools of the trade. This handbook addresses some major tools of the trade in separate chapters.

————Grant Tip————
Funded proposals are in the public domain. You can go to government offices and review successful proposals.

Planning to be Competitive

Deadlines for ongoing grant competitions come around each year, usually at about the same time. Occasionally there are new initiatives for competitions. A small measure of planning and organizing will facilitate the orderly approach to entering the competitions.

Reserve some section of a file for your grants information. This file should contain components you would include as a part of most proposals, so the file will save you the time and effort required to write these segments each time. Some useful items for the files:

- Keep an up-to-date general summary of your organization (school, district, etc.) written in clear, jargon-free prose. This synopsis will introduce a proposal reader to your organization. Be positive. This should sound almost as though the Chamber of Commerce wrote it.

- Have a brief explanation of your organization's capacity to operate a project. Comment on special features, such as computers or cooperative working agreements that can help, such as a college or university or major business or industry. List any special recognitions or awards. Do you have access to libraries or special data bases?

- Demographic information should be easily accessible. Figure 1.3 is a suggested list of the types of information that will help. At the beginning of each year, update a file containing the descriptive items. Keep files for at least three (3) years because some projects require data from previous years (example: local tax rate and per pupil expenditure). Also, data from past years can be used to show changes over time, such as changes in test scores, which may be helpful in evaluation and showing project success. Materials in Figure 1.3 are examples. Keep the data organized in the manner used by your system and state. Keep information in a file system with headings such as System Information, Student Information, etc.

- Keep a handy list of charts and forms that you use in the proposal. These may relate to planning, timelines, showing personnel responsibilities, etc. In the "forms file" keep extra, blank copies of standard forms and "boilerplate/minimal forms" (See last entry of Figure 1.3.)

For the serious grant writer, yet another planning step is important. Write to each grants competition of interest and request the grant

——**Grant Tip**——

Deadlines for ongoing grant competitions come around each year, usually at about the same time. Occasionally there are new initiatives or opportunities for competitions.

Figure 1.3. Demographic Data to Help in Proposal Writing in a Public School System

SYSTEM INFORMATION

1. Map(s) showing location of system in state and location of schools in system.
2. Written description of school system: proximity to major cities; airline service; census data such as population of area; major businesses and industries; education level of adults; organizational structure of school system; square miles in city or county; per capita income (1-2 pages).
3. Federal ID Number (Federal Employer ID Number).
4. Number of schools in system and grades included in each school.
5. Advisory boards, etc.
6. Demographic data on pupils and employees: system-wide and by building units.

STUDENT INFORMATION (Use Numbers and Percents)

1. Total enrollment K-12 and by elementary/secondary, such as K; 1-8; 9-12. Preschool. Adult.
2. Enrollment for each grade by school (monthly attendance report for system) and totals for each.
3. Number and percent of all minorities, by building and, if possible, by programs.
4. Retention rate (failures); absentee rate; dropout rate.
5. Reading and math standardized test scores by school, by grade, and averages for each.
6. Number served by special education.
7. Vocational programs and enrollment.

TEACHER AND PERSONNEL INFORMATION

1. Total number of teachers; total administrative and professional staff.
2. Number of teachers by grade/subject, by school, and totals for each.
3. Level of training: Bachelor's, Master's, Master's + 45, Specialist, Doctorate (include administration).
4. Number of black, white, other minority and percentage (number of male and female).
5. Turnover rate.
6. Average years of experience.
7. Pertinent personnel policies.

FINANCIAL INFORMATION

1. All salary schedules.
2. Fringe benefits rates — social security, hospital, retirement (teacher and non-teacher), life insurance — and how each is computed.
3. Local tax rate.
4. Per pupil expenditure.
5. Percentage of local supplement—percentage of local vs. state funds vs. federal funds.
6. Pertinent fiscal/financial policies.

PRIVATE SCHOOL INFORMATION

1. List of private schools in system—administrators' names, addresses, and phone numbers. Have the private schools been approved by State Education Agency as eligible for federal and state funds?
2. Number of students in private schools in system by grade.

OTHER

1. Forms file: blank standard forms, blank "boilerplate," etc.
2. Copies of timelines, management charts, school organizational chart, etc.
3. Public announcements for newspapers.
4. Copies of any assurance forms for civil rights, Title IX, handicapped.
5. Any information on court orders or important court cases influencing your district.

application package. After you review the application, whether or not you prepare an application, make a note on a master list of (1) the date of the competition, (2) ideas you have for the competition, (3) priority of this grant for your organization, and (4) the address (name and phone of contact, etc.) of the office where you will write for next year's application packet. Next, circulate a general description of the competition, along with a statement of your interest, and solicit from your colleagues their interest/ideas/commitment in developing a project for the next competition. Follow up on this solicitation and get plans started six to ten months in advance of *the usual* application deadline. Know that the regulations and guidelines (and approximate due date for proposals) seldom change much from year to year. Nevertheless, *check the dates each year, and read carefully all new application packets.*

Develop a list of interesting programs, a file of applications, a list of past (and approximate future) due dates, names of people interested in a project, and some good ideas as the basis of planning and preparing a project for the next year. If there is substantial interest, initiate some planning, brainstorming, and writing sessions. Contact the federal office to get names and locations of funded projects. Contact them. Get into the "mainstream" of project ideas. These steps, completed nearly a year in advance of your formal application, will prepare you for the competition.

If you are unsuccessful when you submit your proposal the first time, don't despair. Get the reviewers' comments. Review and study your proposal. (Don't slavishly follow all reviewer comments. There will be new reviewers next year.) Visit a successful project. Find and save good ideas. Speak with program personnel so they will know about your continuing interest. Plan to succeed the next time. Stalk each grant carefully.

Types of Grants: Competitive or Noncompetitive

The *noncompetitive grant* is typically a response to an entitlement established by some formula (e.g., Chapter 1 entitlement). The grant seekers (e.g., Local Education Agency [LEA] personnel) complete forms developed by the funding source (for Chapter 1 this would be the federal agency and State Education Agency [SEA] personnel in the particular state). These forms provide some minimum standards and uniformity to help SEA persons monitor the project to assure that it meets federal and state regulations.

—— **Grant Tip**——

If you are unsuccessful the first time, don't despair. Don't slavishly follow all reviewer comments. There will be new reviewers next year.

These noncompetitive grants require little creativity and not much project development; the proposer completes forms and assurances much like a contract. Most projects will be very similar as they are developed and administered under the SEA master plan (State Plan) that governs how the SEA will handle that particular program.

A *competitive grant,* however, is not awarded until the grant writer develops a proposal that can compete successfully on preset criteria with other proposals submitted in the same competition. The money is available to support projects to carry forth the purposes of the program, but it is *not* earmarked for a particular organization (e.g., LEA) or held as an entitlement based upon a preset formula. Applications for competitive grants extend and test the grantwriter's skills and creativity. Within the broad guidelines of a program's purposes, the competitive grant will support a project developed to serve the needs of a client group. Each project may be quite different as the funding agency only has general guidelines and criteria.

Figure 1.4 provides a brief overview of two major types of grants (competitive and noncompetitive) and some classification of

Figure 1.4. An Outline Summary of Types of Grants

Grant: Award of money or direct assistance to perform an activity or projects whose outcome is seen as less certain than that from a contract, with expected results described in general terms. Application can be submitted without having been solicited (unsolicited proposal) or through a program announcement (Request for Application or RFA). Most federal grants fall into the following categories:

- **Competitive Grants:** awarded for specific types of research, demonstration, training, service to program participants, etc. (These are the grants dealt with in detail in this *Handbook.*)

- **Entitlement or Noncompetitive Grants:** awarded automatically or leased on a minimum "proposal" on the basis of legally defined formula to all agencies or institutions that qualify (state, medical schools, etc.). These are sometimes called formula grants when given to governmental agencies for distribution and monitoring under a state plan or state grant process.

- **Formula Grants:** awarded by federal agencies on the basis of a set formula such as so many dollars for population, per capita income, or enrollment. Chief recipients are state governments.

- **Block Grants:** sometimes called "bloc" grants; refers to grants in which the federal government merely stipulates in broad terms how the state and local government should spend federal aid. The tactical decision on where the money should be spent is left to the discretion of state and local officials. One purpose of block grants is to decentralize federal decision-making powers and let those closest to the problem define how to allocate the available funds. These are not "categorical" in the traditional sense.

- **Categorical Grants:** a restrictive version of the block grant; categorical grants are designated to serve only a specific group (category) specified in the enabling legislation. Examples are funds for handicapped, bilingual education, Chapter 1, etc. Grants may be competitive or noncompetitive.

noncompetitive grants (i.e., some of the vocabulary or terminology for these grants).

The purposes of and approaches to competitive and noncompetitive grants are quite different. In developing a *competitive* proposal the writer undertakes a large writing and development task; in a non-competitive grant the funds are there and the person need only complete the minimal forms (boilerplate) and program descriptions.

Eligible recipients for competitive grants are LEAs, SEAs, Institutions of Higher Education (IHEs), public and private profit and nonprofit agencies, and individuals. Eligible recipients for noncompetitive grants are governmental units or occasionally other nonprofit agencies. Figure 1.5 summarizes some of the differences between competitive and noncompetitive grants.

Figure 1.5. Two Types of Grants: Competitive and Noncompetitive

FACTOR	COMPETITIVE GRANT	NONCOMPETITIVE GRANT
Purpose	Typically supports the cost of special and/ or exemplary project, demonstration and/ or research project, etc.	Typically provides support for conducting—such as block grant—Chapter 1, Chapter 2, etc. This may include salaries, equipment, supplies, etc.
Structure of Document	Development of a narrative document in accordance with general guidelines.	Completion of specific forms.
Eligible Recipients	IHEs, SEAs, community agencies and or individuals. Must check proposal guidelines that you are interested in.	Typically LEAs and SEAs, and some other government agencies.
Creativity	High degree of creativity required.	Little creativity is required.
Length of Document	Long and detailed; perhaps between 20-80 pages, or more.	Several pages.
Amount of Work Required	Requires extensive planning/development of written materials that respond to funding agency established criteria.	Typically involves filling in the blanks (boilerplate forms) and providing support explanations.
Preparation Dates	Notice dates are published in the *FR.* Grant periods are from 1-5 years.	Typically prepared on an annual basis.
Selection Criteria	Criteria established by the Secretary of Education and agency seeking to support innovative projects.	Must meet established guidelines, often a plan developed by another level of government.

Finding Funding. © 1993 Corwin Press, Inc.

Some Tips (and Sobering Thoughts) About Grants

Be familiar with the legislation, regulations, agency, and program. You don't need to be sophisticated, but do your homework.

Understand what has been funded; know what has worked and what has not.

Your idea doesn't need to be brand new, but it should be new to your area or have some distinctive twist.

Relate your idea to current and important theories in your field or in some field of human behavior. If pertinent, rely on accepted theories (e.g., motivation, communication, change) to support what you propose.

Although you will express project need in terms of *your* particular audience, the funding agency is *primarily* interested in how a project such as yours has fairly wide and general application. By relating your project to appropriate theories, you help the agency understand how project ideas can be useful in other sites and with other people. A brief but focused literature review will help you build a conceptual framework to show how your idea fits with current research and thinking.

Although some people explain that your evaluation is related to your objectives, the *real test* of project success is a reduction of the need that precipitated the project. Good projects should put themselves out of business in a few years—or be so successful that hordes flock to your doors. Get and keep good baseline data. At some point three to five years later, a comparison of the original baseline data with new baseline data will show the true measure of your project's success.

If your state has several electoral votes, is politically conservative, has legislators in key positions on key committees, and is located on a coast or near interesting places to visit, you may have an advantage in the proposal chase. In Figure 1.6, for example, the location of the major, federally funded education initiatives (ERIC, R&D Centers, Labs) supported by the Education Department's Office of Educational Research and Improvement (OERI) as taken from OERI sources are plotted on a map (Source: Office of Educational Research and Improvement, 1991). A similar chart using influential congress committee chairs might also be informative.

The "peer review" process is designed to give everyone a fair chance in competitions. On the other hand, some competitions award "performance points" for current projects, so those projects start with a 5-15 point advantage.

If a proposal meets an agency's "fundable" criterion, there is room for considerations other than a project's absolute value as rated by reviewers. Considerations could include past performance, geographic distribution requirements, prior submissions, and even some political influence. Don't panic or be naive. The funding process is generally protected by the peer review process— but not absolutely. A good proposal with influence probably will beat a good proposal with little or no influence.

Figure 1.6. Distribution of OERI's Major Funding[1]

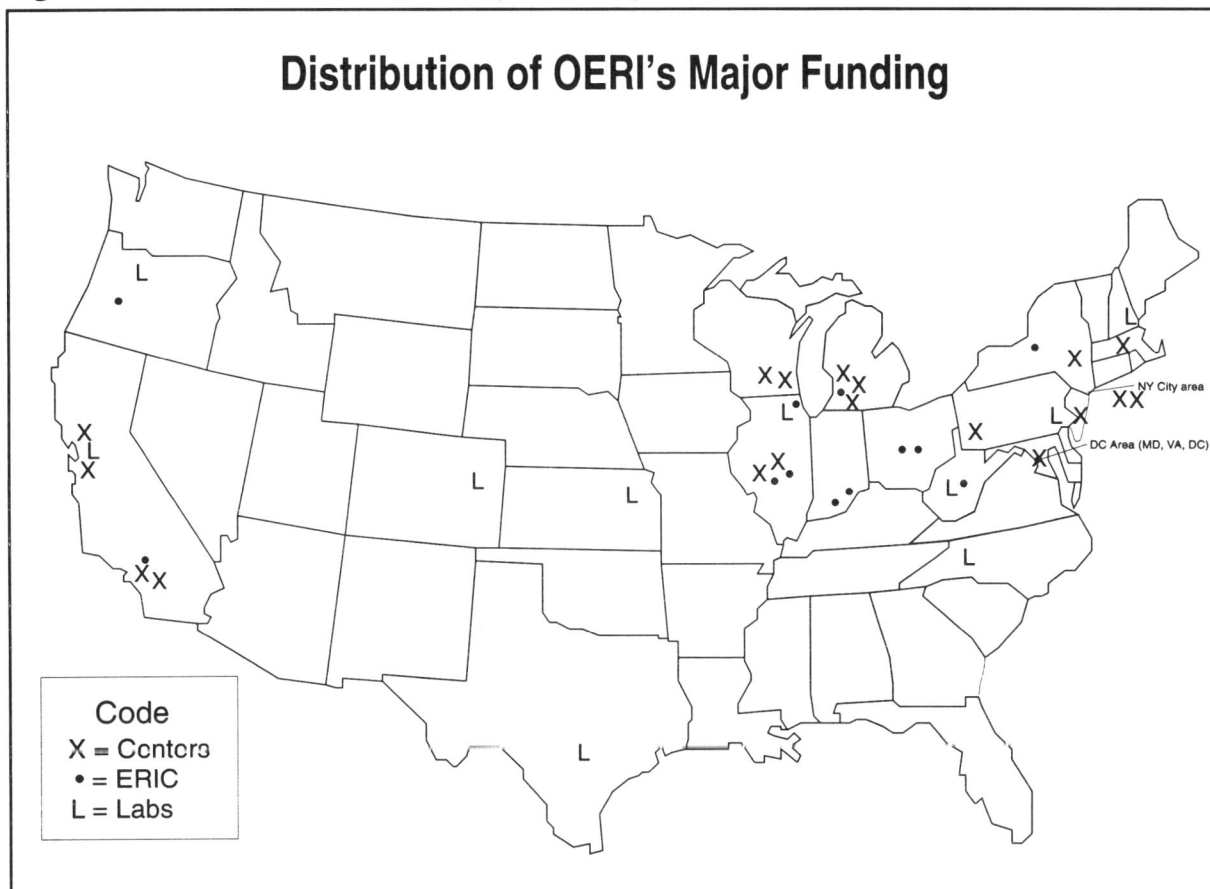

Distribution of OERI's Major Funding

Code
X = Centers
• = ERIC
L = Labs

Source: U.S. Department of Education, OERI, 1991.

[1]Distribution of major OERI-funded Centers/Labs/ERIC prior to Education Leadership Center Competition. The Leadership Centers went to TN, MA, IL, and MI.

Some Concluding Thoughts

────**Grant Tip**────
*Proposal
development is
probably best
approached with a
businesslike effort
buoyed by a sense of
competition and play.*

Much skill and knowledge is involved in successful proposal writing, along with some luck and serendipity. Proposal development is best approached with a businesslike effort buoyed by a sense of competition and play. The Ancient Mariner "stoppeth one in three" and everyone loves a .333 hitter in baseball. Why should you extend the odds? Seek 100 percent, but know that your grant application "hit rate" will begin to average out. That holds true for when you *start*. If you lose the first or second try, you will begin to win as you gain experience. It is not mystique; it is experience, skill, perseverence, and "savvy." It is a serious game.

You can't win if you don't get in the game and play. You can't win with just an idea. You must put "pencil to paper" and express a good idea clearly.

Don't quit after one loss. Winners persevere.

2

How to Explore Grant Possibilities in Education

Introduction

Y ou can become an effective proposal writer for grants in education. However, you must become familiar with the various U.S. Department of Education programs, their purposes and requirements, and their deadline dates before you respond to a Request for Application (RFA). You must be familiar with the various funding sources and the individuals who inform you about solicited education programs, and about the money that has been appropriated and allocated by the federal government. This chapter summarizes some important documents that provide this information. Although this chapter addresses selected basic information sources for grant seekers, Chapters 3 and 4, "Using the *Federal Register* and the *Code of Federal Regulations*" and "Using the *Catalog of Federal Domestic Assistance*," respectively, will cover these key federal documents in more detail. You must identify and use reference materials (the "tools of the trade") in planning for and responding to an RFA effectively. Know about new and old programs, frequent changes in regulations, and deadline dates for submitting the proposals. The Taft Corporation highlights this by saying that "modern fundraising is 90% research, 10% solicitation." In responding to federal grants, research and detailed knowledge are equally important.

Points to Consider Before Responding

Some questions you should consider and answer before you begin to develop a contract or an application can be divided into two major categories: personal and institutional. Examine your areas of interest, your time commitment, and your qualifications and expertise to develop the proposal. Answers to the questions in Figure 2.1 will help you decide if you should proceed. While you may say "yes" to these questions, you must also examine institutional or organizational commitment for the proposal. Figure 2.2 provides some questions you should consider and answer before proceeding to the writing stage.

—— **Grant Tip** ——

Examine your instititional or organizational commitment for the proposal before you commit your own time and resources.

Figure 2.1. Personal Questions Concerning Proposal

•Will I write the proposal?
•Do I have enough time to write the proposal and submit it by the deadline date?
•Can I maintain current job responsibilities and activities while developing a grant proposal?
•Do I have the necessary support personnel—clerical, printing, etc.—to write a competitive proposal?
•Do I have the authority to commit staff to respond quickly to write the proposal?
•Am I willing to put a high level of energy into the proposal to make sure it is competitive and not just mediocre?

Figure 2.2. Institutional Commitment Questions

•Is this grant activity within the scope of my institution or agency?
•Will the institution's priorities be skewed by responding or by conducting the project?
•Does my institution have the necessary facilities and resources to conduct the activities of the project?
•If matching funds are required, can or will my institution meet these requirements?
•How many different people and departments will be involved?
•If the funds are cut off and the program is dropped, what effect would it have on my institution?
•What are the hiring requirements at my institution for soft-money positions?
•Will it take two or three months to hire someone after I have been notified of the grant award?
•Can I still meet the requirements of the grant if I do not hire the personnel in a timely manner?

Individuals who begin to write proposals without considering the above questions often end up not completing the proposal or not meeting the deadline.

Identifying and Using Reference Material

There are over 2,000 daily information sources describing what is going on in the U.S. Capitol. Although one main characteristic of a successful proposal writer is never to leave a stone unturned, there are limits as to which data sources are the most appropriate and how much information you can review, such as federal information sources, subscription services, sources that monitor legislation, and other references and sources that may be appropriate.

Federal Information Sources

Federal Register (FR)

The *Federal Register (FR)* is published every weekday, except on legal holidays, by the Office of the Federal Register, National Archives and Records Administration, under the Federal Register Act and the regulations of the Administrative Committee of the Federal Register. The *FR* is the federal government's uniform system for making available to the public regulations and legal notices issued by federal agencies. It includes presidential proclamations and executive orders, federal agency documents having general applicability and legal effect, documents required to be published by acts of Congress, and other federal agency documents of public interest. The *Federal Register* is available at most major libraries, and its distribution is through the Superintendent of Documents, Government Printing Office, Washington, D.C. 20402. The telephone number is (202) 783-3238. In 1993 the *Federal Register* was furnished by mail to subscribers for $415 per year or $353 per year in microfiche form. Individual copies were $4.50 each. Chapter 3, "Using the *Federal Register* and the *Code of Federal Regulations,*" discusses this important federal information source in more detail.

——**Grant Tip**——
The Federal Register *is the government's uniform system for making available to the public regulations and legal notices issued by federal agencies.*

Catalog of Federal Domestic Assistance (CFDA)

The *Catalog of Federal Domestic Assistance* is a government-wide compendium of federal programs, projects, services, and activities that provide assistance or benefits to the public. This source is published annually by the Office of Management and Budget (OMB) in loose-leaf form, using the most current data available to describe the status of programs at the time the *Catalog* or the *Update* to the *Catalog* are compiled. The basic edition of the *Catalog*, usually published by June, reflects completed congressional action on program legislation. The *Update*, usually published in December, reflects completed congressional action on the President's budget proposals and on substantive legislation as of the date of compilation and includes information on federal programs that was not available

—— **Grant Tip** ——
The CFDA *is a government-wide compendium of federal programs, projects, services, and activities that provide assistance or benefits to the public.*

at the time the latest edition of the *Catalog* was released. This *Catalog*, which is addressed in more detail in Chapter 4, "Using the *Catalog of Federal Domestic Assistance*," describes all federal programs that distribute funds to states, organizations, and individuals. Program descriptions contain uniform, detailed information about individual grant programs. The objectives, types of assistance, and eligibility requirements are provided so applicants can determine whether they are eligible for the assistance and whether it meets their program needs. The *CFDA* is available at most major libraries or by subscription from the Superintendent of Documents, Government Printing Office, Washington, D.C. 20402. The telephone number is (202) 783-3238. The 1993 domestic subscription price was $46 annually, which included periodically updated materials.

Federal Assistance Program Retrieval System (FAPRS)

——**Grant Tip**——
The FAPRS *provides information on federal programs that meet the developmental needs of the applicant and for which the applicant meets basic eligibility criteria.*

The *Federal Assistance Program Retrieval System (FAPRS)* is a computerized question-answer system of rapid access to federal domestic assistance program information. The system provides information on federal programs that meet the developmental needs of the applicant and for which the applicant meets basic eligibility criteria. Program information provided by *FAPRS* is determined from information input supplied by the requestor. Upon receipt of an inquiry specifying the type of organization and its needs, the system can provide a printout of all of the domestic assistance programs that might be useful to that particular applicant. The primary output provided by *FAPRS* consists of a list of the titles and identifying numbers of the applicable programs from the *Catalog of Federal Domestic Assistance (CFDA)*. After you review this list of programs, you can obtain additional program information by (1) requesting the system to print complete program description(s) by program number(s), (2) requesting the system to print selected sections of program description(s), (3) requesting a list of applicable Office of Management and Budget (OMB) circular coordination requirements for each program, or (4) referring directly to the *CFDA* for specific information on a program. Individual FAPRS printouts can be obtained from access points located throughout the country; for volume users, direct access on a cost-reimbursable basis is available through the General Services Administration. For further information and a specific price, call (202) 708-5126 or toll-free answering service: (800) 669-8331, or write to the Federal Domestic Assistance Catalog Staff, General

Services Administration, Ground Floor, Reporters Building, 300 7th Street, SW, Washington, D.C. 20407.

Commerce Business Daily (CBD)

The *Commerce Business Daily (CBD)* is published every weekday, except holidays, by the U.S. Department of Commerce. The *CBD* lists all federal procurement invitations, including the Department of Education's requests for proposals (RFPs) for contracts. Although the *CBD* does not deal with grant competitions directly, some institutions and agencies that traditionally seek grant funds may benefit from materials included in the *CBD*. This publication is available at most major libraries or by subscription from the Superintendent of Documents, Government Printing Office, Washington, D.C. 20402. The telephone number is (202) 783-3238. The 1993 domestic subscription price was $324 annually by first-class priority mail or $275 annually by regular second-class mail. A six-month subscription was $162 by first-class priority mail and $137.50 by regular second-class mail.

------ **Grant Tip**------
The CBD *lists all federal procurement invitations, including the Department of Education's request for proposals (RFPs) for contracts.*

Code of Federal Regulations (CFR)

The *Code of Federal Regulations (CFR)* is published annually by the Office of the Federal Register. This publication is a codification of the general and permanent rules published in the *Federal Register* by the executive departments and agencies of the federal government. The *CFR* is divided into 50 titles that represent broad areas subject to federal regulations. Each title is divided into chapters that usually bear the name of the issuing agency. The *CFR* is kept up-to-date by the individual issues of the *Federal Register*. These two publications must be used together to determine the latest version of any given rule. The price for the *CFR* differs according to the number of books that cover the title of the agency in which you are interested. For example, there are three books for education at a total cost of about $90 per year. This publication is available at most major libraries or by subscription from the Superintendent of Documents, Government Printing Office, Washington, D.C. 20402. The telephone number is (202) 783-3238.

United States Government Manual

The *United States Government Manual* is the official handbook of the federal government. The *Manual* is the best source of information on the activities, functions, organization, and principal officials of the agencies of the legislative, judicial, and executive branches of government. It includes information on quasi-official agencies, international organizations in which the United States participates, and boards, committees, and commissions. A typical agency description includes a list of principal officials, a summary statement of the agency's purpose and role in the federal government, a brief history of the agency, including its legislative or executive authority, a description of its programs and activities, and a "Sources of Information" section. The 1993 price for this annual publication is $27 from the Superintendent of Documents, U.S. Government Printing Office, Washington, D.C. 20402. The telephone number is (202) 783-3238.

Resources in Education

Resources in Education provides up-to-date information about educational research sponsored by the Office of Educational Research and Improvement (OERI), Department of Education. It is designed to keep grant proposal writers, teachers, administrators, research specialists, others in the educational community, and the public informed about findings from educational research. The 1993 price for this annual publication was $26 from the Superintendent of Documents, U.S. Government Printing Office, Washington, D.C. 20402. The telephone number is (202) 783-3238.[1]

Information on Monitoring Upcoming Legislation

Grant seekers must remain up-to-date not only with current programs and new developments and policies within the U.S. Department of Education, but they must also monitor the legislative developments in Congress so they can plan accordingly and respond to changes in a timely manner. Numerous publications and newsletters are helpful here. The *Congressional Record* and *Congressional Quarterly* are two major publications that provide information on legislation.

---

[1]Prices, addresses, phone numbers, publication information, and other details of these sources may change without notice. We have included the most recent information we have, but we cannot be responsible for changes.

Congressional Record

The *Congressional Record* is the daily record of activities conducted within the U.S. Congress. The *Record* contains a verbatim official report of the floor debates and information on new bills being introduced. In 1993 this publication cost $225 per year or $112.50 for six months or $1.50 per issue. Contact Government Printing Office, Washington, D.C. 20402. Phone (202) 783-3238.

Congressional Quarterly

The *Congressional Quarterly* is a weekly report of major action taken in the U.S. Congress. This *Quarterly* documents how members of Congress voted on various bills. Contact Congressional Quarterly, Inc., 1414 22nd Street, NW, Washington, D.C. 20037.

Other Publications Monitoring Legislation

Other publications, such as newspapers, weekly journals, and newsletters of professional lobbying organizations monitor congressional activities and can help the grant seeker find out about new developments. The *Washington Post* and *New York Times* provide daily information on congressional activities, while the *Wall Street Journal* and *USA Today* frequently refer to activities taking place in Congress. Professional publications and subscription newsletters often print timely information on Congress, but the *Congressional Quarterly* and the *Congressional Record* are the most comprehensive publications in this area. Weekly news magazines (e.g., *U.S. News & World Report, Time*, and *Newsweek*) are also excellent sources for monitoring new developments in Congress.

Subscription Service Sources

An almost endless selection of subscription service sources is available on a daily, weekly, and monthly basis. Typically, subscription service sources gather some of their information from the previously-mentioned federal information sources, other sources that monitor legislation, and news releases from departments in the U.S. government. However, some subscription services provide very timely information. Good summaries help you avoid having to read a lot of basic information sources; they screen and abstract the information

———**Grant Tip**———
Not only do you need to keep up with current programs and new developments and policies within the U.S. Department of Education, you must also monitor legislative developments.

———**Grant Tip**———
Subscription service sources typically provide timely information and good summaries that help you avoid having to read basic information sources.

you may be specifically interested in. Some subscription services described here are especially helpful.

Education Daily

————Grant Tip————
Education Daily *provides accurate, timely reports on activities of Congress, the U.S. Department of Education, and the White House.*

Education Daily is the education community's independent news subscription service. It is printed daily, except weekends and legal holidays, and provides accurate, timely reports on activities of Congress, the U.S. Department of Education, and the White House. It also provides weekly legislative updates, reports on the latest educational research findings and activities, and other newsworthy items. The 1993 subscription cost for this daily educational newsletter service was $564 per year or $330 for six months. Contact Capitol Publications, Inc., P.O. Box 1453, Alexandria, Virginia 22314-2053. Phone (800) 327-7203 or (703) 683-4100.

Federal Research Report

The *Federal Research Report* is available on a weekly basis. This report includes federal contract opportunities and federal notes. The 1993 subscription rate was $200 per year. Multiple-year and six-month rates are available on request. Contact Federal Research Report, 951 Pershing Drive, Silver Spring, Maryland 20910-4464. Phone (301) 587-6300.

Federal Grants and Contracts Weekly

The *Federal Grants and Contracts Weekly* is published every Monday except Labor Day and Christmas week. It focuses on project opportunities in research, training, and service. This *Weekly* is a timely and complete newsletter about new federal grants and contracts available. A monthly supplement focuses on foundation funding, profiles of key agencies, and updates on new developments, legislation, and regulations. This highly recommended newsletter helps the grant seeker to keep in touch with various project opportunities. The 1993 price was $359 per year. Contact Capitol Publications, Inc., P.O. Box 1453, Alexandria, Virginia 22314-2053. Phone (800) 327-7203 or (703) 683-4100.

Education Funding News

The *Education Funding News* produced by the Education Funding Research Council is published weekly except the last week in August and the last week in December. This publication provides information on what is happening in Washington and features grant opportunities in the field of education. The 1993 subscription price was $297 per year. Contact Education Funding News, 1611 North Kent Street, Suite 508, Arlington, Virginia 22209. Phone (703) 528-1082.

Report on Educational Research

The *Report on Educational Research* provides up-to-date news of breakthrough programs and studies from around the United States. It includes coverage of federal research activities, research results, and funding. This biweekly newsletter also reports on testing, and evaluation, education reforms, and related topics of interest to individuals who are researchers and/or administrators in education. The 1993 price was $240 per year. Contact Capitol Publications, Inc., 1101 King Street, Alexandria, Virginia 22314. Phone (800) 327-7203 or (703) 739-6444.

The Chronicle of Higher Education

The *Chronicle of Higher Education* is published weekly except during the last two weeks in August and the last two weeks in December. It provides timely news in all fields of higher education, government policies affecting education, grant deadline dates, grant awards, and much more information that will be of interest to the grant seeker. The 1993 price was $75 per year for 49 issues or $40.50 for 24 issues. Contact The Chronicle of High Education, P. O. Box 1955, Marion, Ohio 43306-2055. Phone (202) 466-1050.

Other Publications Concerning Education

Capitol Publications produces a biweekly newsletter entitled *Education of the Handicapped,* which in 1993 cost $257 per year. This newsletter deals with current and pertinent information about federal legislation, regulations, programs, and funding for educating children with handicaps. This newsletter also deals with federal and state litigation on educating handicapped persons and reviews innovations and research in the field. Contact Capitol Publications, Inc., 1101 King Street, Alexandria, Virginia 22314. Phone (800) 327-7203 or (703) 739-6444.

The *Vocational Training News* covers the Federal Job Training Partnership Act (JTPA) and the Carl D. Perkins Vocational Act. This newsletter also covers illiteracy, Private Industry Councils (PICs), and state education and training initiatives. The 1993 cost for this weekly publication was $288 per year. Contact Capitol Publications, Inc., 1101 King Street, Alexandria, Virginia 22314. Phone (800) 327-7203 or (703) 739-6444.

The *Health Grants and Contracts Weekly* contains timely and comprehensive coverage of health-related federal grants and contracts. This weekly also profiles key funding agencies and provides legislative and regulatory updates. The 1993 cost was $339 per year. Contact Capitol Publications, Inc., 1101 King Street, Alexandria, Virginia 22314. Phone (800) 327-7203 or (703) 739-6444.

Annual Resource Documents

——— **Grant Tip** ———
Annual resource documents provide a general overview of programs and grant administration activities, and some may provide information on past and current funding levels.

The following annual resource documents are excellent tools to use in exploring grants in education. They usually provide a general overall view of the programs and grant administration activities. A couple of these publications also provide information on the past and current funding levels, the contact person, and so forth.

Guide to Federal Funding for Education

The annual *Guide to Federal Funding for Education* provides an accurate, detailed description of the federal programs offering financial assistance to local and state educational agencies (LEAs and SEAs), postsecondary institutions, and other public and private organizations and agencies working in the field of education. For each program, the *Guide* provides a program purpose, quick check (eligible applicant, type of aid, and requirements), key facts and any restrictions about the program, the grant-making process (administering agency, application procedure, and selection criteria), award information, and the person to contact for more information about the program. In addition to this 1,287 page document, the *Guide* issues monthly *Grant Updates* that provide information on new funding opportunities and important statutory, regulatory, and budgetary initiatives. The *Updates* include summaries of recent regulations and selected funding invitations published in the *Federal Register* and the *Commerce Business Daily*. This *Guide* and the monthly *Grant Updates* provide convenient and economical access to basic information regarding the various programs being funded in the U.S. Department of Education. The 1993 cost for the *Guide to Federal Funding for Education* with *Grant Updates* was $248 per year plus shipping and handling. The following guides are also provided: *Guide to Federal Funding for Governments and Non-profits* (1,147 pages including monthly *Grant Updates* at $249 plus postage and handling); *Guide to Federal Funding for Anti-Drug Programs* (987 pages including 50 weekly *Anti-Drug Funding Alerts* at $365 plus shipping and handling); and the *Guide Funding for Arts and Culture* (427 pages including monthly newsletter *Arts and Culture Funding Report* at $307 plus handling and postage). Contact Government Information Services, Education Funding Research Council, 1611 North Kent Street, Suite 508, Arlington, Virginia 22209. Phone (703) 528-1000.

Annual Register of Grant Support

The *Annual Register of Grant Support—A Directory of Funding Sources* is a comprehensive compendium of over 3,070 gifts and awards. This annual publication provides grant support information in four major areas: *public funding sources* among government departments and agencies; *private funding sources* that include private and family foundations; *corporate sources* that include corporate foundations and giving programs; and the *nontraditional sources* including educational associations, special interest groups, professional associations, community trusts, etc. The education section deals with the four major headings: *educational projects and research* (general), *elementary and secondary education, higher education projects and research*, and *scholar aid programs* (all disciplines). Each listing comes directly from the source and provides name, address, telephone numbers, fields of interest, names and purposes of grant programs, total funding available, money per award, eligibility requirements, and deadlines. It also notes the number of applicants, recipients, and representative awards in the most recent year. The 1993 cost for the *Annual Register of Grant Support— A Directory of Funding Sources* was $155 plus shipping charges. Contact the Order

Department, R.R. Bowker, P.O. Box 31, New Providence, NJ 07974-9904. Phone (800) 323-6772, or (312) 441-2210 if calling in Illinois.

Federal Grants Management Handbook

The *Federal Grants Management Handbook* is a loose-leaf handbook and monthly update service for individuals who manage federal grants. The *Handbook* outlines the management of a federal grant by providing practical advice and information on the following: how to organize receipt of grants funds; how to administer federal grants; how to develop and maintain a satisfactory grant accounting system; how to develop and negotiate an indirect cost rate; the basic principles in purchasing and procurement under grants; an overview of audit requirements of federal grants; how to comply with "strings attached" to federal grants; and much more grant management information. This *Handbook* also provides monthly page updates and "Current Developments" newsletters that cover a wide range of topics and events that affect federal grants management. The 1993 annual cost was $269 including the monthly updates. Contact Thompson Publishing Group, Subscription Service Center, 1725 K. Street, NW, Suite 200, Washington, D.C. 20006. For instant service, call toll free (800) 677-3789 or (202) 872-4000.

Guide to Department of Education Programs

The *Guide to Department of Education Programs* is published by the Office of Public Affairs, U.S. Department of Education. This annual provides, in compact form, information necessary to begin the process of applying for federal education program funds. The guide's contents include the following offices: Office of Elementary and Secondary Education; Office of Postsecondary Education; Office of Educational Research and Improvement; Office of Bilingual Education and Minority Languages Affairs; Office of Vocational and Adult Education; and Office of Special Education and Rehabilitation Services. Contact the U.S. Department of Education, 400 Maryland Avenue, SW, Washington, D.C. 20202. Phone (202) 245-3792.

Other Information Sources

The Grantsmanship Center

The Grantsmanship Center offers a loose-leaf collection of reprints from *The Grantsmanship Center News* that provides practical advice and information on program planning and proposal writing, funding strategies, and many more areas of interest to nonprofit grant seekers. Contact The Grantsmanship Center, 1125 W. Sixth Street, Fifth Floor, P.O. Box 17220, Los Angeles, CA 90017. Phone (213) 482-9860.

Office of Educational Research and Improvement (OERI)

The U.S. Department of Education's Office of Educational Research and Improvement (OERI) supports and conducts research on education, collects and analyzes education statistics, administers grant and contract programs to improve libraries and library education, and disseminates information to teachers, school administrators, policymakers, researchers, and grant seekers. One avenue that they use is the OERI-funded Regional Educational Laboratories. These laboratories "plan programs through an ongoing assessment of regional needs, a knowledge of the current trends in research and practice, and interaction with the many other agencies and institutions that assist communities and schools with educational improvement" (*Institutional Projects Funded by OERI*, 1992, p. 50). These laboratories and their respective phone numbers are shown in Figure 2.3. Most also have 800 toll-free numbers.

The OERI also oversees and funds an Education Resources Information Center (ERIC) system, a network of clearinghouses and a small number of adjunct clearinghouses, and four support components. "ERIC is the largest education database in the world—containing nearly 700,000 bibliographic records of documents and journal articles; approximately 2,600 records are added monthly. Papers,

——**Grant Tip**——
OERI's Labs, ERIC Centers, and National Research and Development Centers should come in handy when providing a review of literature, a state of the art.

Figure 2.3. Regional Educational Laboratories Funded by OERI

Regional Educational Laboratories
Appalachia Educational Laboratory • Charleston, WV 25325 • 304/347-0400 or 800/624-9120
Far West Lab for Educational Research and Development • San Francisco, CA 94103 • 415/565-3000
Mid-Continent Regional Educational Laboratory • Aurora, CO 80014 • 303/337-0990
North Central Regional Educational Laboratory • Oak Brook, IL 60521 • 708/571-4700
Northwest Regional Educational Laboratory • Portland, OR 97204 • 503/275-9500
Pacific Region Educational Laboratory • Honolulu, HA 96813 • 808/532-1900
Regional Lab for Educational Improvement of the NE & Islands • Andover, MA 01810 • 508/470-0098
Research for Better Schools • Philadelphia, PA 19123 • 215/574-9300
Southeastern Regional Vision for Education • Greensboro, NC 27435 • 800/755-3277
Southwest Educational Development Laboratory • Austin, TX 78701 • 512/476-6861

conference proceedings, literature reviews, and curriculum materials, along with articles from nearly 800 education-related journals, are indexed and abstracted for entry into the ERIC database" (*All About Eric,* 1990, p. 1). Figure 2.4 provides a list of the clearinghouses, addresses, and phone numbers. About 900 locations are designated as ERIC information service providers. ERIC offers free reference and referral services to the grantwriter through its network of clearinghouses and toll-free number. For assistance or more information, call 1-800-USE-ERIC.

In addition to the labs and ERIC centers, the OERI funds and oversees the National Research and Development Centers. These centers conduct research on topics of national significance to educational policy and practice. Each center's role is to exercise leadership in its mission area; conduct research and development that advance theory and practice; attract the sustained attention of expert researchers to concentrate on problems in education; create a long-term interaction between researchers and educators; participate in a network for collaborative exchange in the education community; and disseminate research findings in useful forms to education policymakers

Figure 2.4. ERIC Clearinghouses and System Components

ERIC Clearinghouses and System Components
ACCESS ERIC • 1600 Research Boulevard • Rockville, MD • 800/USE-ERIC
Adjunct ERIC Clearinghouse on Literacy Education • Washington, D.C. • 202/429-9292
Clearinghouse on Adult, Career, and Vocational Education • Columbus, OH • 800/848-4815
Clearinghouse on Counseling and Personnel Services • Ann Arbor, MI • 313/764-9492
Clearinghouse on Educational Management • Eugene, OR • 503/686-5043
Clearinghouse on Elementary and Early Childhood Education • Urbana, IL • 217/333-1386
Clearinghouse on Handicapped and Gifted Children • Reston, VA • 703/620-3660
Clearinghouse on Higher Education • Washington, D.C. • 202/296-2597
Clearinghouse on Information Resources • Syracuse, NY • 315/443-3650
Clearinghouse for Junior Colleges • Los Angeles, CA • 213/825-3931
Clearinghouse on Languages and Linguistics • Washington, D.C. • 202/429-9551
Clearinghouse on Reading and Communication Skills • Bloomington, IN • 812/855-5847
Clearinghouse on Rural Education and Small Schools • Charleston, WV • 800/344-6646
Clearinghouse for Science, Mathematics, & Environmental Education • Columbus, OH • 614/292-6717
Clearinghouse for Social Studies/Social Science Education • Bloomington, IN • 812/855-3838
Clearinghouse on Teacher Education • Washington, D.C. • 202/293-2450
Clearinghouse on Tests, Measurement, and Evaluation • Washington, D.C. • 202/342-5060
Clearinghouse on Urban Education • New York, NY • 212/678-3433
Document Reproduction Service • Alexandria, VA • 800/227-3742
Processing and Reference Facility • Rockville, MD • 301/258-5500

and practitioners. Figure 2.5 lists each center and provides respective addresses and phone numbers.

The OERI also funds such things as the Leadership in Educational Administration Development (LEAD) Programs (one per state), the National Diffusion Network State Facilitator Projects (one per state), Development/Demonstration Projects, and four Star School Demonstration Projects.

Figure 2.5. National Research and Development Centers

National Research and Development Centers

Center for Learning and Teaching of Elementary Subjects • East Lansing, MI • 517/353-6470
Center for Research on Context of Secondary School Teaching • Stanford, CA • 415/723-4972
Center for Research on Effective Schooling for Disadvantaged Students • Baltimore, MD • 301/338-7570
Center for Technology in Education • New York, NY • 212/222-6700
Center on Families, Communities, Schools, & Children's Learning • Boston, MA • 617/353-3909
Center on Organization and Restructuring of Schools • Madison, WI • 608/263-7575
Finance Center of the Consortium for Policy Research in Education • Los Angeles, CA • 213/740-3450
Nat'l Center for Adult Literacy • Philadelphia, PA • 215/898-2100
Nat'l Center for Educational Leadership • Cambridge, MA • 617/495-3575
Nat'l Center for Research in Mathematical Sciences Education • Madison, WI • 608/263-4285
Nat'l Center for Research on Educ. Accountability & Teacher Evaluation • Kalamazoo, MI • 616/387-5895
Nat'l Center for Research on Teacher Learning • East Lansing, MI • 517/355-9302
Nat'l Center for School Leadership • Urbana, IL • 217/244-1122 or 800/356-0069
Nat'l Center for Science Teaching & Learning • Columbus, OH • 614/292-3339
Nat'l Center for the Study of Writing & Literacy • Berkeley, CA • 415/643-7022
Nat'l Center on Education in the Inner Cities • Philadelphia, PA • 215/787-3001
Nat'l Center on Educational Quality of the Workforce • Philadelphia, PA • 215/898-4585
Nat'l Center on Postsecondary Teaching, Learning, & Assessment • University Park, PA • 814/865-5917
Nat'l Research Center on Cultural Diversity & Second Language Learning • Santa Cruz, CA • 408/549-3501
Nat'l Research Center on Literature Teaching & Learning • Albany, NY • 518/442-5026
Nat'l Research Center on Student Learning • Pittsburgh, PA • 412/624-7450
Nat'l Research Center on the Gifted & Talented • Storrs, CT • 203/486-5279
Policy Center of the Consortium for Policy Research in Education • New Brunswick, NJ • 908/828-3872
Reading Research and Education Center • Champaign, IL • 217/333-2552

The OERI provides publications available from OERI's Education Information Branch (EIB) or from the Government Printing Office (GPO). Contact the Education Information Branch, Capitol Plaza Building, Suite 300, 555 New Jersey Avenue, SW, Washington, D.C. 20208. Phone (800) 424-1616 or (202) 357-6556.

Depository Library Program

Information from the federal government is available at Depository Libraries around the U.S. and its territories. Each working day, federal agencies provide these libraries with information. As noted in Figure 2.6, there are two Depository Libraries designated in any part the state by each Senator, two in each congressional district, one at each land-grant university. According to Joint Committee Print (*A Directory of U.S. Government Depository Libraries,* 1990), almost 1,400 libraries have been designated as depositories. These libraries participate in the Depository Library Program established by Congress to allow the public free access to government publications. Each year Depository Libraries select titles from more than 25,000 new government publications. Fifty regional Depository Libraries receive every unclassified government publication of interest to the public and have undertaken the responsibility of retaining this material permanently, on paper or microfiche. Figure 2.7 is a map with the number of Depository Libraries per state. Inter-library loan and reference services are also provided. To find the Depository Library in your area, contact your local library or write to the Superintendent of Documents, Washington, D.C. 20402.

Figure 2.6. Types of Libraries Designated

	Types of Libraries Designated
870	2 libraries for each congressional district designated by the Representative
200	2 libraries for each state designated by each Senator
2	2 libraries designated by the Resident Commissioner from Puerto Rico
2	2 libraries designated by the Mayor of the District of Columbia
1	1 library designated by the Governor of American Samoa
1	1 library designated by the Governor of Guam
2	2 libraries designated by the Governor of the Virgin Islands
55	Highest state appellate court libraries
50	State libraries
72	Libraries of the land-grant colleges
14	Libraries of the executive departments in Washington
125	Libraries of the independent agencies and of major bureaus/divisions of departments and agencies
5	Libraries of the U.S. military academies
175	Law school libraries

Figure 2.7. Number of Depository Libraries Per State

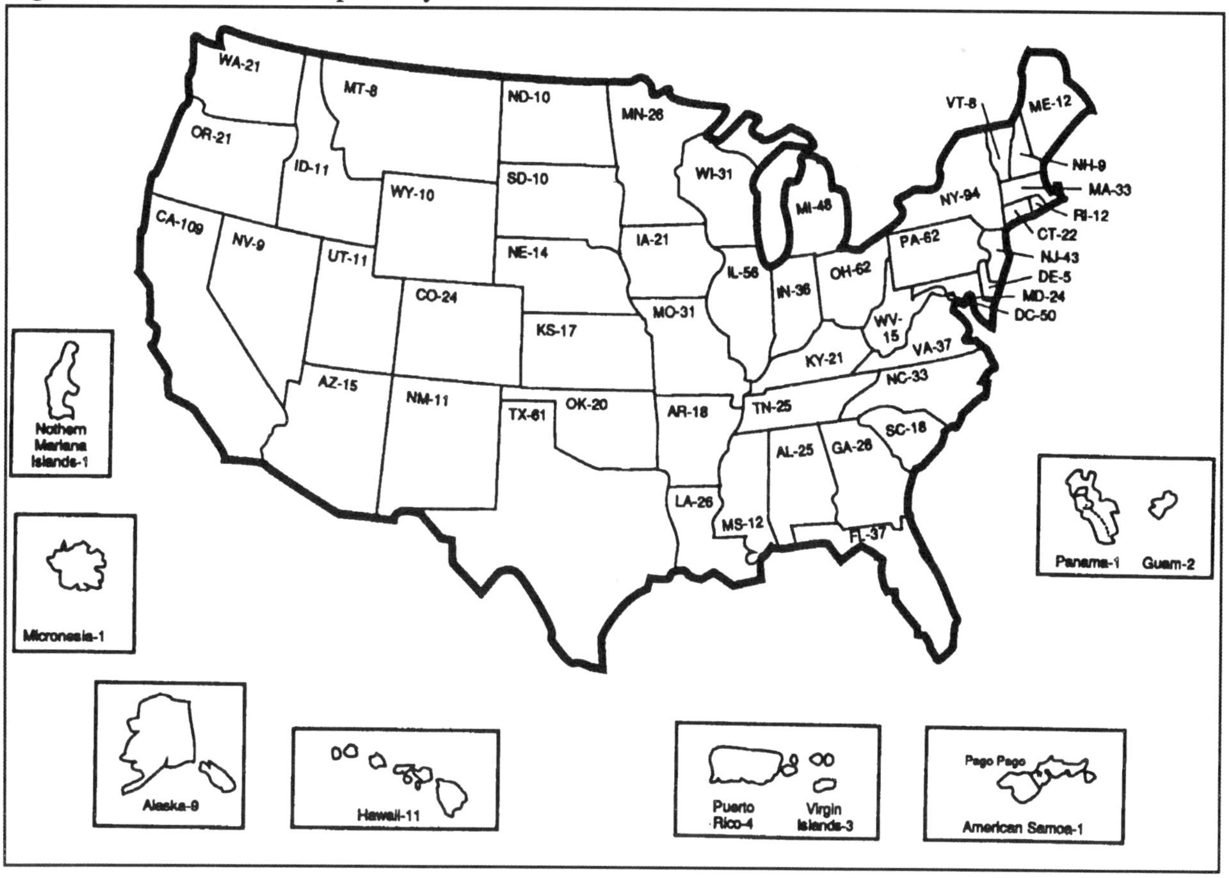

Foundation and Corporation Directories

Many foundation and corporation directories are on the market. *The Foundation Directory* is a major publication describing over 4,000 of the largest foundations in the U.S. Financial data (assets, number of grant awards, etc.) are provided along with information on the types of support generally awarded, geographic and other giving restrictions, application deadlines, etc. There is also a *Foundation Directory Supplement* that provides updates six months after publication of the *Directory* itself. To make this set complete, *The Foundation Directory Part 2* is available and provides information on midsize foundations ($25,000 to $100,000) whereas the other publication ad-dresses those foundations with annual grants totaling at least $100,000. The 1993 costs for these publications were $185 for *The Foundation Directory,* $110 for *The Foundation Directory*

Supplement, and $160 for *The Foundation Directory Part 2.* The Foundation Center produces a variety of publications (*National Data Book of Foundations, Foundation Grants Index, The National Directory of Corporate Giving, Grant Guides,* etc.). Write The Foundation Center, 79 Fifth Avenue, New York, New York 10003. Phone (800) 424-9836 or (212) 620-4230.

The Taft Corporation publishes a two-volume set of reference directories that combines information on corporate and foundation funding sources. *The Directory of Corporate and Foundation Givers* provides information on approximately 8,000 private foundations, corporate foundations, and corporate direct giving programs. The *Foundation Reporter* gives detailed information (foundation philosophy, financial summaries, typical recipients, enumerates recent grants, etc.) on the 588 leading foundations in the U.S. The 1993 cost for the *Directory* was $195 and $327 for the *Reporter.* For more information on these publications, contact The Taft Group, 835 Penobscot Building, Detroit, MI 48226. Phone (800) 877-8238.

National Science Foundation (NSF)

The National Science Foundation (NSF) funds many educational programs. The NSF's *Grants for Research and Education in Science and Engineering Guide* provides guidance for the preparation of unsolicited proposals to NSF. Some NSF programs operate from more specific program announcements or solicitations. The general provisions of this *Guide* apply to all NSF programs to the extent that they are not modified by individual program announcements or solicitations. Information about program deadlines and target dates for proposals appears in the *NSF Bulletin,* issued monthly except July and August; copies may be obtained from the Editior, *NSF Bulletin,* NSF, Washington, D.C. 20550. General information about NSF programs may be found in the *Guide to Programs,* available from the Forms and Publications Unit of NSF. Information about special requirements of NSF programs may be obtained from the appropriate program offices.

For information about the NSF grant process, refer to the NSF *Grant Policy Manual,* NSF 77-47, or Chapter VI of Title 45 of the *Code of Federal Regulations.* The *Manual* is a compendium of basic NSF policies and procedures for use by the grant community and NSF staff. NSF grants are subject to the specific provisions contained in the grant instruments, including Grant General Conditions. The *Manual* is available only by subscription for $15.00 from the Superintendent of Documents, Government Printing Office, Washington, D.C. Copies of the Grant General Conditions may be obtained from Forms and Publications, National Science Foundation, Washington, D.C. 20550. Phone (202) 357-7861.

National Endowment for the Arts (NEA)

The *National Endowment for the Arts Guide to Programs* provides, step-by-step instructions on who is eligible, how to apply, deadlines, and amounts available. Contact the appropriate NEA Program Director. Get the *Guide* free of charge by writing to the National Endowment for the Arts, Public Information Office, 1100 Pennsylvania Avenue NE, Washington, D.C. 20506. Phone (202) 682-5400.

National Endowment for the Humanities (NEH)

The *National Endowment for the Humanities Overview of Endowment's Programs* is the sister publication to the NEA's *Guide*. It provides information about the history, purposes, policies, and organization of NEH to help individuals and organizations determine whether proposed projects and activities in the humanities may be eligible for support. It provides information on the activities supported by the Endowment's grant-making programs, as well as a current schedule of application deadlines. The publication is available free by writing to the National Endowment for the Humanities, 1100 Pennsylvania Avenue, SW, Washington, D.C. 20506. Phone (202) 786-0438.

Institutional or Agency Grants Newsletter

Many large institutions and agencies have a grants and research office that disseminates a monthly newsletter to other personnel in the organization. The agency usually abstracts information on upcoming grants, deadlines, etc., to advertise potential funding sources and new programs. However, information may not be all that helpful because the reporting is remote from the original source.

——**Grant Tip**——

The NEA Guide *and the* NEH Overview *are both* free *and they provide valuable information for developing proposals to* NEA and NEH.

Word-of-Mouth

Word-of-mouth sources can be helpful. Professional conventions and visits to institutions, agencies, or both, are excellent avenues to pertinent grant information. Talk to people who have been successful in obtaining grants. Scan professional newsletters and journals but be aware that this may be old information and not as helpful as other sources identified in this chapter.

Summary

This chapter has provided selected information regarding various reference sources to aid in the processes of grant seeking and grant administration. The chapter does not include all sources on the market; it concentrates on the sources most frequently used by proposal writers and administrators in education. The listing is not intended to be comprehensive, and omission or inclusion of a source does not imply endorsement or rejection. The most essential and basic. publications for federal sources of grant support and administration requirements are the *Federal Register, Code of Federal Regulations,* and the *Catalog of Federal Domestic Assistance,* which are explained in more detail in subsequent chapters.

Many good newsletters and grant information services cover government funding sources; however, the government is the original source for its information. Because information on grants is so widely disseminated, do not get absorbed with information that is outdated or of little value. It is sometimes difficult to ascertain what information is pertinent or what the full scope is of an anticipated program coming up for funding. If that is the case, contact the U.S. Department of Education directly for answers to specific questions. The grant application package is the comprehensive word and serves as the main resource for directions that will help you respond to a program with a competitive proposal document.

——**Grant Tip**——
Sometimes it is difficult to ascertain what information is correct. Contact the U.S. Department of Education directly. The application package is comprehensive and will serve as your main resource.

3

Using the *Federal Register (FR)* and the *Code of Federal Regulations (CFR)*

Introduction

Chapter 2, "How to Explore Grant Possibilities in Education," identified and provided a brief description of some basic information sources that are important in responding to requests for federal educational grants. Some sources, such as the *Federal Register (FR), Code of Federal Regulations (CFR),* and the *Catalog of Federal Domestic Assistance (CFDA),* deserve more attention because they are the official federal government documents to inform the public and, more specifically, the grant seeker and grant administrator of the various grant programs. This chapter provides detailed information both on the *Federal Register* and the *Code of Federal Regulations,* which often must be used together. Chapter 4 covers the *Catalog of Federal Domestic Assistance* in more detail and explains how to use the *CFDA* effectively in responding to federal grants in education.

There are many excellent commercial newsletters and information services regarding federal grants in education. However, the federal government is the original source for their information. Therefore, the *Federal Register* and the *Code of Federal Regulations* are the two most essential publications for federal sources of support and grant administration requirements.

The Federal Register System

The Federal Register System is composed mainly of two major publications, the daily *Federal Register* and the annual *Code of Federal Regulations*, which are described in this chapter. These two publications together provide a current version of any federal agency's regulations. Congress established the Federal Register Publication System as a unified method of informing the public of regulations. In the surge of New Deal legislation enacted in the 1930s, Congress delegated more responsibility to federal departments and agencies in

---

the form of authority to issue detailed regulations dealing with complex social and economic issues. As programs were in the making and more regulations were written, a serious communications problem evolved. With no central publication system, there was no efficient way for the public to know about the various regulations that affected them. Therefore, a central publication system was established to manage effectively the increased number and expanded scope of federal regulations.

Federal Register Act

The Federal Register Act (became law on July 26, 1935) established a systematic approach for handling agency regulations (44 U.S.C. Chapter l5). Prior to l935 you would have to go directly to the federal agency and review a couple of typed or written pages. The act established a uniform system for handling agency regulations by requiring the following:

- Submitting and filing documents with the Office of the Federal Register.
- Placing documents on public inspection.
- Publishing documents in the *Federal Register.*
- After a 1937 amendment to the Act, codifying rules in the *Code of Federal Regulations.*

Administrative Procedure Act

The Administrative Procedure Act (became law on June 11, 1946) added several new dimensions to the Federal Register System (5 U.S.C. 55l et seq.). This act specifically provided for

- Giving the public (but with some stated exceptions) the right to participate in the rulemaking process by commenting on proposed rules.
- Requiring that the effective date for a regulation be not less than 30 days from the date of publication of the final rules unless there was good cause for an earlier date.
- Providing for publication of agency statements of organization and procedural rules.

The Federal Register Act and the Administrative Procedure Act, as outlined above, define the basic functions of the Federal Register System and provide the framework for the promulgation of

——— Grant Tip———
The daily FR *and the annually revised* CFR *work together to provide an up-to-date version of any agency's regulations.*

government regulations. As mentioned before, the System is composed primarily of two major publications, the daily *Federal Register* and the annually revised *Code of Federal Regulations*. These two publications work together to provide an up-to-date version of any agency's regulations. To understand the system, one needs to understand each separate publication as well as the relationship between the two publications. Figure 3.1 displays how this total system works together.

Figure 3.1. The Federal Register System Flowchart

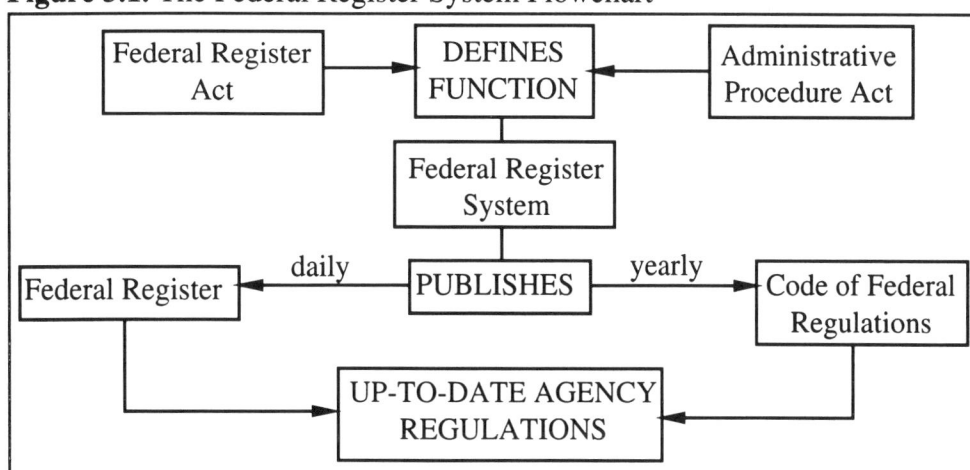

The *Federal Register (FR)*

The executive branch's two official dailies are the *Federal Register* and the *Commerce Business Daily*. Typically, grant programs are announced in the *Federal Register* and contract solicitations appear in the *Commerce Business Daily*. In harmony with the scope of this book, we do not go into great detail discussing the *Commerce Business Daily* but focus our attention on the *Federal Register*.

The *Federal Register* is published every federal working day by the Office of the Federal Register (OFR), National Archives and Records Administration in Washington, D.C. The *Federal Register* provides a uniform system for making available to the public regulations and legal notices issued by federal agencies and the President. These include presidential proclamations and executive orders and federal agency documents having general applicability and legal effect, documents required to be published by act of Congress, and other federal agency documents of public interest. Documents are on file for public inspection in the Office of the Federal Register (OFR) the day before publication, unless earlier filing is requested by the issuing agency. Distribution is made only by the Superintendent of Documents, U.S. Government Printing Office.

To provide a uniform system, the documents are categorized and published under the five main title headings: Presidential, Rules and Regulations, Proposed Rules, Notices, and Sunshine Act Meetings. These document categories are reviewed in the following paragraphs.

Document Categories of the *Federal Register*

Presidential Document

These are documents signed by the President and submitted to the Office of the Federal Register (OFR) for publication. Documents in this category include the following:

- Proclamations,
- Executive orders,
- Memorandums,
- Orders,
- Presidential determinations, and
- Reorganization plans.

There is an example of a proclamation (Figure 3.2) on page 53. This document was issued by the President of the United States and put in the *Federal Register* immediately after it was signed.

Rules and Regulations

These are regulatory documents that have general applicability and legal effect. The *Federal Register* publication system considers the terms "rules" and "regulations" as similar. According to the OFR's *Document Drafting Handbook* (Fox, Nanovic, & Sowada, 1986), documents in this category are classified as follows:

1. **Documents that amend the CFR.** These documents amend the *Code of Federal Regulations (CFR)* by adding new text or by revising or removing existing text. A document that

Figure 3.2. An Example of a Presidential Document

3401

Federal Register	**Presidential Documents**

Vol. 54, No. 13

Monday, January 23, 1989

Title 3 —   Proclamation 5935 of January 18, 1989

The President   National Day of Excellence, 1989

By the President of the United States of America

A Proclamation

On this third anniversary of the Space Shuttle Challenger's tragic accident, the lines of Tennyson in his poem "Ulysses" seem most appropriate:

Come, my friends,
"Tis not too late to seek a newer world.
It may be that the gulf will wash us down;
It may be that we touch the Happy Isles,
And see the great Achilles, whom we knew.
Tho' much is taken, much abides; . . .

Indeed, much was taken when we lost Challenger's brave crew. Yet much abides, because the American people will forever remember them and salute the devotion to excellence that characterized them and continues to characterize the members of the U.S. space program. That spirit has manifested itself again and again as we have journeyed to the moon and probed planets, our solar system, and beyond. It thrives today as we seek a permanent base in space and further manned exploration.

The Challenger crew made the supreme sacrifice on their quest to extend man's horizons. As we resolve to go forward in space, let us always take with us the spirit of vision, skill, and excellence.

That spirit was evident on September 29, 1988, when the Space Shuttle Discovery lifted off from the launch pad. There could be no more fitting testimony to the Challenger crew and the excellence they personified than this mission, which returned our Nation to manned space flight. May our boundless dreams continue to inspire us in the pursuit of excellence—in space and in every endeavor.

The Congress, by Public Law 100-681, has designated January 28, 1989, as "National Day of Excellence" and authorized and requested the President to issue a proclamation in observance of that day.

NOW, THEREFORE, I, RONALD REAGAN, President of the United States of America, do hereby proclaim January 28, 1989, as National Day of Excellence. I call upon the people of the United States to observe that day with appropriate ceremonies and activities.

IN WITNESS WHEREOF, I have hereunto set my hand this eighteenth day of January, in the year of our Lord nineteen hundred and eighty-nine, and of the Independence of the United States of America the two hundred and thirteenth.

[FR Doc. 89-1577
Filed 1-19-89; 11:00 am]
Billing code 3195-01-M

amends *CFR* text must publish each change to the *CFR* in full and state the effective date for any change.

2. **Documents that are interim or temporary rule.** Interim or temporary rule documents are effective immediately for a short or definable period of time. They have the same effect as a final rule in that they amend the *CFR* and give an effective date. However, in issuing an interim or temporary rule, the agency often asks for public comment. After the comment period expires, the agency may consider adjustments to the interim or temporary rule before issuing the final rule.

3. **Documents that affect other documents.** These documents affect other documents previously published in the rules and regulations section and typically include the following:

   • Corrections to previously published rules.
   • Any change of the effective date of a previously published rule.
   • Any document changing the comment period of an interim or temporary rule.
   • Suspension of a previously published rule.
   • Withdrawal of a previously published rule not yet in effect.
   • Petition for reconsideration of a previously published rule.

4. **Documents that have no regulatory text.** These documents have no regulatory text and do not amend the *CFR* but either affect the agency's handling of its regulations or are of continuing interest to the public in dealing with an agency. The Administrative Conference of the United States, in Recommendation No. 76-2, recommends that these documents be preserved in the *CFR*. These types of documents are as follows:

   • General policy statements.
   • Interpretations of agency regulations.
   • Statements of organization and function.

On pages 55 and 56, Figure 3.3 is a copy of this type of document. This rules and regulations document issued by the U.S. Department of Education identifies the specific office (Office of Elementary and Secondary Education), the *CFR* number, the title, and the action taken in reference to the regulations.

Figure 3.3. An Example of a Rules and Regulations Document

6858   Federal Register / Vol. 54, No. 29 / Tuesday, February 14, 1989 / Rules and Regulations

DEPARTMENT OF EDUCATION

Office of Elementary and Secondary Education

34 CFR Part 222

Assistance for Local Educational Agencies in Areas Affected by Federal Activities and Arrangements for Education of Children Where Local Educational Agencies Cannot Provide Suitable Free Public Education

AGENCY: Department of Education.

ACTION: Final Regulations.

SUMMARY: The Secretary removes a regulatory provision, 34 CFR 222.95(d)(2) (53 FR 5556, February 24, 1988), promulgated under the Impact Aid law, Pub. L. 81-874 (the Act). That regulatory provision denies eligibility for funds under section 2 of the Act to a local educational agency (LEA) in a State with an equalized program of State aid meeting the requirements of section 5(d)(2) of the Act if that State, in allocating State aid, takes into consideration payments received by the LEA under section 2 of the Act. The Secretary removes this provision because of changes to the Impact Aid law made by the Augustus F. Hawkins-Robert T. Stafford Elementary and Secondary School Improvement Amendments of 1988 (the Hawkins-Stafford Amendments), enacted April 28, 1988. The removal is effective beginning with payments to be made from fiscal year (FY) 1988 Impact Aid funds.

EFFECTIVE DATE: This regulatory change takes place either 45 days after publication in the Federal Register or later if the Congress takes certain adjournments. If you want to know the effective date of these final regulations, call or write the Department of Education contact person.

FOR FURTHER INFORMATION CONTACT: Mr. Charles Hansen, Director, Impact Aid Program, U.S. Department of Education, 400 Maryland Avenue, SW., Room 2079, Washington, DC 20202-6272. Telephone: (202) 732-3637.

SUPPLEMENTARY INFORMATION:

Background

Final Regulations governing eligibility and entitlement determinations under section 2 of the Impact Aid program (Pub. L. 81-874) were published in the Federal Register on February 24, 1988 (53 FR 5552). Section 222.95(d)(2) of the regulations provides, in effect, that an LEA in a State that has an equalized program of State aid qualifying under section 5(d)(2) of the Act is not eligible for section 2 assistance if the State takes into consideration the LEA's section 2 payments in determining that LEA's eligibility for or amount of State aid. (53 FR 5556). Prior to the publication of those regulations, a State certified under section 5(d)(2) could take into consideration any Impact Aid funds (except the additional funds paid for certain handicapped children, heavily-impacted school districts, or school districts with unusual geographical factors) with no penalty to either the State or its LEAs.

The Secretary now removes § 222.95(d)(2) of the regulations, because the Secretary interprets provisions in the Hawkins-Stafford Amendments as effectively nullifying the policy underlying that regulatory provision. First, in the Hawkins-Stafford Amendments, Congress overturned a policy embodied in a regulatory provision to which § 222.95(d)(2) was tied. Under the related provision, 34 CFR 222.100 (53 FR 5552, 5557-58) (February 24, 1988), the computation of the maximum section 2 payment was to be changed so that, beginning with FY 1988 payments, it would be based upon only the "unequalized" portion of an LEA's local real property tax rate.

Many states "equalize" part or all of the local real property tax rate, so that an LEA receives from the State the difference between a guaranteed State aid amount and its local real property tax revenues generated from a mandated tax levy. To the extent such equalization exists, when the Department uses the LEA's full tax rate to compute the section 2 maximum entitlement, the LEA arguably does not experience a revenue loss attributable to the Federal property because State aid compensates for any lack of property tax

revenues. In that situation, a State's deduction of section 2 revenues under section 5(d)(2) of the Act justifiably would further the State's equalization efforts.

In order not to pay section 2 funds where State aid already compensates for a lack of property tax revenues, beginning with FY 1988 under the Department's regulations the section 2 maximum payment was to be based only on the unequalized portion of the LEA's tax rate, i.e., the portion producing revenues not deducted from the State guarantee because they are raised voluntarily in addition to the required amount. The State's consideration of the section 2 funds, when thus calculated, would prevent those funds from compensating a true loss. The Department therefore provided in § 222.95(d)(2) of the regulations that if a State did consider the section 2 revenues in allocating State aid, the LEAs in that State would not be eligible for further section 2 payments. See 53 FR 552, 5562 (February 24, 1988).

In the Hawkins-Stafford Amendments, however, Congress specifically overturned the policy in § 222.100 regarding the calculation of the maximum section 2 payments, effective beginning with FY 1989 Impact Aid payments (Pub. L. 100-297, section 2013). Section 222.100 was effective beginning with FY 1988 funds and would therefore have been effective for only one fiscal year. As a result of the anticipated burden on States and LEAs of a one-year implementation, the Department suspended the use of the unequalized tax rate methodology for FY 1988. 53 FR 26772 (July 15, 1988). With the suspension of § 222.100, which provided the major rationale for § 222.95(d)(2), the basis for § 222.95(d)(2) is effectively eliminated.

Further, in the Hawkins-Stafford Amendments, Congress prohibited States certified under section 5(d)(2) of the Act from taking into consideration certain *other* Impact Aid payments. (Pub. L. 100-297, section 2015(f), amending section 5(d)(2) of Pub. L. 81-874). The omission of "section 2 payments" from the list of prohibited State deductions in the Hawkins-Stafford Amendments can be seen as evidence that Congress intended that "section 5(d)(2)" States be permitted to continue their consideration of section 2 funds.

Figure 3.3 Continued. An Example of a Rules and Regulations Document

Federal Register / Vol. 54, No. 29 / Tuesday, February 14, 1989 / Rules and Regulations   6859

Because the Hawkins-Stafford Amendments are effective for FY 1989 payments (see Pub. L. 100-351 (June 27, 1988)), while the regulations published on February 24, 1988, were effective for FY 1988, § 222.95(d)(2) could be implemented for FY 1988 payments. However, the Secretary is removing § 222.95(d)(2) of the regulations effective for payments from FY 1988 appropriations that have not been made as of the effective date of these final regulations. The application of this provision for only one year would cause fiscal disruption to LEAs and their States, as well as an administrative burden to States should they seek to avoid the penalty to their LEAs by readjusting their FY 1988 State aid payments so as not to consider section 2 funds. If, however, a State has already taken that action, the removal of the regulatory provision does not penalize the State or LEAs, but preserves for the State the choice of whether to consider section 2 funds in allocating State aid in any fiscal year.

The Department has not yet made any FY 1988 section 2 payments to LEAs in States certified under section 5(d)(2) of the Act that would be affected by the provision. The removal of the provision for FY 1988 will therefore preserve the pre-existing status quo, under which "section 5(d)(2)" States are able to consider section 2 funds in allocating State aid.

Waiver of Notice of Proposed Rule-making

In accordance with section 431(b)(2)(A) of the General Education Provisions Act (20 U.S.C. 1232(b)(2)(A)), and the Administrative Procedure Act, 5 U.S.C. 553, it is the Secretary's practice to offer interested parties the opportunity to comment on proposed regulations. In this case, however, the Secretary interprets recent legislation (the Hawkins-Stafford Amendments) as overturning the policy in 34 CFR 222.95(d)(2), effective beginning with FY 1989 funding. The Secretary has determined that it would be administratively burdensome and fiscally disruptive to applicants and States to apply that regulatory provision for only one year, i.e., to FY 1988 payments. It is important that the removal of the regulatory provision take effect immediately to enable the Secretary to make FY 1988 section 2 pay-

ments to the LEAs in affected States.

Removing the regulatory provision effective for FY 1988 payments would have the effect of allowing "section 5(d)(2)" States to continue deducting section 2 payments in allocating State aid and permitting eligible LEAs in those States to continue receiving their section 2 payments. The Secretary therefore anticipates that the removal of the provision will have no adverse impact on States or LEAs. Because this action is in accordance with the public comment received when this provision was published as a proposed regulation in 1987 (52 FR 16144, 16152 (May 1, 1987)), and is beneficial to applicants, the Secretary does not anticipate that any further comment period would provide the Department with additional information or new comments.

Therefore, the Secretary has determined that publication of a proposed rule is impracticable, unnecessary, and contrary to the public interest under 5 U.S.C. 553(b)(B).

Executive Order 12291

These regulations have been reviewed in accordance with Executive Order 12291. They are not classified as major because they do not meet the criteria for major regulations established in the order.

Regulatory Flexibility Act Certification

The Secretary has determined that these regulations will not have the type of impact on a sufficient number of small entities that would require analysis under the Regulatory Flexibility Act. The small entities that would be affected by these final regulations are small LEAs receiving Federal funds under this program. However, only those LEAs entitled to section 2 funds would be affected, and of those, LEAs in no more than three States would be affected, and only for FY 1988 payments.

Paperwork Reduction Act of 1980

These regulations have been examined under the Paperwork Reduction Act of 1980 and have been found to contain no information collection requirements.

List of Subjects in 34 CFR Part 222

Education, Elementary and secondary education, Federally affected areas, Grant programs—education.

Dated: February 6, 1989.

Lauro F. Cavazos,

Secretary of Education.

(Catalog of Federal Domestic Assistance No. 84.041, School Assistance in Federally Affected Areas—Maintenance and Operations.)

The Secretary amends Part 222 of Title 34 of the Code of Federal Regulations as follows:

PART 222—ASSISTANCE FOR LOCAL EDUCATIONAL AGENCIES IN AREAS AFFECTED BY FEDERAL ACTIVITIES AND ARRANGEMENTS FOR EDUCATION OF CHILDREN WHERE LOCAL EDUCATIONAL AGENCIES CANNOT PROVIDE SUITABLE FREE PUBLIC EDUCATION

1. The authority citation for Part 222 continues to read as follows:

    Authority: 20 U.S.C. 236-241-1 and 242-244, unless otherwise noted.

2. Section 222.95 is amended by revising paragraph (d) and the authority citation to read as follows:

§ 222.95 What constitutes a substantial and continuing financial burden?
*   *   *   *   *

(d) The Secretary determines that a substantial and continuing burden does not exist if the amount obtained in paragraph (b) of this section is zero or less.

(Authority: 20 U.S.C. 237(a)(2).)

[FR Doc. 89-3466 Filed 2-13-89; 8:45 am]

BILLING CODE 4000-01-M

Proposed Rules

These documents notify the public of the issuance of proposed rules and regulations. The OFR classifies the following types of documents as proposed rules for publication in the *Federal Register:*

- •Documents that suggest changes to agency regulations in the *CFR* and request public comments on those suggested changes. Most of the documents in this section are required to be published as proposals by section 553 of the Administrative Procedure Act (APA) or other statutory authority. Some regulations are exempted from notice an comment requirements. Many agencies voluntarily publish these regulations in proposed form to allow public comment.

- •Documents that affect other documents previously published in the proposed rule section. These documents may do the following:

  —Extend the comment period
  —Announce a public hearing
  —Publish or announce the availability of supplemental
    information
  —Withdraw a proposed rule or terminate a proposed
    rule proceeding
  —Correct a previously published proposed rule document.

- •Any document that serves as the first public notice that a rulemaking proceeding is anticipated. These include the following documents:

  —Advance Notices of Proposed Rulemaking
  —Notices of Inquiry
  —Notices of Intent

Federal agencies issue these documents early in the rulemaking process to receive public reaction as early as possible. These documents describe a problem or situation that implies the possibility of regulatory action by the agency. In accordance to the following, they seek public response concerning the necessity for regulations in the area and the adequacy of the agency's potential regulatory response.

- •Certain petitions for rulemaking are placed in the proposed rule section because the petition proposes to amend, revise, add to, or remove existing regulations in the *CFR,* and the agency requests public comment.

•A document that announces a meeting or hearing that may be the first step in a rulemaking proceeding is placed in the proposed rule section.

•The documents also provide the public with advance notice of anticipated agency rulemaking and allows for comments.

Figure 3.4, page 59, shows the first page of four pages of a Proposed Rules Document issued by the Office of Special Education and Rehabilitation Services. Notice the *action (Notice of proposed rulemaking)* that is to be taken on this document. The Department of Education is proposing to amend the regulations and is seeking comments concerning these proposed regulations. Comments must be received on or before March 31, 1989.

Notices

These are documents other than rules and proposed rules that are applicable to the public and are published for public information. The typical notice documents announce the following:

•Grant application deadlines
•Meetings
•Applications
•Issuance or revocation of licenses
•Availability of environmental impact statements
•Certain petitions
•Orders or decisions affecting named parties

Figure 3.5 on page 63 is a Notice Document. The notice document example states that the deadline to submit this application is March 31, 1989. It also provides valuable information such as deadline date for intergovernmental review, date when applications are available, the amount of funds available, the estimated range of awards, and the estimated number of grants to be funded under this program.

Sunshine Act Meetings

These are notices of meetings published as required by thegovernment in the Sunshine Act (5 U.S.C. 552b(e)(3)).

——**Grant Tip**——

Notice Documents provide valuable information, ranging from deadline dates to estimated number of grants to be funded under this program.

Figure 3.4. An Example of a Proposed Rules Document

6808	Federal Register / Vol. 54, No. 29 / Tuesday, February 14, 1989 / Proposed Rules

DEPARTMENT OF EDUCATION

Office of Special Education and Rehabilitative Services

34 CFR Part 379

Projects With Industry

AGENCY: Department of Education.
ACTION: Notice of proposed rulemaking.

SUMMARY: The Secretary proposes to amend the regulation in Part 379 governing the Projects With Industry (PWI) program by amending existing regulations, and by adding regulations in a new Subpart F to implement requirements in sections 621(f) and 621(h) of the Rehabilitation Act (Act) as added by Pub. L.99-506, the Rehabilitation Act Amendments of 1988. The amendments require: that indicators of minimum compliance with program evaluation standards approved by the National Council on the Handicapped be published in the **Federal Register**; that, beginning with fiscal year 1989, each PWI grantee report to the Secretary at the end of each project year the extent to which it meets the compliance indicators; that continuation funding be provided only to grantees who are carrying out the provisions of their approved grant application and who meet the compliance indicators; and that the Secretary consider geographical distribution of projects and, beginning in fiscal year 1991, past performance of projects in making new grant awards.
DATE: Comments must be received on or before March 31, 1989.
ADDRESSES: All comments concerning these proposed regulations should be addressed to Ann Weinheimer, Acting Director, Policy and Planning Staff, Rehabilitation Services Administration, Mary E. Switzer Building, Room 3220, 330 C Street SW., Washington, DC 20202-2550.

A copy of any comments that concern information collection requirements should also be sent to the Office of Management and Budget at the address listed in the Paperwork Reduction Act section of this preamble.
FOR FURTHER INFORMATION CONTACT: Suzanne Choisser, Rehabilitation Services Administration, Mary E.

Switzer Building, Room 3216, 330 C Street SW., Washington, DC 20202-2550. Telephone (202) 732-1337.

SUPPLEMENTARY INFORMATION:
Development of Evaluation Standards and Proposed Compliance Indicators

In accordance with section 621(d) (1), (3) and (4) of the Act, PWI evaluation standards, based on statutory provisions and successful project practices, were developed by the Rehabilitation Services Administration (RSA) and approved by the National Council on the Handicapped. The evaluation standards are published for information purposes only as an appendix to the proposed regulations. As required by section 621(d)(2) of the Act, an evaluation of the PWI program, using the approved evaluation standards, was conducted in 1985. A report on the evaluation was forwarded to Congress in February 1986.

In the Rehabilitation Act Amendments of 1986, Congress added the requirement that the Secretary develop indicators of what constitutes minimum compliance with the evaluation standards. Proposed indicators have been developed based on the PWI evaluation standards and the results of the national PWI program evaluation. Compliance indicators were developed only for those standards that were determined to be measurable: standard 2—individuals served; standard 4—provision of services at minimum cost to the Federal government; and standard 7—project results. The remaining standards (standard 1—project objectives and activities, standard 3—provision of appropriate services, standard 5—advisory council, and standard 6—project relationships) are already implemented in program regulations as application requirements and were determined not to be susceptible to quantifiable measurement.

The National Association of PWI Grantees (I-NABIR) conducted an unofficial mailing of draft PWI indicators to all current program grantees in January 1988. As a result of this mailing RSA received 35 comments on the draft indicators and made some modifications to the indicators based on the comments. RSA then field tested the draft indicators on a sample of PWI projects in March 1988 and made additional changes based

on the test results.

Following development of the proposed compliance indicators, a Notice of Information Collection Request was published in the **Federal Register** on July 1, 1988 (53 FR 25105). The purpose of the notice was to collect data from the current PWI grantees that would enable RSA to develop a proposed minimum performance level for each compliance indicator. Data, varying in completeness, was received form all 108 PWI grantees. Sixty-two grantees submitted complete data.

A proposed performance level was developed for each compliance indicator based upon analysis of the grantee data, consideration of the data collected in the program evaluation in 1985, and the Department's views as to satisfactory grantee performance. A proposed weight was developed for each compliance indicator based on the Department's assessment of the relative importance of each indicator.

Proposed Compliance Indicators, Performance Levels, and Weights

The purpose of these proposed regulations is to propose compliance indicators, and a weight and minimum level of performance for each indicator, to measure the effectiveness of individual projects in critical performance areas. The proposed indicators would be used to evaluate performance to determine whether a grantee's application for continuation funding should be approved. As a measure of past performance, compliance with the indicators would also be a factor in making new awards beginning in fiscal year 1991.

The principles used by the Department in developing the proposed weights and performance levels for the compliance indicators are:

Principles for Weighting (Assigning Points)

• The most important indicators of a PWI project's success are the placement of individuals in competitive jobs at a reasonable cost to the Federal Government. The proposed regulations therefore allocate the greatest number of points to the four indicators measuring placement and cost.

Figure 3.4 Continued. An Example of a Proposed Rules Document

• The proposed regulations put slightly more emphasis on the placement of persons with severe disabilities than on the placement of recipients of Social Security Insurance or Social Security Disability Insurance (SSI or SSDI) and unemployed persons. While it is recognized that some persons who are receiving SSI or SSDI or who are unemployed for at least six months at the time of project entry will also be counted as persons with severe disabilities, the Secretary believes special and separate emphasis needs to be placed on serving persons from all three of these groups because these individuals are the most difficult to place into competitive employment.

• The actual placement rate and the actual cost per placement achieved by a PWI project are more important than a project meeting the placement and cost projections stated in its grant application; however, sufficient weight is placed on projected performance to discourage applicants from proposing overly meager or ambitious project goals.

• The proposed regulations place less emphasis on compliance indicators involving the number and types of persons with disabilities who are served since the results of the services rendered are considered more important and are measured by the project performance (results) indicators.

Principles for Scoring (Minimum Performance Levels)

• A composite scoring system is proposed. This approach would allow projects with different strengths, the principle upon which the PWI program is based, to continue to receive funding. The maximum possible composite score would be 100 points. A minimum composite score of 60 is proposed. This minimum total passing score would allow projects who perform poorly on a few indicators to be eligible for continuation funding or a new award based on past performance if they have met most of the indicators.

• A minimum performance level would be established for each indicator (for example, serve 60 percent of persons who have severe disabilities). If a project meets the minimum performance level for an indicator, it would receive a specified number of points. If it fails to meet the minimum performance level for an indicator, it would receive no points. Thus, grantees would know exactly what minimum level of performance is expected for each compliance indicator, as well as the relative emphasis placed by the Secretary on each indicator.

• A project's performance would be determined by the data it submits from the most recent complete project year. For those PWI projects that do not meet the minimum passing score on the basis of the previous year's performance, the proposed regulations at $379.46(b) provide an additional opportunity for grantees to meet the compliance indicators, and thus qualify for continuation funding, by submitting data from the first six months of the current project year to demonstrate improved performance.

Application of the Compliance Indicators

• Since grant awards under this program are made near the end of the fiscal year with project periods that run concurrent with the following fiscal year, grantees would receive two years of funding before their performance is measured against the compliance indicators. This is because at the time a grantee receives its second year of funding, or its first continuation award, it will not have available a full project year of data. When a grantee submits its application for its third year of funding, or its second continuation award, it must submit project data from the first year of funding.

• The proposed indicators and minimum performance levels would be first applied to continuation grants funded from fiscal year 1990 appropriations, which will be made by September 30, 1990 and will cover the project year that begins October 1, 1990 and ends September 30, 1991. The awards will be based, in part, on grantee compliance with the indicators. The data used to measure performance will be the twelve months of data from the project year running from October 1, 1988 to September 30, 1989 or, if necessary six months of data from October 1, 1989 through March 31, 1990. Grantees were advised in the July 1, 1988 notice that collection of this data was necessary.

Consideration of Prior Performance and Geographical Location

In making new awards, the proposed regulations provide for giving priority to geographic areas among the States that are currently not served or are underserved by PWI projects and for consideration of past performance, if appropriate. This is consistent with statutory language in sections 621 (h)(3) and (i) of the Act.

Executive Order 12291

These proposed regulations have been reviewed in accordance with Executive Order 12291. They are not classified as major because they do not meet the criteria for major regulations established in the order.

Regulatory Flexibility Act Certification

The Secretary certifies that these proposed regulations would not have a significant economic impact on a substantial number of small entities. The small entities that would be affected by these proposed regulations are nonprofit organizations providing services to or conducting activities for persons with disabilities. However, the regulations would not have a significant economic impact on the organizations affected because the regulations would not impose excessive regulatory burdens or require unnecessary Federal supervision. The regulations would impose minimal requirements to ensure the proper expenditure of program funds.

Paperwork Reduction Act of 1980

Section 379.46 contains information collection requirements. As required by the Paperwork Reduction Act of 1980, the Department of Education will submit a copy of this section to the Office of Management and Budget (OMB) for its review. (44 U.S.C. 3504(h))

Organizations and individuals desiring to submit comments on the information collection requirements should direct them to the Office of Information and Regulatory Affairs, Room 3002, New Executive Office Building, Washington, DC 20503; Attention: James D. Houser.

Figure 3.4 Continued. An Example of a Proposed Rules Document

6810   Federal Register / Vol. 54, No. 29 / Tuesday, February 14, 1989 / Proposed Rules

Invitation to Comment

Interested persons are invited to submit comments and recommendations regarding these proposed regulations.

All comments submitted in response to these proposed regulations will be available for public inspection, during and after the comment period, in Room 3220, Switzer Building, 330 C Street SW., Washington, DC, between the hours of 8:30 a.m. and 4:00 p.m., Monday through Friday of each week except Federal holidays.

To assist the Department in complying with the specific requirements of Executive Order 12291 and the Paperwork Reduction Act of 1980 and their overall requirement of reducing regulatory burden, the Secretary invites comment on whether there may be further opportunities to reduce any regulatory burdens found is these proposed regulations.

List of Subjects in 34 CFR Part 379

Education, Grant programs— education, Grant programs—social programs, Reporting and recordkeeping requirements, Vocational rehabilitation.

Dated: December 27, 1988.
(Catalog of Federal Domestic Assistance Number: 84.128 Projects With Industry)
Lauro F. Cavazos,
Secretary of Education.

The Secretary proposes to amend Part 379 of Title 34 of the Code of Federal Regulations as follows:

PART 379—PROJECTS WITH INDUSTRY

1. The authority citation for Part 379 continues to read as follows:
Authority: 29 U.S.C. 711(c) and 795g, unless otherwise noted.

§ 379.32 [Redesignated from § 379.31]

2. Section 379.31 is redesignated as § 379.32 and a new § 379.31 is added to read as follows:

§379.31 What other factors does the Secretary consider in reviewing an application?

In addition to the selection criteria in § 379.30, the Secretary, in making awards

under this program, considers—
(a) The geographical distribution of projects among the States and gives priority to geographic areas which are currently not served or are underserved by the Projects With Industry program; and

(b) Beginning with fiscal year 1991, the past performance of the applicant in carrying out a similar Project With Industry under previously awarded grants, as indicated by such factors as compliance with grant conditions, soundness of programmatic and financial management practices, and meeting the requirements of Subpart F of this part.

(Authority: Secs. 621(h)(3) and 621(i) of the Act, 29 U.S.C. 795g(h)(3) and 795g(i))

3. Section § 379.46 is revised to read as follows:

§ 379.46 What are the reporting requirements?

(a) Beginning with fiscal year 1990, each application for continuation funding for the third or any subsequent year of a PWI grant must include data for the most recent complete project year in order for the Secretary to determine if the grantee has met the program compliance indicators established in Subpart F of this part.

(b) If the data for the most recent complete project year provided under paragraph (a) shows that any grantee has failed to achieve the minimum composite score required in § 379.52(e) to meet the program compliance indicators, a grantee may, at its option, submit data from the first six months of the current project year to demonstrate that is project performance has improved sufficiently to meet the minimum composite score.
(Authority: Section 621(f)(2) of the Act; 29 U.S.C. 795g(f)(2))

4. Part 379 is amended by adding a new Subpart F, consisting of § § 379.50 through 379.53, to read as follows:

Subpart F—What Requirements Must a Grantee Meet to Receive Continuation Funding?

Sec.
379.50   What are the requirements for continuation funding?
379.51   What are the program compliance indicators?

379.52   Are the compliance indicators weighted?
379.53   What are the weights and minimum performance levels for each compliance indicator?

Subpart F—What Requirements Must a Grantee Meet to Receive Continuation Funding?

§ 379.50 What are the requirements for continuation funding?

Beginning with fiscal year 1990, in order to receive a continuation award for the third or any subsequent year of a PWI grant a grantee shall adhere to the provisions of its approved application and shall receive a minimum composite score of at least 60 points on the program compliance indicators contained in § 379.53.
(Authority: Section 621(h)(4)(B) of the Act; 29 U.S.C. 795g(h)(4)(B))

§ 379.51 What are the program compliance indicators?

The program compliance indicators implement program evaluation standards, which are contained in an appendix to this part, by establishing minimum performance levels in essential project areas to measure the effectiveness of individual grantees.
(Authority: Secs. 621(d)(1) and 621(f)(1) of the Act; 29 U.S.C. 795g(d)(1) and 795g(f)(1))

§ 379.52 Are the compliance indicators weighted?

(a) Each compliance indicator is assigned a certain number of points.

(b) If a grantee meets the minimum performance level for a compliance indicator, it will receive the assigned number of points.

(c) If a grantee does not meet the minimum performance level for a compliance indicator, it will receive no points.

(d) The maximum possible score for meeting the minimum performance level in every compliance indicator is 100 points.

(e) A grantee must receive a composite score of at least 60 points to qualify for continuation funding.
(Authority: 621(h)(4)(B) of the Act; 29 U.S.C. 795g(h)(4)(B))

§ What are the weights and minimum performance levels for each compliance

Figure 3.4 Continued. An Example of a Proposed Rules Document

Federal Register / Vol. 54, No. 29 / Tuesday, February 14, 1989 / Proposed Rules   **6811**

indicator?

(a) *Percent of persons served whose disabilities are severe.* (4 points) A minimum of 60 percent of persons served by the project are persons who have severe disabilities.

(b) *Percent of persons served who have been unemployed for at least six months at time of project entry.* (3 points) A minimum of 60 percent of persons served by the project have been unemployed for at least six months at time of project entry.

(c) *Percent of persons served who received Social Security Insurance (SSI) or Social Security Disability Insurance (SSDI) benefits in the month prior to project entry.* (3 points) A minimum of 25 percent of persons served by the project have received SSI or SSDI benefits in the month prior to project entry.

(d) *Cost per placement.* (20 points) The average cost of placement of individuals served by the project does not exceed $1350.00.

(e) *Projected cost per placement.* (10 points) The actual average cost per placement of persons served by the project does not exceed 125 percent of the projected average cost per placement in the grantee's application.

(f) *Placement rate.* (20 points) A minimum of 60 percent of persons served by the project are placed in competitive employment.

(g) *Projected placement rate.* (10 points) The actual number of persons served by the project that are placed into competitive employment is at least 75 percent of the number of persons that the grantee, in the grant application, projected would be placed.

(h) *Change in earnings.* (10 points) The earnings of persons served by the project who are placed into competitive employment have increased by an average of at least $125.00 a week over earnings at project entry.

(i) *Percent placed who have severe disabilities.* (10 points) At least 60 percent of persons served by the project who are placed into competitive employment are persons who have severe disabilities.

(j) *Percent unemployed placed.* (5 points) At least 60 percent of persons served by the project who are placed into

competitive employment are persons who were unemployed for at least six months at time of project entry.

(k) *Percent SSI or SSDI placed.* (5 points) At least 25 percent of persons served by the project who are placed into competitive employment are persons who received SSI or SSDI benefits in the month prior to project entry.

(l) *Composite chart of weights and minimum performance levels.* The weights and performance levels for each compliance indicator are shown on the following composite chart.

Minimum Scores and Performance Levels for Indicators

Indicator	Weight (points)	Performance level
Persons with severe disabilities served...	4	60%
Unemployed served..	3	60%
SSI or SSDI served...	3	25%
Cost per placement (maximum average).................	20	$1350.00
Projected cost per placement (maximum)............	10	125%
Placement rate.........	20	60%
Projected placement rate......................	10	75%
Change in earnings..	10	$125
Percent with severe disabilities placed..	10	60%
Percent unemployed placed....................	5	60%
Percent SSI or SSDI placed....................	5	25%

Minimum passing composite score is 60 points.

(Authority: Section 621(f)(1) of the Act; 29 U.S.C. 795g(f)(1))

5. An appendix is added to Part 379 to read as follows:

Appendix to Part 379—Evaluation Standards

Standard 1: The primary objective of the project shall be to assist individuals with disabilities to obtain competitive employment. The activities carried out by the project shall support the accomplishment of this objective.

Standard 2: The project shall serve individuals with disabilities that impair their capacity to obtain competitive employment.

In selecting persons to receive services, priority shall be given to individuals with severe disabilities.

Standard 3: The project shall ensure the provision of services that will assist in the placement of persons with disabilities.

Standard 4: Funds shall be used to achieve the project's primary objective at minimum cost to the federal government.

Standard 5: The project's advisory council shall provide policy guidance and assistance in the conduct of the project.

Standard 6: Working relationships, including partnerships, shall be established with agencies and organizations in order to expand the project's capacity to meet its objectives.

Standard 7: The project shall obtain positive results in assisting individuals with disabilities to obtain competitive employment.

[FR Doc. 89-3350 Filed 2-13-89; 8:45 am]
BILLING CODE 4000-01-M

Figure 3.5. An Example of a Notice Document

Federal Register / Vol. 54, No. 29 / Tuesday, February 14, 1989 / Notices   **6741**

DEPARTMENT OF EDUCATION

[CFDA NO. 84.029H1]

Invitation of Applications for New State Grant Awards for Fiscal Year 1989

Title of Program: Training Personnel for the Education of the Handicapped—Grants to State Education Agencies or Institutions of Higher Education.

Purpose of Program: Grants made under this program are for the purpose of assisting States in establishing and maintaining preservice and inservice programs to prepare personnel to meet the needs of handicapped infants, toddlers, children, and youth or supervisors of such persons, consistent with the personnel needs identified in the State's comprehensive system of personnel development.

Deadline For Transmittal of Applications: March 31, 1989.

Deadline For Intergovernmental Review: June 1, 1989.

Applications Available: February 15, 1989.

Total Available Funds: $5,584,500.

Estimated Range of Awards: $75,000—$250,000.

Estimated Number of Awards: 45.

Note.—The Department is not bound by any estimates in this notice.

Average Project Period: 12 months.

Applicable Regulations: [a] The Education Department General Administrative Regulations [EDGAR] in 34 CFR Part 74 [Administration of Grants to Institutions of Higher Education, Hospitals, and Nonprofit Organizations],Part 75 [Direct Grant Programs], Part 77 [Definitions that Apply to Department Regulations], Part 79 [Intergovernmental Review of Department of Education Programs and Activities], Part 80 [Uniform Administrative Requirements for Grants and Cooperative Agreements to State and Local Governments], and Part 85 [Governmentwide Debarment and Suspension[Nonprocurement]; and [b] the regulations for this program in 34 CFR Part 319.

Note.—Part 319 applies only to applications from State educational agencies [SEAs].

Eligible Applicants: Applications for State grants may be submitted by SEAs and, in any State in which the SEA does not apply for such a grant, any institution of higher education [IHE] within such State for those purposes may apply. SEAs that apply for a continuation grant are not eligible for a new State grant in fiscal year 1989. If an SEA chooses not to apply for any State grant award in fiscal year 1989, it must notify all IHEs within the State of this intention by March 3, 1989. Applications by IHEs will be considered only if no new or continuation proposal is received from the SEA.

Description of Program: If applications are submitted by more than one IHE within a State, the Secretary will use the selection criteria in EDGAR [34 CFR 75.210] to evaluate the applications. These regulations authorize the Secretary to distribute an additional 15 points among the selection criteria in 34 CFR 75.210 to bring the total possible points to a maximum of 100 points. For the purpose of this competition, the Secretary will distribute the additional points as follows:

Quality of key personnel, 34 CFR 75.210[b][4]: Three [3] additional points will be added for a possible total of 10 points for this criterion.

Evaluation plan, 34 CFR 75.210[b][6]: Ten [10] additional points will be added for a possible total of 15 points for this criterion.

Adequacy of resources, 34 CFR 75.210[b][7]: Two [2] additional points will be added for a possible total of 5 points for this criterion.

A grant of at least $75,000 will be awarded to meet the needs of each State from which an eligible application is submitted. To determine the amount of a grant the Secretary considers the State's need for assistance and the quality of the application using the criteria published in 34 CFR Part 319. In addition, as required by the Handicapped Programs Technical Amendments Act of 1988, Pub. L. 100—630, the Secretary will ensure that each grant awarded is of sufficient size and scope

to assist States in meeting the requirements of section 632[c] of the Education of the Handicapped Act, as amended.

Funds available for new awards under this program exceed those available for new awards in fiscal year 1988. Therefore, it is anticipated that no State will receive a smaller award than during fiscal year 1988.

For Applications or Information Contact: Frank S. King, U.S. Department of Education, Office of Special Education Programs, Division of Personnel Preparation, 400 Maryland Avenue SW., [Switzer Building, Room 3094—M/S 2651], Washington, DC 20202. Telephone: [202] 732-1086.

Program Authority: 20 U.S.C. 1432.

Dated: February 9, 1989.

[Catalog of Federal domestic Assistance No. 84.029: Training Personnel for the Education of the Handicapped]

Madeleine Will,

Assistant Secretary, Office of Special Education and Rehabilitative Services.

[FR Doc. 89-3467 Field 2-13-89; 8:45 am]

BILLING CODE 4000-01-M

Figure 3.6 on page 65 is a Sunshine Act Meeting Document. This section of the *Federal Register* contains notices of meetings published under the Government in the Sunshine Act.

Structure of the Federal Register

The *Federal Register* is cataloged according to date, day, volume, numbers, and pages. For example, the volume for the 1990 calendar year was 55, with numbers 1 to 251, meaning that the *Federal Register* was issued 251 days in 1990, with the pages being cumulative from 1 to 33,553 throughout the calendar year. Each issue of the *Federal Register* contains the following elements:

- Preliminary pages of finding aids concerning the contents of that issue.

- Documents arranged under the headings of

    — Presidential documents (see example on page 53)
    — Rules and regulations (see example on pages 55 and 56)
    — Proposed rules (see example on pages 59-62)
    — Notices (see example on page 63)
    — Sunshine Act meetings (see example on page 65)
    — Corrections.

- Documents published as separate parts to allow the issuing agency to order reprints.

- Pages of general reader aids.

Steps to Using the *Federal Register*

To use the *Federal Register* effectively to respond to requests for federal applications for grants in education, you need access to the daily *Federal Register*. This could be obtained through the research and grants' office at your institution or through the nearest depository library that receives the *Federal Register*. Because the *Federal Register* is not received the day it is issued, you may want to set aside time each week to review daily *Federal Registers* for that week. The following steps are a good format to follow:

Step 1 • Set an hour per week aside to review the most current daily *Federal Register* documents.

Figure 3.6. An Example of a Sunshine Act Meeting Document

6802

Sunshine Act Meetings

Federal Register

Vol. 54, No. 29

Tuesday, Feburary 14, 1989

This section of the FEDERAL REGISTER contains notices of meetings published under the "Government in the Sunshine Act" (Pub. L. 94-409) 5 U.S.C. 552b(e)(3).

FEDERAL RESERVE SYSTEM BOARD OF GOVERNORS

TIME AND DATE: 1:00 a.m., Tuesday, February 21, 1989.
PLACE: Marriner S. Eccles Federal Reserve Board Building, C Street entrance between 20th and 21st Streets, NW., Washington, DC 20551.
STATUS: Closed.
MATTERS TO BE CONSIDERED:
 1. Personnel actions (appointments, promotions, assignments, reassignments, and salary actions) involving individual Federal Reserve System employees.
 2. Any items carried forward from a previously announced meeting.

CONTACT PERSON FOR MORE INFORMATION: Mr. Joseph R. Coyne, Assistant to the Board; (202) 452-3204. You may call (202) 452-3207, beginning at approximately 5 p.m. two business days before this meeting, for a recorded announcement of bank and bank holding company applications scheduled for the meeting.
 Date: February 10, 1989.
Jennifer J. Johnson,
Associate Secretary of the Board.
[FR Doc. 89-3560 Filed 2-10-89; 4:07 pm]
BILLING CODE 6210-01-M

COMMISSION ON MERCHANT MARINE AND DEFENSE

SUMMARY: The Commission on Merchant Marine and Defense was established by Pub. L. 98-525 (as amended), and the Commission was constituted in December 1986. The Commission's mandate is to study and report on problems relating to transportation of cargo and personnel for national defense purposes in time of war or national emergency, the capability of the Merchant Marine to meet the need for such transportation, and the adequacy of the shipbuilding mobilization base to support naval and merchant ship construction. In accordance with the Federal Advisory Committee Act, Pub. L. 92-463, as amended, the Commission announces the

following meeting:
DATES AND TIMES: Thursday, February 16, 1989, Beginning 9:00 a.m.
PLACE: Suite 520, 4401 Ford Avenue, Alexandria, Virginia, 22302-0268.
TYPE OF MEETING: Closed.
CONTACT PERSON: Allan W. Cameron, Executive Director, Commission on Merchant Marine and Defense, Suite 520, 4401 Ford Avenue, Alexandria, Virginia 22302-0268, Telephone (202) 756-0411.
PURPOSE OF MEETING: To discuss the work of the Commission and to deliberate facts and opinions obtained from briefings and public hearings.
SUPPLEMENTARY INFORMATION: The executive meetings of the Commission will be closed to the public pursuant to 5 U.S.C. 552b(c)(1) and 552b(c)(4) in the interests of national security and to protect proprietary information provided to the Commission in confidence.
Allan W. Cameron,
Executive Director, Commission on Merchant Marine and Defense.
[FR Doc. 89-3559 Filed 2-10-89; 4:06 pm]
BILLING CODE 3820-01-M

NATIONAL MEDIATION BOARD
"FEDERAL REGISTER" CITATION OF PREVIOUS ANNOUNCEMENT: 54 FR 1470.
PREVIOUSLY ANNOUNCED TIME AND DATE OF THE MEETING: 2:00 P.M., Wednesday, February 15, 1989.
SUPPLEMENTARY INFORMATION: Chairman Walter C. Wallace and Board Member Joshua M. Javits have determined by recorded vote that Agency business required this change and that no earlier announcement of such change was possible.
CONTACT PERSON FOR MORE INFORMATION: Mr. Charles R. Barnes, Executive Director, Tel: (202) 523-5920.
 Date of notice: February 7, 1989.
Charles R. Barnes,
Executive Director, National Mediation Board.
[FR Doc. 89-3496 Field 2-10-89; 11:16 am]
BILLING CODE 7550-01-M

NUCLEAR REGULATORY COMMISSION
DATE: Weeks of February, 13, 20, 27, and March 6, 1989.
PLACE: Commissioners' Conference Room, 11555 Rockville Pike, Rockville, Maryland.
STATUS: Open and Closed.

MATTERS TO BE CONSIDERED:

Week of February 13

Friday, February 17

11:30 a.m.
 Affirmation/Discussion and Vote (Public Meeting) (if needed).

Week of February 20—Tentative

Tuesday, February 21

2:00 p.m.
 Oral Argument on Sanction Issued in Shoreham Proceedings (Public Meeting) (postponed from February 10)

Wednesday, February 22

10:00 a.m.
 Briefing on Final Rule on Early Site Permits; Standard Design Certification; and Combined Licenses for Nuclear Power Reactors (Public Meeting)

Week of February 27—Tentative

Monday, February 27

10:00 a.m.
 Briefing on the Status of NUREG-1150 (Public Meeting)
2:00 p.m.
 Briefing on Final Report on BWR Mark I Containment Issues (Public Meeting)

Wednesday March 1

9:30 a.m.
 Briefing on Status of Performance Indicator Development (Public Meeting)

Thursday, March 2

10:00 a.m.
 Briefing on Importing and Exporting of Radioactive Waste (Public Meeting)

Week of March 6—Tentative

Monday, March 6

2:30 p m
Briefing on Status of Generic Issues (Public Meeting)
 Note.—Affirmation sessions are initially scheduled and announced to the public on a time-reserved basis. Supplementary notice is provided in accordance with the Sunshine Act as specific items are identified and added to the meeting agenda. If there is no specific subject listed for affirmation, this means that no item has as yet been identified as requiring any Commission vote on this date.

TO VERIFY THE STATUS OF MEETINGS CALL (RECORDING): (301) 492-0292.

— Grant Tip —

The Contents section of the Federal Register *can immediately inform you if there are any proposed rules, regulations, and notices that affect the federal agency that you may be interested in.*

Step 2 • Write down items in the *Federal Register* that are of special interest to you. For example: deadline dates, pages you want to photocopy, etc.

Step 3 • Check the Contents pages to see if that particular issue contains information about the department in which you are interested. For example, review the Contents to see if the Education Department has documents in the issue. The Contents is a comprehensive alphabetical listing by *agency* of all documents in the issue. Under each agency the documents are arranged by classification—Rules, Proposed Rules, or Notices. Each entry includes the page number on which the document begins and a brief description of the document. Figure 3.7 on pages 68 and 69 is Contents of the *Federal Register* issued on February 14, 1989. Examine this page in more detail

—Notice the Education Department *subheading.*
—Notice what is listed under *rules.*
—Notice what is listed under *proposed rules.*
—Notice what is listed under *notices.*

This issue of the *Federal Register* has even more information a proposal writer in the field of education needs. However, the other four or five daily documents you may have reviewed during this hour may have less under the Education Department subheading, or they may have even more than this particular example.

Step 4 • On the second page (page 69) of the Contents section, you will notice the subheading, *Separate Parts in This Issue.* The *Federal Register* prints separate parts at the request of submitting agencies so they can have copies to mail out to individuals requesting information on a specific program. The Department of Education has three separate parts (Part II, Part VI, and Part VIII). Part VI, noted as Figure 3.8, pages 70-72, shows an example of a Separate Part.

Step 5 • After reviewing the *Federal Registers,* you may want to contact the person included on the document and seek answers to specific questions. Usually you must write the contact person to receive an application package in order to respond to a grant notice.

Code of Federal Regulations (CFR)

Documents published in the *Federal Register* as codified regulations keep the *Code of Federal Regulations* current. These documents make changes to the appropriate *Code of Federal Regulations* volume.

How to Use the *Code of Federal Regulations*

To determine whether a *CFR* volume has been amended since its revision date (in this case, July 1, 1989), consult the *List of CFR Sections Affected (LSA)*, which is issued monthly, and the *Cumulative List of Parts Affected*, which appears in the Reader Aids section of the daily *Federal Register*. These two lists will identify the *Federal Register* page number of the latest amendment of any given rule.

The *Federal Register* includes at the end of each issue a Reader Aids section. This section is designed to help the reader find specific information in the Federal Register System, as distinguished from the finding aids in the preliminary pages which are oriented toward one particular issue. Refer to Figure 3.9 on pages 73-74. This section addresses the following:

> •*Information and Assistance.* Appearing first is the list of Office of the *Federal Register* telephone numbers to call for specific information (see page 73).

> •Federal Register *Pages and Dates.* This is a table of the inclusive pages and corresponding dates for the current month's *Federal Register* (see page 73).

> •CFR *Parts Affected During (respective month).* This is a cumulative list of *CFR* parts affected by rules and proposed rules published during the current month in the *Federal Register*, in this case for the first 14 days of February 1989 (see pages 73-74).

> •*List of Public Laws.* This is a continuing list of bills from the current session of Congress that have become federal law (see pages 73-74).

> •CFR *Parts Affected in the Respective Issue.*

Figure 3.7. An Example of a Table of Contents

III

Federal Register

Vol. 54, No. 29

Tuesday, February 14, 1989

Contents

Advisory Council on Historic Preservation
See Historic Preservation, Advisory Council

Agricultural Marketing Service
PROPOSED RULES
Dairy products; grading, inspection, and standards:
  User fees and administrative changes, 6682

Agriculture Department
See Agricultural Marketing Service; Federal Crop Insurance
  Corporation; Food Safety and Inspection Service; Forest
  Service

Alcohol, Drug Abuse, and Mental Health Administration
NOTICES
Meetings; advisory committees:
  March, 6754

Army Department
NOTICES
Meetings:
  Science Board, 6741

Centers for Disease Control
NOTICES
Grants and cooperative agreements; availability, etc:
  Immunization demonstration projects, 6755

Commerce Department
See Export Administration Bureau; International Trade
  Administration; Minority Business Development
  Agency National Oceanic and Atmospheric
  Administration; Patent and Trademark Office

Commission on Merchant Marine and Defense
NOTICES
Meetings, 6802

Consumer Product Safety Commission
RULES
Voluntary standards activities; Commission participation
  and employee involvement, 6646

Defense, Commission on Merchant Marine and
See Commission on Merchant Marine and Defense

Defense Department
See Army Department

Drug Enforcement Administration
NOTICES

Applications, hearings, determinations, etc:
  Kingsolver, Daryl L., D.D.S., 6777
  Penick Corp., 6778

Education Department
RULES
Elementary and secondary education:
  Local educational agencies assistance, 6858
PROPOSED RULES
Special education and rehabilitative services:
  Projects with industry program, 6808
NOTICES
Grants and cooperative agreements; availability, etc.:
  Handicapped education program—
    Training personnel, 6741
  Minority science improvement program, 6742
  Vocational and adult education cooperative
      demonstration program
    Funding priorities, 6846

Energy Department
See also Energy Information Administration; Federal Energy
  Regulatory Commission; Southeastern Power
  Administration
NOTICES
Atomic energy agreements; subsequent arrangements, 6742

Energy Information Administration
NOTICES
Agency information collection activities under OMB review,
  6742, 6743
  (2 documents)
Reporting and recordkeeping requirements, 6743

Environmental Protection Agency
RULES
Air quality implementation plans; approval and
    promulgation; various States:
  Test methods and procedures; clarification, 6660
Water pollution control:
  Critical aquifer protection areas identification criteria,
    6836
PROPOSED RULES
Air pollution; standards of performance for new stationary
    sources:
  Rubber tire manufacturing industry; revisions, 6850
Air quality planning purposes; designation of areas:
  Ohio, 6733
NOTICES
Environmental statements; availability, etc.:
  Pascagoula, MS, 6748
Grants, State and local assistance:
  Municipal wastewater treatment works construction

Figure 3.7 Continued. An Example of a Table of Contents

| VI | Federal Register / Vol. 54, No. 29 / Tuesday, February 14, 1989 / Contents |

programs—
    Allotments; correction, 6804
Meetings:
    Asbestos-containing materials in schools, 6749
    Science Advisory Board, 6749
Water pollution control:
    Disposal site determinations—
        Hurricane Creek, Bacon County, GA, 6749
Water quality criteria:
    Water quality standards program documents; availability, 6750

Export Administration Bureau
RULES
Export licensing:
    Forms; revisions, 6643

Federal Aviation Administration
RULES
Airworthiness directives:
    Canadair, 6641
    Pacific Stock Exchange, Inc., 6793
    Philadelphia Stock Exchange, Inc., 6793
Applications, hearings, determinations, etc.:
    Aegon N.V., 6793
    Northeastern Capital Corp, 6795
    Prudential-Bache Global Fund, Inc., et al., 6796

Small Business Administration
NOTICES
Applications, hearings, determinations, etc.:
    Flushing Capital Corp., 6797
    Western General Capital Corp., 6798

Social Security Administration
PROPOSED RULES
Organization and procedures:
    Social security numbers for newborn children, 6707

Southeastern Power Administration
NOTICES
Power rates:
    Cumberland Basin Projects, 6747

State Department
NOTICES
Senior Executive Service:
    Performance Review Board; membership, 6798

Transportation Department
See Federal Aviation Administration

Treasury Department
See also Internal Revenue Service
NOTICES
Agency information collection activities under OMB review,
    6800
        (2 documents)

United States Information Agency
NOTICES
Art objects, importation for exhibition:
    Seventeenth Century Netherlandish Paintings from
        Switzerland: Work of the Briner Foundation and the
        Kuntsmuseum, Winterthur and the Musee D'Art et
        D'Histoire, Geneva, 6801

Separate Parts in This Issue

Part II
Department of Education, 6808

Part III
Department of Health and Human Services, Food and Drug
    Administration, 6814

Part IV
Department of Health and Human Services, Public Health
    Service, 6830

Part V
Environmental Protection Agency, 6836

Part VI
Department Education, 6846

Part VII
Environmental Protection Agency, 6850

Part VIII
Department Education, 6858

Reader Aids
Additional information, including a list of public laws,
telephone numbers, and finding aids, appears in the Reader
Aids section at the end of this issue.

Figure 3.8. An Example of a Separate Part of a *Federal Register* Issue

federal register

Tuesday
February 14, 1989

Part VI

Department of Education

Office of Vocational and Adult Education

Cooperative Demonstration Program;
Notice of Proposed Priority, Required
Activities, and Selection Criteria for
Fiscal Year 1989; Notice

Figure 3.8 Continued. An Example of a Separate Part of a *Federal Register* Issue

6846   Federal Register / Vol. 54, No. 29 Tuesday, February 14, 1989 / Notices

DEPARTMENT OF EDUCATION

Office of Vocational and Adult Education

Cooperative Demonstration Program

AGENCY: Department of Education.

ACTION: Notice of proposed priority, required activities, and selection criteria for fiscal year 1989.

SUMMARY: The Secretary of Education proposes to establish an absolute priority for a fiscal year 1989 grant competition under the Cooperative Demonstration Program. Under the priority, funds would be reserved for applications proposing to conduct high technology training projects in vocational education that involve cooperation between the private sector and public agencies in vocational education. The Secretary also proposes to require applicants to submit certain written assurances, as described under the Activities section of this priority, as part of their applications for this program and to prohibit the use of Federal funds to cover the costs of equipment used for project activities. Lastly, the Secretary proposes to use new selection criteria in evaluating applications submitted for this competition only.
DATE: Comments must be received on or before March 16, 1989.
ADDRESS: Comments should be addressed to Richard F. DiCola or Robert L. Miller, Program Improvement Branch, Division of National Programs, Office of Vocational and Adult Education (Room 4512, Switzer Building), 400 Maryland Avenue SW., Washington, DC 20202-7242. Telephone (202) 732-2362 or 732-2428.

SUPPLEMENTARY INFORMATION:

Program Information

Recent data compiled by the Bureau of Labor Statistics indicate faster than average growth in the demand for skilled technicians in high technology fields through the year 2000. The data also indicate that these emerging technologies will have a significant impact on the efficiency and flexibility of a well-trained work force.

High technology training can be conducted most effectively with the active involvement and cooperation of the private sector. Effective partnerships between the private sector and public agencies in vocational education are an important aspect of the Cooperative Demonstration Program which is designed, in part, to demonstrate ways in which public agencies in vocational education and the private sector can work together to assist students to attain the advanced level of skills needed to make the transition from school to work.

Priority

In accordance with Department of Education General Administrative Regulations at 34 CFR 75.105(c)(3), the Secretary proposes to establish an absolute priority for the fiscal year 1989 grant competition under the Cooperative Demonstration Program for projects that focus on high technology training efforts that are also models of cooperation between the private sector and public agencies in vocational education. In order to maximize the use of Federal funds for the direct training of students, the Secretary proposes that no Federal funds be used to purchase or lease equipment to conduct project activities. Any necessary equipment costs may be counted toward the cost-sharing requirement for this program.

Specifically, the Secretary proposes to support projects that—

(1) Train persons to become skilled workers or technicians in high technology occupations (including providing related instruction to individuals undergoing apprenticeship training) or to become skilled workers or technicians involved in the production, installation, operation, and maintenance of high technology equipment, systems, and processes;

(2) Are examples of successful cooperation between the private sector (including employers, consortia of employers, labor organizations, building trade councils, and other private agencies, organizations, and institutions) and public agencies in vocational education (including State and local educational agencies, postsecondary educational institutions, institutions of higher education, and other public agencies, organizations, and institutions). For the purpose of this competition the military and publicly funded laboratories are considered employers that could be used as private sector partners in a proposed project; *and*

(3) Expend no Federal funds for equipment, as defined in 34 CFR 74.132.

Activities

In support of this priority, an applicant would be required to submit, as part of its application, a written assurance that it will cooperate, if selected, with a planned national evaluation study of projects funded under this competition.

An applicant would also be required to submit, as part of its application, written assurances from each public agency in vocational education and each private sector entity that they will participate in the planning and operation of the proposed project as described in the application.

Criteria for Evaluating Applications

For the Fiscal Year 1989 grant competition under the Cooperative Demonstration Program, the Secretary proposes to use the following selection criteria and to assign points to the selection criteria as indicated:

(a) Need. (15 points)
(1) The Secretary reviews each application for information that shows the need for and the soundness of the rationale for the project.
(2) The Secretary looks for information that shows—
(i) A clear description of the need for the proposed project;
(ii) Specific evidence of the need for the project;
(iii) A description of any ongoing and planned activities in the community relative to the need, including, if appropriate, the relationship of any local, regional or State economic development plan;
(iv) Evidence that demonstrates the vocational training to be provided is designed to meet current and projected occupational needs;
(v) A clear statement of what the project seeks to demonstrate; and
(vi) Evidence that the project is likely to serve as a model in the future.
(b) *Plan of Operation.* (25 points)
(1) The Secretary reviews each application for information that shows the quality of the plan of operation for the project.
(2) The Secretary looks for information that shows—
(i) High quality in the design of the project;

Figure 3.8 Continued. An Example of a Separate Part of a *Federal Register* Issue

(ii) An effective plan of management that ensures proper and efficient administration of the project;

(iii) A clear description of how the objectives of the project relate to the purpose of the program;

(iv) The way the applicant plans to use its resources and personnel to achieve each objective; and

(v) A clear description of how the applicant will provide equal access and treatment for eligible project participants who are members of groups that have been traditionally underrepresented, such as—

(A) Members of racial or ethnic minority groups;

(B) Women;

(C) Handicapped persons; and

(D) The elderly.

(c) *Quality of Key Personnel.* (10 points)

(1) The Secretary reviews each application for information that shows the qualifications of the key personnel the applicant plans to use on the project.

(2) The Secretary looks for information that shows—

(i) The qualifications of the project director (if one is to be used);

(ii) The qualifications of each of the other key personnel to be used in the project;

(iii) The time that each person referred to in paragraphs (c)(2)(i) and (ii) of this section will commit to the project; and

(iv) The extent to which the applicant, as part of its nondiscriminatory employment practices, encourages applications for employment from persons who are members of groups that have been traditionally underrepresented, such as—

(A) Members of racial or ethnic minority groups;

(B) Women;

(C) Handicapped persons; and

(D) The elderly.

(3) To determine personnel qualifications, the Secretary considers experience and training in fields related to the objectives of the project, as well as other information that the applicant provides.

(d) *Budget and Cost Effectiveness.* (10 points)

(1) The Secretary reviews each application for information that shows the project has an adequate budget and is cost effective.

(2) The Secretary looks for information that shows—

(i) The budget for the project is adequate to support the project activities; and

(ii) Costs are reasonable in relation to the objectives of the project.

(e) *Evaluation Plan.* (10 points)

The Secretary reviews each application to determine the quality of the project's evaluation plan for the project, including the extent to which—

(1) The plan includes activities during the formative stages of the project to help to guide and improve the project, as well as a final evaluation that includes summary data and recommendations; and

(2) The plan includes, at a minimum, a description of the participant data to be collected based on the project objectives; tracking and follow-up of progress by all project participants throughout the project period; and outcome measures to be used for each objective.

(f) *Adequacy of Resources.* (5 points)

(1) The Secretary reviews each application for information that shows that the applicant plans to devote adequate resources to the project.

(2) The Secretary looks for information that shows—

(i) The facilities that the applicant plans to use are adequate; and

(ii) The equipment and supplies the applicant plans to use are adequate.

(g) *Private Sector Involvment.* (10 points)

(1) The Secretary reviews each application for information that shows the involvement of the private sector.

(2) The Secretary looks for information that shows—

(i) Private sector involvement in the planning of the project; and

(ii) Private sector involvement in the operation of the project.

(h) *Employment Opportunities.* (5 points)

The Secretary looks for information and documentation to the extent to which trainees, upon completion of their training, will be either employed in jobs related to their training or enrolled in postsecondary vocational education programs related to the training received during the project. Acceptable documentation includes letters of commitment from employers to hire training completers or descriptions of postsecondary vocational education programs that would be appropriate for subsequent training.

(i) *Dissemination.* (10 points)

(1) The Secretary reviews each applica-

tion for information that shows that the applicant has an effective and efficient plan for disseminating information about the demonstration project, including the results of the project and any specialized materials developed by the project.

(2) The Secretary looks for information that shows—

(i) High quality in the design of the dissemination plan and procedures for evaluating the effectiveness of the dissemination plan;

(ii) A description of the types of materials the applicant plans to make available and the methods for making the materials available;

(iii) Provisions for demonstrating the methods and techniques used by the project;

(iv) Provisions for assisting others to adopt and successfully implement the project or methods and techniques used by the project; and

(v) Provisions for publicizing the findings of the project at the local, State or national level.

Invitation to Comment

Interested persons are invited to submit comments and recommendations regarding (a) the proposed priority for high technology projects that involve cooperation with the private sector and prohibit the expenditure of Federal funds for equipment and related requirements; and (b) the proposed selection criteria.

All comments submitted in response to this notice will be available for public inspection during and after the comment period in Room 4512 Switzer Building, 330 C Street SW., Washington, DC, between the hours of 9:30 a.m. and 3:00 p.m. Monday through Friday of each week except Federal holidays.

Authority: 20 U.S.C. 2411
Dated: February 2, 1989.
Lauro F. Cavazos,
Secretary of Education.
[FR Doc. 89-3470 Field 2-13-89; 8:45 am]
BILLING CODE 4000-01-M

Figure 3.9 Continued. An Example of the Reader Aids Section of the *Federal Register*

i

Reader Aids

Federal Register

Vol. 54, No. 29

Tuesday, February 14, 1989

INFORMATION AND ASSISTANCE

Federal Register

Index, finding aids & general information	523-5227
Public inspection desk	523-5215
Corrections to published documents	523-5237
Document drafting information	523-5237
Machine readable documents	523-5237

Code of Federal Regulations

Index, finding aids & general information	523-5227
Printing schedules	523-3419

Laws

Public Laws Update Service (numbers, dates, etc.)	523-6641
Additional information	523-5230

Presidential Documents

Executive orders and proclamations	523-5230
Public Papers of the Presidents	523-5230
Weekly Compilation of Presidential Documents	523-5230

The United States Government Manual

General Information	523-5230

Other Services

Data base and machine readable specifications	523-3408
Guide to Record Retention Requirements	523-3187
Legal staff	523-4534
Library	523-5240
Privacy Act Compilation	523-3187
Public Laws Update Service (PLUS)	523-6641
TDD for the deaf	523-5229

FEDERAL REGISTER PAGES AND DATES, FEBRUARY

5071-5206	1
5207-5404	2
5405-5582	3
5583-5920	6
5921-6114	7
6115-6262	8
6263-6380	9
6381-6502	10
6503-6640	13
6641-6860	14

CFR PARTS AFFECTED DURING FEBRUARY

At the end of each month, the Office of the Federal Register publishes separately a List of CFR Sections Affected (LSA), which lists parts and sections affected by documents published since the revision date of each title.

1 CFR

305	5207

3 CFR

Administrative Orders:
Memorandums

Dec. 22, 1988	6237

Presidential Determinations:
No. 89-10 of

Jan. 18, 1989	5071

5 CFR

Proposed Rules:

550	5494

7 CFR

1	5073
26	5921
68	5923
405	6381
800	5924
802	5925
919	5584
932	5585
981	5408
1006	6382
1012	6382
1013	6382
1124	5587
1125	5587
1150	6263
1413	6232
1735	5925
1980	5409
3017	6363

Proposed Rules:

29	5494
58	6681
905	6136
1933	6532
1944	6532
1980	6417

8 CFR

101	5927
235	6365
245a	6504

9 CFR

201	5073
307	6388
350	6388
351	6388

381	6388
391	6388

Proposed Rules:

92	5089
113	5939
307	6684
310	6684

10 CFR

62	5409
430	6062
1036	6363

Proposed Rules:

20	5089, 6296
430	6364
600	6296
710	5376

11 CFR

Proposed Rules:

110	6684
113	6684
114	6684
116	6684

12 CFR

208	6115
516	6363
525	6112
569c	6109
578	6108

Proposed Rules:

229	5495
543	5629
544	5629
546	6685
552	5629
561	6685
563	6685
570	6685
571	6685
584	6689

13 CFR

101	6512
108	6265
121	6267
123	6268
142	6271
145	6363

Proposed Rules:

121	6298

Figure 3.9. An Example of the Reader Aids Section of the *Federal Register*

ii   Federal Register / Vol. 54, No. 29 / Tuesday, February 14, 1989 / Reader Aids

14 CFR
71............. 5214-5219, 5929
91.................................. 5580
97...................... 5587, 6515
241.................................. 5588
1265................................ 6363
Proposed Rules:
Ch. 1............................... 5637
30.....5637, 6549, 6689-6692
71............. 5246, 6233, 6301
399.................... 5497, 6475
15 CFR
26.................................... 6363
770.................................. 6643
771.................................. 6643
772.................................. 6643
16 CFR
13.................................... 5929
305.................................. 6517
1031................................ 6646
1032................................ 6646
Prposed Rules:
13.................................... 6141
414.................................. 5090
17 CFR
4...................................... 5597
231.................................. 5600
241.................................. 5600
Proposed Rules:
1...................................... 5576
3...................................... 5576
31.................................... 5576
18 CFR
157.................................. 6120
201.................................. 5424
271.................................. 5075
284.................................. 5219
381.................................. 5424
Proposed Rules:
410.................................. 5638
19 CFR
122.................................. 5427
148.................................. 5076
162.................................. 5076
207...................... 5077, 5220
356.................................. 5930
Proposed Rules:
134.................................. 6418
141.................................. 5091
20 CFR
204.................................. 5223
235.................................. 5225
302.................................. 5226
404.................................. 5603
Proposed Rules:
422.................................. 6707
21 CFR
5...................................... 6517
107.................................. 6804
133.................................. 6120
Proposed Rules:
50.................................... 6060
56.................................... 6060
106.................................. 6804
22 CFR

137.................................. 6363
208.................................. 6363
310.................................. 6363
513.................................. 6363
1006................................ 6363
1508................................ 6363
Proposed Rules:
503.................................. 6420
24 CFR
24.................................... 6363
125.................................. 6492
25 CFR
2...................................... 6478
26CFR
1...................................... 5577
601.................................. 6363
Proposed Rules:
1................ 5577, 5939, 6710
53.................................... 6060
56.................................... 6060
28 CFR
67.................................... 6363
Proposed Rules:
34.................................... 6098
29 CFR
1...................................... 5303
5...................................... 5303
98.................................... 6363
2704................................ 6284
Proposed Rules:
530........................ 5303, 5500
1602................................ 6551
1627................................ 6551
30 CFR
5...................................... 6365
Proposed Rules:
250.................................. 6302
761.................................. 5577
935.................................. 5940
31 CFR
19.................................... 6363
500.................................. 5229
515.................................. 5229
32 CFR
199.................................. 5604
280.................................. 6363
286b................................ 5235
351.................................. 5607
Proposed Rules:
169.................................. 5640
33 CFR
100.......... 5432, 6392, 6519
165.................................. 5432
173.................................. 5608
34 CFR
73.................................... 6364
222.................................. 6858
Proposed Rules:
379.................................. 6808
35 CFR
253.................................. 6364
36 CFR
1190................................ 5434
1209................................ 6363
Proposed Rules:

Ch. VII.......................... 6425
222.................................. 6425
37 CFR
10...................... 6520, 6659
Proposed Rules:
211.................................. 5942
38 CFR
1...................................... 6520
2...................................... 5610
3........................... 5235, 5610
8...................................... 5931
39 CFT
Proposed Rules:
111.................................. 5641
40 CFR
32.................................... 6363
52.... 5236, 5448, 5449, 6125
               6286, 6287
81.................................... 5237
82.................................... 6376
162.................................. 6288
Proposed Rules:
257.................................. 5746
271.................................. 5500
300.................................. 6153
500.................................. 5746
41 CFR
101-17............................ 6291
101-50............................ 6363
105-68............................ 6363
Proposed Rules:
201-1...................... 5904, 5905
201-2.............................. 5905
42 CFR
57.................................... 5615
413....................... 5316, 5619
433.................................. 5452
Proposed Rules:
405.................................. 5946
415.................................. 5946
43 CFR
4...................................... 6483
12.................................... 6363
Public Land Orders:
6696................................ 5302
6706................................ 6232
6707................................ 5932
Proposed Rules:
11.................................... 5093
44 CFR
17.................................... 6363
67.................................... 5240
Proposed Rules:
67........................... 5971, 5979
45 CFR
76.................................... 6363
400.................................. 5463
620.................................. 6363
1080................................ 6368
1169................................ 6363
1185................................ 6363
1229................................ 6363
2016................................ 6363
Proposed Rules:
704.................................. 5504

46 CFR
25.................................... 6396
58.................................... 6396
147.................................. 6396
221.................................. 5382
252.................................. 5085
282.................................. 5086
Proposed Rules:
31.................................... 5642
71.................................... 5642
91.................................... 5642
550........................5253,5506
580.................................. 5506
581.................................. 5506
47 CFR
25.................................... 5483
69.................................... 6292
73..... 5243-5245, 5623, 5624
        5932, 5933, 6132-6134,
               6294
97.................................. 5933
Proposed Rules:
73.... 5979-5983, 6154, 6155,
            6307, 6308
48 CFR
204.................................. 5484
219.................................. 5484
1837................................ 5625
Proposed Rules:
25.................................... 6251
52.................................... 6251
505.................................. 5516
509.................................. 6308
552.................................. 6308
49 CFR
29.................................... 6363
192...................... 5484, 5625
218.................................. 5485
1312................................ 6403
1314................................ 6403
Proposed Rules:
392.................................. 5516
393.................................. 5516
396.................................. 5518
544.................................. 5519
50 CFR
17.................................... 5935
380.................................. 6407
611.................................. 6526
646.................................. 5938
652.................................. 6415
672.................................. 6524
675.................................. 6134
683.................................. 6531
Proposed Rules:
17............. 5095, 5983, 5986
672.................................. 6734

LIST OF PUBLIC LAWS
Note: No public bills which
have become law were received
by the Office of the Federal
Register for inclusion in today's
List of Public Laws.
Last List February 10, 1989

Monthly, the Office of the Federal Register publishes separately a *List of* CFR *Sections Affected (LSA)*, which lists sections and parts affected by documents published since the revision date of each title (see pages 73-74). The *CFR* number for EDUCATION is 34; a person writing grant proposals for education would mainly be interested in noting any changes in this area.

Code of Federal Regulations

The *Code of Federal Regulations (CFR)* is a basic component of the Federal Register publication system. The *CFR* is a codification of the regulations of the various federal agencies.

Structure

The *CFR* is divided into 50 titles according to subject matter. Titles are divided into chapters, chapters into parts, and parts into sections. The Office of the Federal Register (OFR) assigns each federal agency the title, chapter, and parts in which it publishes its regulations.

Titles • Chapters • Parts • Sections

Title

Each title represents a broad area that is subject to federal regulation. For example, Title 34 deals with Education; Title 7 deals with Agriculture; Title 29 deals with Labor; Title 45 deals with Public Welfare. Subtitles, lettered consecutively in capitals (A, B, C, etc.), are sometimes used to distinguish between department-wide regulations and the regulations of the department's various units. Subtitles are also used to group related chapters. For example, Title 34— Education, has the following subtitles:

Subtitle A—Office of the Secretary, Department of Education
Subtitle B—Regulations of the Offices of the Department of Education

Chapter

Each chapter is numbered in Roman capitals (I, II, III, etc.) and usually is assigned to a single agency, which may be an entire department or one of its units. Chapters are sometimes divided into subchapters, lettered in capitals (A, B, C, etc.) to group related parts. For example, Title 34—Education, has seven (7) chapters.

Figure 3.10. Chapters of the *CFR* for Title 34, Education

Chapter I	Office for Civil Rights, Department of Education
Chapter II	Office of Elementary and Secondary Education
Chapter III	Office of Special Education and Rehabilitation Services
Chapter IV	Office of Vocational and Adult Education
Chapter V	Office of Bilingual Education and Minority Languages Affairs
Chapter VI	Office of Postsecondary Education
Chapter VII	Office of Educational Research and Improvement

Part

Each chapter is divided into parts, numbered in Arabic throughout each title. A part consists of a unified body of regulations applying to a single function of the issuing agency or devoted to specific subject matter under control of the issuing agency. Parts are usually assigned to chapters as follows: Chapter I, Parts 1 to 199; Chapter II, Parts 200 to 299; Chapter III, Parts 300 to 399, etc. Subparts, usually lettered in capitals, sometimes group related sections within a part.

Section

The section is the basic unit of the *CFR* and consists of a short, simple presentation of one proposition. Each section number includes the number of the part followed by a period and a sequential number. For example, the first section in Part 25 is expressed as "§ 25.1".

CFR *Indexes and Tabular Guides*

A subject index to the *Code of Federal Regulations* is contained in a separate volume, revised annually as of January 1, entitled *CFR Index and Finding Aids*. This volume contains the Parallel Table of Statutory Authorities and Agency Rules (Table I), and Acts Requiring Publication in the *Federal Register* (Table III). A list of *CFR* titles, chapters, and parts and an alphabetical list of agencies publishing in the *CFR* are also included in this volume.

The *Federal Register Index* is issued monthly in cumulative form. This index is based on a consolidation of the Contents entries in the daily *Federal Register*. A *List of CFR Sections Affected (LSA)* is published monthly, keyed to the revision dates of the 50 *CFR* titles.

Inquiries and Sales

For a summary, legal interpretation, or other explanation of any regulation in the volumes, contact the issuing agency. Inquiries concerning editing procedures and reference assistance with respect to the *Code of Federal Regulations* may be addressed to the Director, Office of the Federal Register, National Archives and Records Administration, Washington, D.C. 20408 (telephone 202-523-3517). Sales are handled exclusively by the Superintendent of Documents, Government Printing Office, Washington, D.C. (telephone 202-783-3238).

Summary Caution

Just reading through this chapter is not particularly exciting. Nevertheless, its content is of tremendous importance because it is a guide to the heart of grant proposal writing. Unless you thoroughly understand this area, you are likely to commit grave errors: deadlines missed, proposals mailed to the wrong agency, and inquiries made to the wrong office.

——**Grant Tip**——
The content of this chapter is a guide to the heart of proposal writing. Unless you thoroughly understand this area, you are likely to commit grave errors.

4

Using the *Catalog of Federal Domestic Assistance (CFDA)*

Introduction

In spite of its formidable and rather uninspired name, the *Catalog of Federal Domestic Assistance (CFDA)* is an essential tool for the proposal writer. As one can guess from its physical size, the *CFDA* includes a considerable array of information. A creative person can find ways to combine information in the *CFDA* to reveal some hidden utilities. The *CFDA* is one of three or four required "tools of the trade" for a person seeking federal assistanc. Much of the information in this chapter is taken directly from the *CFDA*.

What is the *CFDA*?

The *CFDA* is often referred to as "The Mother Lode of Information." It is a compilation of the federal government's domestic assistance programs that are "on the books." That is, the *CFDA* includes the names and pertinent information about the vast range of programs the federal government has enacted and administers to offer some kind of assistance to particular groups. The 1993 *Catalog* contains 1,261 assistance programs administered by 51 federal agencies. The U.S. Department of Education administers 172 of these programs. The standard, but abbreviated, information provided with each program entry is enough to give the user an overview of the

---

> **1,261 Programs Administered By 51 Federal Agencies**

---

program and the directions to more particular or specific information. The *CFDA* includes information on all federal domestic assistance programs (direct payments with unrestricted use, formula grants, insured loans, project grants, and direct loans). As noted in Figure 4.1, of the 1,261 programs listed in the *CFDA,* six percent (6%) are project grants, and 20% are formula grants.

Figure 4.1. Major Federal Assistance Programs

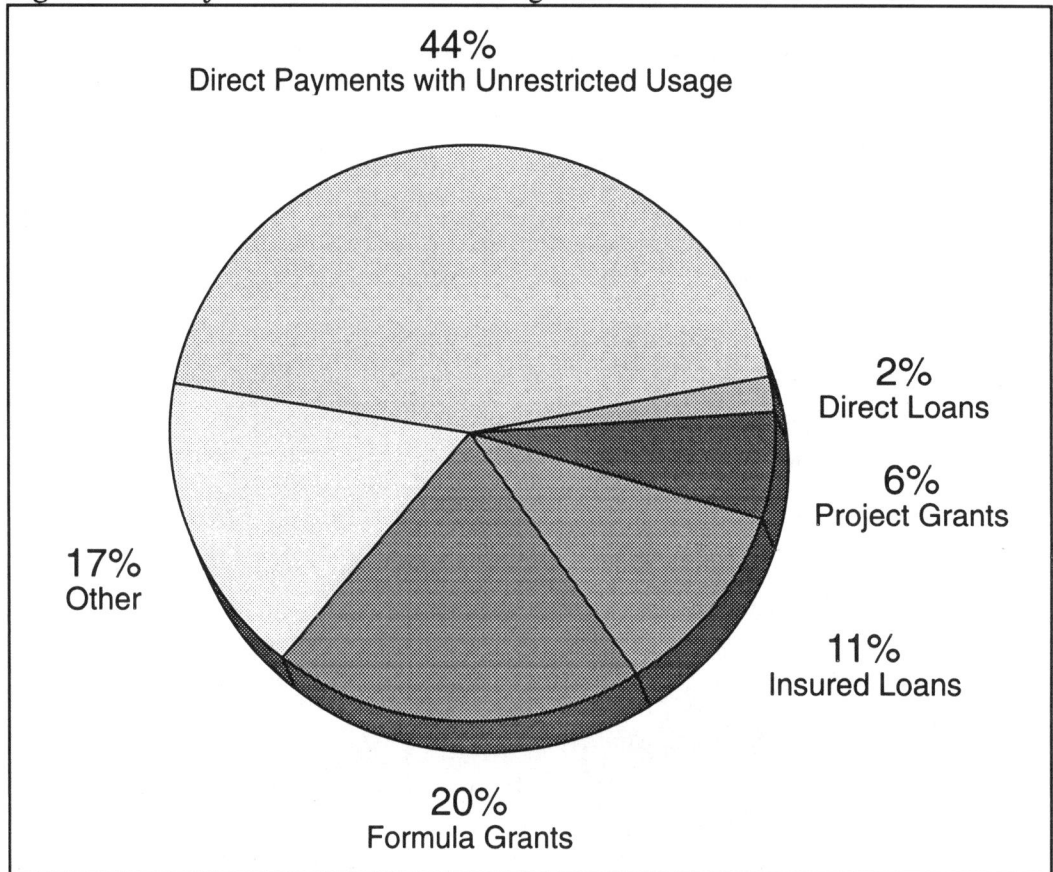

44%
Direct Payments with Unrestricted Usage

2%
Direct Loans

6%
Project Grants

11%
Insured Loans

20%
Formula Grants

17%
Other

————**Grant Tip**————

A listing in the CFDA *does not guarantee that a program has funds at the present time.*

Thus, *caveat emptor!* A listing in the *CFDA* does not guarantee that a program has funds at the present time. The *CFDA* has three major sections: the indexes, the program descriptions, and a series of helpful appendixes. The six indexes are designed to help the user locate a particular program.

Indexes • Program Descriptions • Appendixes

The six indexes are as follows:

•**Agency Index Summary:** Summarizes the overall functions and activities of agencies responsible for administering programs in the *CFDA*.

•**Agency Program Index:** Lists a program by the agency that administers it.

• **Functional Index:** Includes 20 basic categories (e.g., agriculture, education, housing) and the 176 subcategories that identify specific areas of interest.

• **Subject Index:** Is similar to the *Functional Index* but is more detailed as programs may be listed in several ways (i.e., popular names, general functional terms, categories of services).

• **Applicant Eligibility Index:** Is arranged with columns to indicate who is eligible to apply for assistance.

• **Deadline Index:** Provides the deadline date(s) by which the federal agencies must receive applications.

Although the *CFDA* originated with the Office of Economic Opportunity in 1965, the Federal Program Information Act (P.L. 95-220) of 1977 mandated dissemination of this considerable volume of federal program information. In 1977, responsibility for the *CFDA* passed to the Executive Office of the President, Office of Management and Budget (OMB). In 1984 responsibility for *CFDA* was again transferred, this time to the General Services Administration (GSA) under the oversight of the OMB. The *CFDA* was produced in 1965, 1967, 1969, and then each year thereafter. The basic edition is usually available in June, with updates available in December.

Purpose of *CFDA* and Types of Assistance

The *CFDA* will help grantseekers match potential sources of assistance with needs, facilitate the grant application process, and coordinate interaction between the federal government and state and local governments. The value of the *CFDA* is easily inferred from the major sections in its Table of Contents. Figure 4.2 is a Table of Contents of the *CFDA*.

Major highlights of the *CFDA* are topics of prominence in the Table of Contents. Note, for example, the following:

1. Catalog highlights, updating information, and how-to-use instructions.

2. Indexes of agencies, programs, application eligibility, deadlines, functional categories, and subjects.

Figure 4.2. Table of Contents of the *CFDA*

Table of Contents

3. Information on modified programs: programs that were deleted or added and a crosswalk of changes to program numbers and titles.

4. Program descriptions of over 1,200 programs.

5. Appendixes include information on such topics as Programs Requiring Executive Order 12372 Review, Authorization, Budget Functional Code, Agency Regional and Local Office Addresses, Sources of Additional Information Contacts, and Historical Profile of Programs.

The *CFDA* contains a detailed list of types of assistance with a description of each. Included are financial and nonfinancial assistance of the following kinds:

1. Grants, loans, loan guarantees, scholarships, mortgage loans, insurance, cooperative agreements and other types of financial assistance.

2. Property, technical assistance, counseling, statistical, and other expert information.

3. Service activities of regulatory agencies.

Distribution of *CFDA* and Ordering Information

The *CFDA* is distributed free to government offices at various levels of government. A grantwriter can visit these agencies and use the *CFDA* there, possibly copying specific pages for later use. The following usually receive the *CFDA* at no cost each time a new edition is produced.

•**Federal and National Level:** Members of Congress, congressional staff, federal offices of the U.S. government, federal information centers, federal regional councils, federal executive boards, and most federal agency field offices.

•**State Level:** Governors, state coordinators of federal-state relations, directors of state departments of administration and budget offices, directors of state departments of community affairs, directors of state planning agencies, directors of state agricultural extension services, state municipal leagues, state association of counties, chief state school officers, and state employment security agencies.

•**Local Level:** Mayors, county chairpersons, chairs of boards of commissioners, and city planners.

In addition, the *CFDA* is provided to other state and local government agencies with a population of 250 or more. Some well-connected agencies obtain the *CFDA* from their representatives in Congress. The agency for which you work may choose to buy the *CFDA* annually either in hard copy or by subscribing to the *CFDA* information in other forms. The *CFDA* is so basic a "tool of the trade" that an individual may wish to own a personal copy. As of 1993 the cost for the *CFDA* was $46 per year, including periodic updates. You can order the *CFDA* from the Government Printing Office, Superintendent of Documents, Washington, DC 20402 (Phone: 202-783-3238).

Federal Assistance Program Retrieval System

Federal Assistance Programs Retrieval System (FAPRS) provides federal domestic assistance program information via an interactive computerized process. It is fast, easy-to-use, on-line, low-cost, comprehensive, and is a key-word search. To obtain information on *FAPRS* and state access points, contact Federal Domestic Assistance Catalog Staff. *CFDA* program information on machine-readable magnetic tape may also be purchased from the Federal Domestic Assistance Catalog Staff (WKU), General Services Administration, Reporters Building, 300 7th Street, SW, Washington, DC 20407. Phone: (202) 708-5126 or (800) 669-8331.

Ways to Use the *CFDA*

The basic steps in using the *CFDA* are:

Step 1 • Locate program by working through one or more of the indexes (agency, functional, subject).

Step 2 • Determine the type of assistance and the type of assistance definitions.

Step 3 • Consult the *Catalog Update* (usually published in December) for changes.

Step 4 • Determine if you and/or your agency are eligible.

Step 5 • Determine program objectives and uses. In some cases, go directly to preparation and submission of application.

Step 6 • Obtain required preliminary clearances. Note that some programs *require* intergovernmental review accordance with Executive Order 12372 (refer to Appendix I in the*CFDA*);others *require* clearances from a state or regional office. (It is a good idea to inform pertinent offices any time you develop a proposal.) On occasion, a letter of support from that office will be useful.

Step 7 • Gather supporting documentation (contact grantor agency).

Step 8 • Determine application timing requirements.

Step 9 • Obtain application forms from grantor agency. (It may be necessary at this time to reconsider program location accomplished in Step 1.)

Step 10• Prepare and submit application.

Step 11• Request more information as needed from additional information sources.

———**Grant Tip**———
Inform pertinent offices any time you develop a project proposal. On occasion, a letter of support from that office will be useful.

Figure 4.3 is a flowchart provided in the *CFDA* to aid the grant seeker in using the *Catalog*. Each box in the flowchart is divided into three sections: the top section describes the type of action to take, the middle section identifies the appropriate *CFDA* section, and the bottom section details important procedures and requirements.

The Basics

The listing of programs in *CFDA* in education can provide a general indication if a particular program is "in the ball park" to do what the grant seeker wants (see Figure 4.4). In this listing each education program that receives federal assistance is shown with key information, such as the type of assistance and the eligibility index— a summary of the type of agency eligible to apply for assistance under that program. For example, the College Assistance Migrant Program (CAMP) is a project grant (note "B" at the end of title in Figure 4.4, Index #84.149) and is opened to nonprofit organizations.

Figure 4.3. Flowchart in Using the *Catalog of Federal Domestic Assistance (CFDA)*

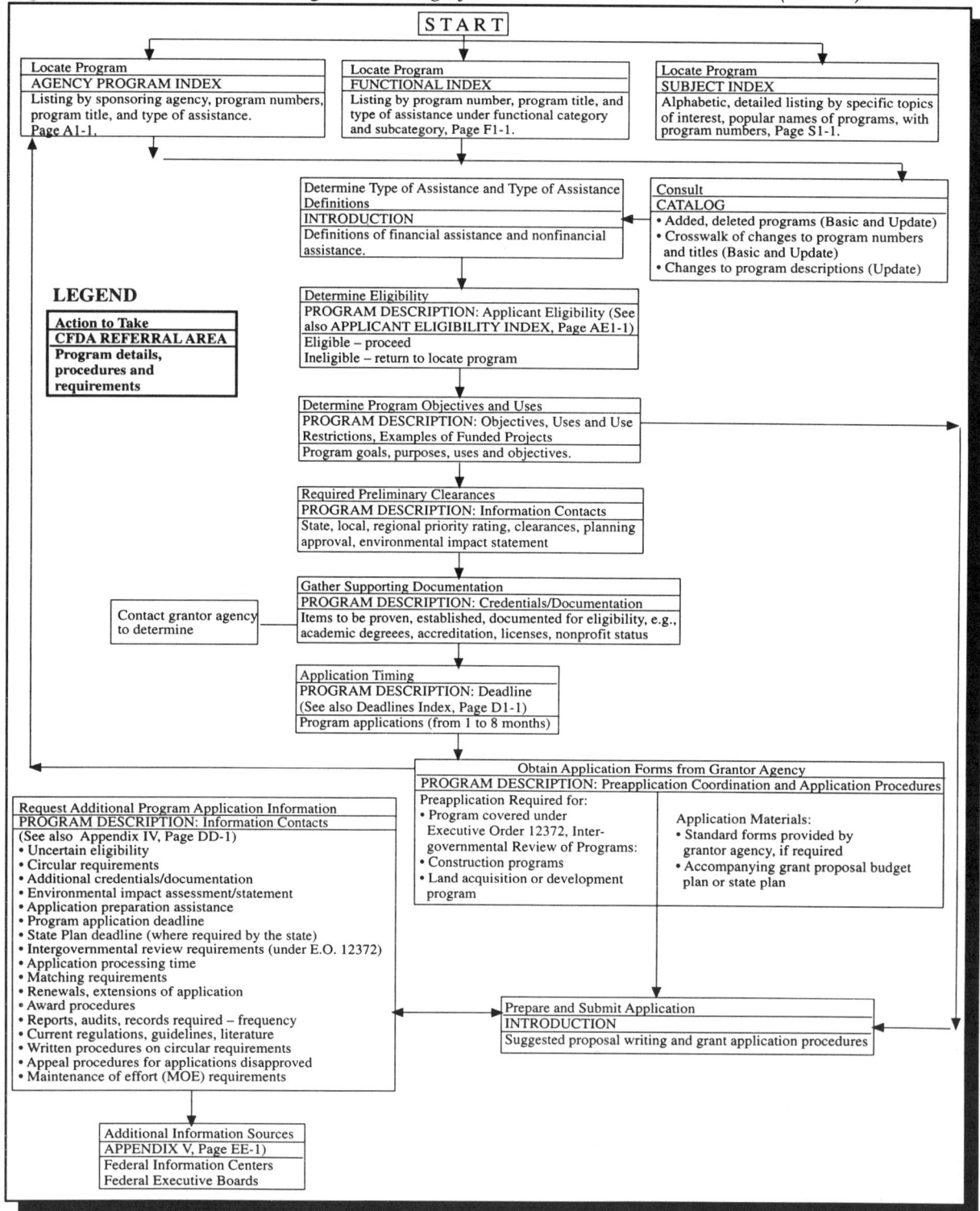

Figure 4.4. Department of Education Programs That Receive Federal Assistance

INDEX #	PROGRAM DESCRIPTION	ELIGIBILITY INDEX					
		IND	LOC	N/P	ST	UST	FTG
84.002	Adult Education-State Administered Basic Grant Program (A)		x	x	x		
84.003	Bilingual Education (B,C)	x	x	x	x		x
84.004	Desegregation Assistance, Civil Rights Training, & Advisory Services (B)		x	x	x		
84.007	Supplemental Educational Opportunity Grants (C)			x	x		
84.009	Educ. of Handicapped Children in State Operated/Supported Schools (A)		x		x	x	
84.010	Chapter 1 Programs—Local Educational Agencies (A)				x		x
84.011	Migrant Education—Basic State Formula Grant Program (A)				x		
84.012	Educationally Deprived Children—State Administration (A)				x		
84.013	Chapter 1 Programs for Neglected and Delinquent Children (A)				x	x	
84.014	Follow Through (B)		x	x	x		
84.015	National Resource Centers and Fellowships Program for Language and Area or Language and International Studies (B)			x			
84.016	Undergraduate International Studies & Foreign Language Programs (B)			x	x		
84.017	International Research and Studies (B)	x		x			
84.018	Fulbright-Hays Seminars Abroad—Bilateral Projects (B)	x					
84.019	Fulbright-Hays Training Grants—Faculty Research Abroad (B)			x		x	
84.021	Fulbright-Hays Training Grants—Group Projects Abroad (B)		x	x	x		
84.022	Fulbright-Hays Training Grants—Doctoral Dissertation Res. Abroad (B)			x		x	
84.023	Disabled—Innovation and Development (B)		x	x	x		
84.024	Early Education for Children with Disabilities (B)		x	x	x		
84.025	Services for Children with Deaf-Blindness (B)			x			
84.026	Media and Captioning for Individuals with Disabilities (B)		x	x	x	x	
84.027	Special Education—State Grants (A)		x	x	x	x	
84.028	Disabled—Regional Resource and Federal Centers (B)		x	x	x		
84.029	Special Education—Special Educ. Personnel Development/Parent Trng (B)		x	x	x		
84.030	Clearinghouses for Individuals with Disabilities (B)	x		x			
84.031	Higher Education—Institutional Aid (B)			x	x	x	
84.032	Guaranteed Student Loans (F)	x	x	x	x	x	x
84.033	College Work-Study Program (C)		x	x	x		
84.034	Public Library Services (A)				x		
84.035	Interlibrary Cooperation and Resource Sharing (A)				x		
84.036	Library Career Training (B)		x	x	x		
84.037	National Defense/National Direct/Perkins Loan Cancellations (C,D)			x	x		
84.038	Perkins Loan Program—Federal Capital Contributions (C)			x	x		
84.039	Library Research and Demonstration (B)	x	x	x	x		
84.040	Impact Aid—Construction (B)		x	x			
84.041	Impact Aid—Maintenance and Operation (D)		x	x			
84.042	Student Support Services (B)		x	x	x		
84.044	Talent Search (B)		x	x	x		
84.047	Upward Bound (B)		x	x	x		
84.048	Vocational Education—Basic Grants to States (A)				x		
84.049	Vocational Education—Consumer & Homemaking Education (A)				x	x	
84.051	National Vocational Education Research (B)	x	x	x	x		
84.053	Vocational Education—State Councils (A)				x		
84.055	Higher Education—Cooperative Education (B)		x	x	x		
84.060	Indian Education—Formula Grants to Local Educational Agencies (A, B)		x	x			x
84.061	Indian Education—Special Programs and Projects (B)		x	x	x		
84.062	Indian Education—Adult Education (B)		x				x
84.063	Pell Grant Program (C)	x					
84.064	Higher Education—Veterans Education Outreach Program (C)		x	x	x		
84.066	Educational Opportunity Centers (B)		x	x	x		
84.069	Grants to States for State Student Incentives (A)		x		x	x	
84.072	Indian Education—Grants to Indian Controlled Schools (B)		x				x
84.073	National Diffusion Network (B)		x	x	x		
84.077	Bilingual Vocational Training (B,C)	x	x	x	x		

Finding Funding. © 1993 Corwin Press, Inc.

Figure 4.4 Continued. Department of Education Programs That Receive Federal Assistance

INDEX #	PROGRAM DESCRIPTION	ELIGIBILITY INDEX					
		IND	LOC	N/P	ST	UST	FTG
84.078	Postsecondary Education Programs for Persons with Disabilities (B)		x	x			
84.083	Women's Educational Equity (B)	x	x	x	x		
84.086	Special Education—Severely Disabled Program (B)	x	x	x	x		
84.087	Indian Education—Fellowships for Indian Students (B)	x					
84.091	Strengthening Research Library Resources (B)		x	x	x		
84.094	Patricia Roberts Harris Fellowships (B)		x	x			
84.097	Law School Clinical Experience Program (B)		x	x			
84.099	Bilingual Vocational Instructor Training (B,C)	x		x	x		
84.100	Bilingual Vocational Materials, Methods, and Techniques (B)	x		x	x		
84.101	Vocational Education—Indian and Hawaiian Natives (B)						x
84.103	Training for Special Programs Staff and Leadership Personnel (B)		x	x	x		
84.116	Fund for the Improvement of Postsecondary Education (B)		x	x			
84.117	Educational Research and Development (B)	x		x			
84.120	Minority Science Improvement (B)	x		x		x	
84.123	Law-Related Eduation (B)		x	x	x		
84.124	Territorial Teacher Training Assistance Program (B)					x	
84.125	Clearinghouse on Disability Information (L)	x	x	x	x	x	x
84.126	Rehabilitation Services—Basic Support (A)				x	x	
84.128	Rehabilitation Services—Service Projects (B)		x	x	x	x	
84.129	Rehabilitation Training (B)		x	x	x	x	
84.132	Centers for Independent Living (B)		x	x	x	x	
84.133	National Institute on Disability and Rehabilitation Research (B)	x	x	x	x		
84.136	Legal Training for the Disadvantaged (B)	x	x	x	x	x	x
84.141	Migrant Education—High School Equivalency Program (B)		x	x			
84.142	College Housing and Academic Facilities Loans (E)			x			
84.144	Migrant Education—Coordination Program (B)				x		
84.145	Federal Real Property Assistance Program (H)		x	x	x		
84.149	Migrant Education—College Assistance Migrant Program (B)			x			
84.151	Federal, State, and Local Partnerships for Educational Improvement (A)	x		x	x		
84.153	Business and International Education (B)			x			
84.154	Public Library Construction and Technology Enhancement (A)				x		
84.158	Secondary Educ. & Transitional Services for Youth with Disabilities (B)		x	x	x		
84.159	Disabled—Special Studies and Evaluation (B)		x	x	x		
84.160	Training Interpreters for Deaf Individuals (B)		x	x	x	x	
84.161	Rehabilitation Services—Client Assistance Program (A)				x	x	
84.162	Emergency Immigrant Education (A)				x	x	
84.163	Library Services for Indian Tribes and Hawaiian Natives (B)						x
84.164	Eisenhower Mathematics and Science Education—State Grants (A)				x	x	x
84.165	Magnet Schools Assistance in Desegregating Districts (B)		x				
84.167	Library Literacy (B)		x		x		
84.168	Dwight D. Eisenhower Nat'l Program for Mathematics & Science Educ. (B)		x	x	x		
84.169	Comprehensive Services for Independent Living (A)				x	x	
84.170	Jacob K. Javits Fellowships (B)	x	x	x	x	x	x
84.173	Special Education—Preschool Grants (A)				x	x	
84.174	Vocational Education—Community Based Orgainzations (A)		x	x	x	x	
84.176	Douglas Teacher Scholarships (A)		x		x	x	
84.177	Rehab. Services—Independent Living Services for Older Blind Ind. (B)				x	x	
84.178	Leadership in Educational Administration Development (B)		x	x	x		
84.180	Technology, Educ. Media & Materials for Individuals with Disabilites (B) .	x	x	x	x		
84.181	Infants and Toddlers with Disabilities(B)				x	x	
84.184	Drug-Free Schools and Communities—National Programs (B)		x	x	x		
84.185	Robert C. Byrd Honors Scholarships (A)				x		
84.186	Drug-Free Schools and Communities—State Grants (A)				x	x	
84.187	Supported Employment Serv. for Individuals with Severe Handicaps (A)				x		
84.188	Drug-Free Schools and Communities—Regional Centers (B)			x			
84.190	Christa McAuliffe Fellowships (B)		x	x	x		

Figure 4.4 Continued. Department of Education Programs That Receive Federal Assistance

		ELIGIBILITY INDEX					
INDEX #	**PROGRAM DESCRIPTION**	**IND**	**LOC**	**N/P**	**ST**	**UST**	**FTG**
84.191	National Adult Education Discretionary Program (B)	x		x			
84.192	Adult Education for the Homeless (B)		x	x	x		
84.193	Demonstration Centers for the Training of Dislocated Workers (B)			x			
84.194	Bilingual Education Support Services (B)		x	x	x		
84.195	Bilingual Education Training Grants (B)	x	x	x	x		
84.196	Educ. of Homeless Children & Youth—Grants for State/Local Activities (A)				x	x	
84.197	College Library Technology (B)			x	x		
84.198	National Workplace Literacy Program (B)	x	x	x	x		
84.199	Vocational Education—Cooperative Demonstration (B)		x	x	x		
84.200	Graduate Assistance in Areas of National Need (B)			x			
84.201	School Dropout Demonstration Assistance (B)		x	x			
84.202	Grants to Inst. to Encourage Minority Participation in Grad. Educ. (B)	x		x			
84.203	Star Schools Program (B)		x	x	x		
84.204	School, College, and University Partnerships (B)	x	x	x			
84.206	Jacob K. Javits Gifted and Talented Students Educ. Grant Program (B)		x	x	x		x
84.207	Educational Personnel Training (B)		x	x	x		
84.208	Native Hawaiian Model Curriculum Development (C)	x		x	x		
84.209	Native Hawaiian Family Based Education Centers (C)	x		x	x		
84.210	Native Hawaiian Gifted and Talented (C)			x			
84.211	FIRST Schools and Teachers (B)		x	x	x		
84.212	FIRST Family School Partnerships (B)		x				
84.213	Even Start—State Education Agencies (A)				x		
84.214	Even Start—Migrant Education (B)				x		
84.215	The Secretary's Fund for Innovation in Education (B)		x	x	x		
84.216	Capital Expenses (A, B)		x		x		
84.217	Ronald E. McNair Post-Baccalaureate Achievement (B)			x	x		
84.218	State Program Improvement Grants (A)				x		
84.219	Student Literacy Corps (B)			x	x		
84.220	Center for International Business Education (B)			x			
84.221	Native Hawaiian Special Education (B)			x	x		
84.223	English Literacy Program (B)			x			
84.224	State Grants for Tech.-Related Assist. to Individuals with Disabilities (B, L)				x	x	
84.226	Income Contingent Loan Program (C)	x					
84.228	Educational Partnerships (B)		x	x			
84.229	Language Resource Centers (B)		x	x	x		
84.230	Technology Education Demonstration (B)		x	x	x		
84.231	Demonstration and Innovation Projects of National Significance in Technology-Related Assistance for Individuals with Disabilities (B)	x		x			
84.232	Mid-Career Teacher Training (B)			x	x		
84.233	Drug-Free Schools and Communities—Emergency Grants (B)		x				
84.234	Projects with Industry (B)	x		x			
84.235	Special Projects and Demonstrations for Providing Vocational Rehabilitation Services to Individuals with Severe Disabilities (B)			x	x		
84.236	Training and Public Awareness Projects in Technology Related Assistance for Individuals with Disabilities (B)	x		x			
84.237	Children and Youth with Serious Emotional Disturbance (B)		x	x	x		
84.238	Training Programs for Educators—Alcohol Abuse (B)	x	x	x	x		
84.239	Foreign Language Materials Acquisition (B)		x		x		
84.240	Program of Protection and Advocacy of Individual Rights (B)				x		
84.241	Counselor Training (B)		x	x	x		
84.242	National Science Scholars (C)	x					
84.243	Tech-Prep Education (A)				x		
84.244	Business and Education Standards (B)	x		x			
84.245	Tribally Controlled Postsecondary Vocational Institutions (B)				x		
84.246	Rehabilitation Short-Term Training (B)		x	x	x	x	
84.247	Commerical Drivers Education (B)	x	x	x	x		

Figure 4.4 Continued. Department of Education Programs That Receive Federal Assistance

INDEX # PROGRAM DESCRIPTION	IND	LOC	N/P	ST	UST	FTG
84.248 Demonstration Projects for the Integration of Voc. & Academic Learning (B)		x	x	x		
84.249 Foreign Languages Assistance (A)				x		
84.250 Rehabilitation Services—American Indians with Disabilities (B)		x		x		x
84.251 Periodicals Published Outside the United States (B)		x	x	x		
84.252 Urban Community Services (B)			x	x		
84.253 Supplementary State Grants for Facilities, Equipment, & Other (A)				x		
84.254 State Literacy Resource Centers (A)				x		
84.255 Literacy for Incarcerated Adults (B)		x		x		
84.256 Territories—Freely Associated States Education Grant Program (B)					x	

Source: *Catalog of Federal Domestic Assistance (CFDA),* 1993.

The letter(s) in parenthesis following the program title, shows the type(s) of assistance available through that program. The letter codes with accompanying types of assistance are as follows: A—Formula Grants; B—Project Grants; C—Direct Payments for Specified Use; D—Direct Payments with Unrestricted Use; E—Direct Loans; F—Guaranteed/Insured Loans; G—Insurance; H—Sale, Exchange, or Donation of Property and Goods; I—Use of Property, Facilities, and Equipment; J—Provision of Specialized Services; K—Advisory Services and Counseling; L—Dissemination of Technical Information; M—Training; N—Investigation of Complaints; O—Federal Employment.

Definitions of the types of applicants used in this Eligibility Index are given below.

IND: Individual—Any person or persons, as individuals, groups, or profit making organizations. Such persons and groups do not represent Federally Recognized Indian Tribal Governments. Includes Indians or other Native Americans who apply as individuals rather than as a member of a tribe or other Indian organization.

LOC: Local—Agencies or instrumentalities of political subdivisions within a state, to include cities, towns, townships, parishes, municipalities, villages, counties, and school districts. Included under local are Indian tribes on state reservations, Indian bands and groups, Pueblos, Indian school boards, and state-designated Indian tribes. Local does *not* include institutions of higher education and hospitals.

N/P: Nonprofit—A public or private agency or organization established by charter to perform specialized functions or services for the benefit of all or part of the general public. Functions or services are provided without charge or at cost, and earn no profit. The agency or organization has no shareholders to receive dividends..

ST: State—Any agency or instrumentality of the 50 states of the United States and the District of Columbia. State does not include the political subdivisions of the state, but does include institutions of higher education and hospitals.

UST: U.S. Territories—Any agency or instrumentality of the Commonwealth of Puerto Rico, the Virgin Islands, Guam, American Samoa, the Trust Territories of the Pacific Islands, and Mariana Islands. Included are the political subdivisions of the territories, institutions of higher education, and hospitals.

FTG: Federally Recognized Indian Tribal Organizations—The governing body or a governmental agency of an Indian tribe, nation, or other organized group or community recognized and certified by the Secretary of the Interior.

Functional Index Number

Each federal domestic assistance program in the *CFDA* is identified by a five-digit *CFDA* number. The first two digits identify the federal department or agency that administers the program, and the last three digits identify a specific program. For example, program number 10.001 is administered by the Department of Agriculture, 17.802 by the Department of Labor, 13.103 by the Department of Health and Human Services, 84.149 by the Department of Education, and so on. The *CFDA* number will appear on grant application packets and in notices in the *Federal Register* referring to the assistance program. The following is an example.

84.XXX	Education. Programs in Education are in the Functional Index as 84.XXX.
84.149	Specifically, Education's Migrant Education CAMP Program was assigned XX.149 or 84.149, which indicates that the federal agency administrating this program is the U.S. Department of Education.
84.044	Education's Talent Search Program was assigned XX.044.

> **A Listing of Department of Education Programs from the *CFDA* Appears in Figure 4.4.**

—— **Grant Tip** ——

Each federal domestic assistance program in the CFDA *is identified by a five-digit "CFDA Number." The first two digits identify the federal department or agency that administers the program, and the last three digits identify a specific program.*

Program Description

A "typical" *CFDA* program entry includes nearly one page of information about the program and the processes of applying for the assistance (Figure 4.5 is a typical example of a *CFDA* Program Description). This specific program relates to the sample grant proposal presented in Chapter 7, "Reviewing a Funded Proposal." The entry in Figure 4.5 provides a full range of information to assist the grant seeker in determining if this is a correct source, if the grant seeker is an eligible applicant, and how and where to get additional information. Some program information and examples are provided. The first information in the entry is the *CFDA* number, the program title, and the agency administering the assistance program. Other information includes abbreviated topics to help a grant seeker determine whether or not this particular program will support what the grant seeker needs or is planning to propose.

A list of topic headings found in a typical education entry is presented in Figure 4.6. For some programs the entry *Related Programs* will provide considerable additional and important information; for some programs the entry simply is "none."

Figure 4.5. Sample of a Program Description in the *CFDA*

84.149 MIGRANT EDUCATION—COLLEGE ASSISTANCE MIGRANT PROGRAM (CAMP)

FEDERAL AGENCY: SECRETARY FOR ELEMENTARY AND SECONDARY EDUCATION, DEPARTMENT OF EDUCATION

AUTHORIZATION: Higher Education Act of 1965, Section 418A, 20 U.S.C. 1070d-2.

OBJECTIVES: To assist students that are engaged, or whose families are engaged in migrant and other seasonal farmwork, and are enrolled or are admitted for enrollment on a full-time basis in the first academic year at an institution of higher education.

TYPES OF ASSISTANCE: Project Grants.

USES AND USE RESTRICTIONS: Project funds may be used to provide supportive and instructional services including tutoring and counseling services and assistance in obtaining student financial aid (including stipends, tuition, and room and board) to first-year college students, and assist those students in obtaining financial aid for their remaining undergraduate years.

ELIGIBILITY REQUIREMENTS:

Applicant Eligibility: Institutions of higher education or private non-profit agencies in cooperation with institutions of higher education may apply.

Beneficiary Eligibility: First-year college students that are engaged, or whose families are engaged, in migrant and other seasonal farmwork will benefit.

Credentials/Documentation: To be eligible to participate in a CAMP project, a migrant or other seasonally employed farmworker or dependent must: (1) Be enrolled or admitted for enrollment as a full-time student at a participating institution of higher education; (2) not be beyond the first academic year of a program of study at the institution of higher education, as determined under the standards of the institution; and (3) be determined by the grantee to need the academic and supporting services and financial assistance provided by the project in order to complete an academic program of study at the institution of higher education.

APPLICATION AND AWARD PROCESS:

Preapplication Coordination: This program is eligible for coverage under E.O. 12372, 'Intergovernmental Review of Federal Programs.' An applicant should consult the office or official designation as the single point of contact in his or her State for more information on the process the State requires to be followed in applying for assistance, if the State has selected the program for review.

Application Procedure: Application forms are available from the Department of Education. An applicant submits its application to the Department of Education no later than the date announced by the Department in the Federal Register. An application must be prepared and submitted in accordance with the regulations, instructions, and forms included in the grant application package. The applications are reviewed and evaluated by a panel for possible selection for funding.

Award Procedure: The Department of Education notifies successful applicants of awards. Actual negotiation and awarding of grants is done by the Department of Education's Grants and Contracts Service.

Deadlines: Contact the Department of Education for application deadlines.

Range of Approval/Disapproval Time: Three months.

Appeals: None

Renewals: Grants are awarded for three years.

ASSISTANCE CONSIDERATIONS:

Formula and Matching Requirements: This program has no statutory formula or matching requirements.

Length and Time Phasing of Assistance: The project period is up to 36 months; funds are awarded for a twelve month budget period.

POST ASSISTANCE REQUIREMENTS:

Reports: Annual financial and performance reports are required.

Audits: In accordance with the Education Department General Administration Regulations in the Appendix to 34 CFR 80, State and local governments that receive financial assistance of $100,000 or more within the State's fiscal year shall have an audit made for that year. State and local governments that receive between $25,000 and $100,000 within the State's fiscal year shall have an audit made in accordance with the Appendix to Part 80, or in accordance with Federal laws and regulations governing the programs in which they participate. If such entities are excluded, audits of these entities shall be made in accordance with statutory requirements and the provisions of 34 CFR Part 74.

Records: In accordance with the General Education Provisions Act and the Education Department General Administrative Regulations (34 CFR 74, 75, and 80), grantees must maintain certain project records for five years.

FINANCIAL INFORMATION:

Account Identification: 91-0900-0-1-501.

Obligations: (Grants) FY 91 $1,952,000; FY $2,265,000; and FY est. $2,265,000. (Additional authorizing legislation is required for this program to operate in FY 93).

Range and Average of Financial Assistance: $212,768 to $354,504; $278,857.

PROGRAM ACCOMPLISHMENTS: During fiscal year 1991, approximately 350 students in seven institutions were served.

REGULATIONS, GUIDELINES, AND LITERATURE: 34 CFR 206

INFORMATION CONTACTS:

Regional or Local Office: Not applicable.

Headquarters Office: Office of Migrant Education, Office of Elementary and Secondary Education, Department of Education, 400 Maryland Avenue, Roomm 2145, Washington, D.C. 20202. Contact: W. L. Stormer. Telephone: (202) 401-0742.

RELATED PROGRAMS: 84.011, Migrant Education—Basic State Formula Grant Program; 84.042, Student Support Services; 84.141, Migrant Education—High School Equivalency Program; 84.144, Migrant Education—Coordination Program; 93.246, Migrant Health Centers Grants.

EXAMPLES OF FUNDED PROJECTS: Project funds are used to recruit potential participants and to provide services to students in such areas as: tutoring; academic, career, and personal counseling; health services; housing support; exposure to academic programs, cultural events, and other activities not usually available to migrant youth; and appropriate in-service training activities for project staff members.

CRITERIA FOR SELECTING PROPOSALS: Program Regulations (34 CFR 206) include the criteria for selecting proposals, as follows: Plan of operation (25 points); objectives and activities (20 points); evaluation plan (15 points); quality of key personnel (10 points); budget and cost-effectiveness (10 points); interagency consultation and coordination (10 points); adequacy of resources (5 points); recruitment (5 points); and prior experience (15 points).

Source: *CFDA*, 1992, pages 825-826.

Figure 4.6. Topic Headings for *CFDA* Program Description

•Federal agency administering a program
•Authorization upon which a program is based
•Objectives and goals of a program
•Types of financial and nonfinancial assistance offered under a program
•Uses and restrictions placed upon a program
•Eligibility requirements
•Application and award process
•Amount of obligations for the past, current, and future fiscal years
•Regulations, guidelines, and literature relevant to a program
•Information contacts at the headquarters, regional, and local offices
•Programs that are related based upon program objectives and uses
•Examples of funded projects
•Criteria for selecting proposals
•Individual agency policies and federal management policy directives
 pertaining to a program

Beyond the Basics

If entries under the *Related Programs* heading are plentiful, review the other programs to determine how well their purposes fit with your idea. This analysis may lead to programs whose general categories may not at first seem directly applicable. For example, if you are interested in education programs for handicapped persons, you may find applicable programs under parks, recreation, or community services.

If the related program is out of your field (Example: You are in education but the related program is in recreation), check carefully the rules of eligibility. People seldom look outside their own primary area of interest. If a related program is out of your primary field, but another very cooperative agency is an eligible applicant, plan to submit a proposal through that agency, not through the usual one.

——**Grant Tip**——
Identify related programs that allow you to be innovative in tying your ideas to a program's objectives or in being an applicant who is "different."

1. Work cooperatively with representatives of the related field (e.g., recreation) that really is the primary category for this program.

2. Develop a strong, innovative proposal using recreation and education resources.

3. Submit the proposal through your agency (education) rather than through the primary agency (recreation).

By submitting the proposal through your agency (education) rather than through the primary agency (recreation), and assuming that not many others have used that procedure, your proposal may generate interest and a "second look" as it will be different from the majority of proposals the agency receives for that competition. (It will be out of the ordinary and may catch the attention of the readers.)

In Conclusion

——Grant Tip——
The CFDA *is of utmost importance to the grantwriter. It provides access to information about all assistance programs administered by federal departments and agencies.*

The *CFDA* is a governmentwide compendium of federal programs, projects, services, and activities of utmost importance to the grantwriter. In a single publication the *CFDA* provides access to information about all assistance programs administered by federal departments and agencies. The program information in the *CFDA* is cross-referenced by functional classification (Functional Index), subject (Subject Index), applicant (Applicant Index), deadline(s) for program application (Deadlines Index), and authorizing legislation (Authorization Index). This *Catalog* is the grantwriter's most valuable "tool of the trade." If used carefully and skillfully, the *CFDA* can make it easier for you to identify specific areas of program interest more efficiently.

PART II

Writing Grant Proposals

In Part II, Chapters 5-9, we address the specifics of writing grant proposals. Information on the basic components of a standard proposal, tips on reviewing and responding to a request for proposal (RFP), and a sample funded proposal are presented. In addition, we outline the various steps an application goes through and introduce key players who are vital participants in the grant-making process.

5

What Are the Components of a Proposal?

Introduction and Some Background

In Chapter 5 we explore some ideas, tips, and strategies for developing proposals in *general;* in Chapter 6 we use *in detail* one specific Department of Education program and analyze the process of writing a proposal to that program. Chapters 1, 5, and 6 together offer a roadmap for developing successful proposals for external funding excluding the private sector where a foundation or group may have specific requirements.

This chapter emphasizes developing competitive proposals and offers some samples and examples. The grantwriter will compile a file of forms and formats that suit the writer's own style and needs. A proposal must be well written; the proposal is the bridge between (a) the funding agency with its goals, priorities, and regulations and (b) your agency with its abilities, interests, staff, and approach to problems of concern to the funding source.

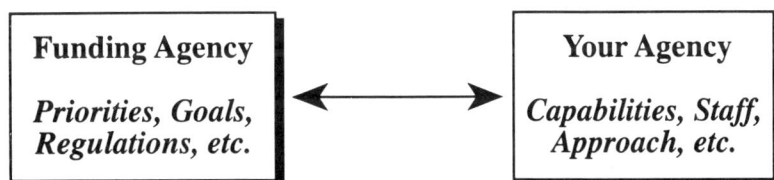

Funding Agency		**Your Agency**
Priorities, Goals, Regulations, etc.	◄──────►	*Capabilities, Staff, Approach, etc.*

The proposal should be *clear, concise, cogent, compelling,* and *correct*—the *"five Cs"* of carefully crafted proposals. The language should be reasonably free of jargon. The ideas should be presented succinctly with minimum repetition. Use short sentences and the active voice. The plan should be clear and forceful. Your ideas should be refreshing and attractive with direct ties both to a major problem and to the key interests of the agency to which you will submit the proposal. Finally, the proposal should be as error free as possible: Attend well to tense, agreement, and other rules of grammar.

——**Grant Tip**——
The proposal should be clear, concise, cogent, compelling, and correct—the "five Cs" of carefully crafted proposals.

This chapter reviews the background of the "standard" federal proposal and explains each section briefly. Some explanations are pertinent for recent proposal formats that are reviewed later in the chapter, but the chapter has a special slant toward a "standard" federal proposal.

Although still directed toward Department of Education programs, Chapter 5 has relevance across other federal agencies. This is possible, in part, due to the general similarity among many federal proposal formats and other requirements. The desire for some commonality among federal program proposal requirements led, in 1974, to Federal Management Circular (FMC) 74-7 (9/13/74) "Uniform administrative requirements for grants-in-aid to state and local governments." In part, FMC 74-7 stated, "On March 27, 1969, the President ordered a 3-year effort to simplify, standardize, decentralize and otherwise modernize the Federal grant machinery." FMC 74-7 temporarily replaced Office of Management and Budget (OMB) Circular No. A-102 while standardization occurred. On 9/12/77 the OMB issued a new Circular A-102 as Part VII of the *Federal Register*. Figure 5.1 shows the "standard" proposal format as described in OMB

Figure 5.1. Parts of a Standard Proposal (OMB A-102, 1977)

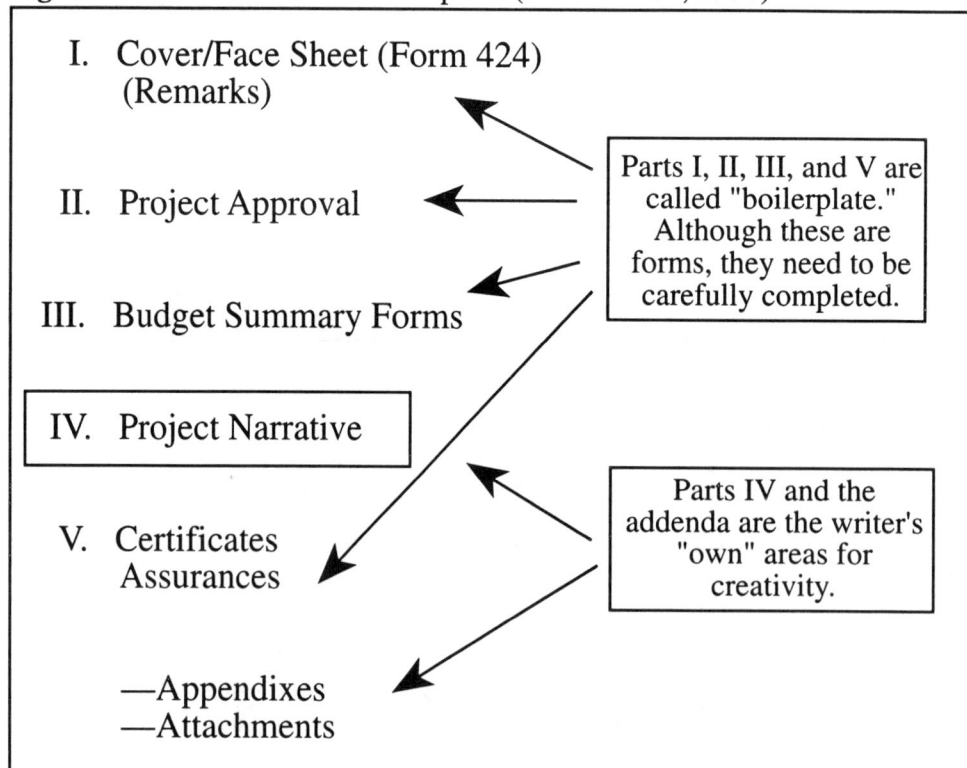

I.   Cover/Face Sheet (Form 424)
     (Remarks)

II. Project Approval

III. Budget Summary Forms

Parts I, II, III, and V are called "boilerplate." Although these are forms, they need to be carefully completed.

IV. Project Narrative

V.   Certificates
     Assurances

Parts IV and the addenda are the writer's "own" areas for creativity.

—Appendixes
—Attachments

A-102; standard forms, including the face sheet (Form 424), a project approval form, budget summary forms, and various certifications and assurances become part of each proposal application. Between 1977 and the present, there have been some modest changes in the forms and the formats, but the 1977 standardization instilled the idea that the various agencies might be able to work from a similar proposal design. *The original (1977) plan is shown here for perspective. Newer examples are provided a few pages later.*

In proposal-preparation parlance, the standard forms that become part of the proposal package are collectively called "boilerplate." These are Parts I, II, III and V of the A-102 format. The boilerplate provides a similarity and continuity that assist in categorizing, comparing, and codifying the proposals at the agency, and it facilitates multiple-agency proposals and/or interagency funding of large projects. The boilerplate is usually completed last, or near last, in the proposal-writing process.

Part IV of the 1977 A-102 format is the Narrative, the opportunity for the writer to express what the project is all about. Each proposal application may have some specific instructions, but the general parts of the narrative (9/77) are those shown in Figure 5.2. Some programs *require* an *Abstract,* usually about 250 words. You will probably write this last. Although not required, a brief *Introduction/Background* may be useful, especially if your agency is not well known. Here you might *briefly* describe your agency and something of your (and the agency's) history, experience, and interest in the project being proposed. Comment on special strengths. Be brief and concise—try to keep this to less than two pages. The parts of the narrative required in A-102 are briefly described here. (Later Education Department proposal applications have slightly different formats and follow (a) specifics for the program and (b) Education Division General Administrative Regulations, or *EDGAR,* as set forth in 34 *CFR,* Part 74 [Administration of Grants; Part 75; Direct Grant Programs], and Part 77 [Definitions that apply to Department Regulations]. See Chapter 3 of this book for information on the *CFR, EDGAR,* etc.)

Objectives and Need for Assistance

You should work first on the needs, because the needs will help structure the objectives, the project activities, and the evaluation. Needs should be specific, employing compelling data. Move from

Figure 5.2. General Federal Proposal Format, Part IV: Program Narrative for Standard Grant Applications

---

ABSTRACT

INTRODUCTION/BACKGROUND*

1. OBJECTIVES AND NEED FOR THIS ASSISTANCE

   Need (National, Regional, State, or Local). Get and use data. Objectives will be stated to show that progress toward them will be measurable.

2. RESULTS OR BENEFITS EXPECTED (GENERAL)

   This is a "philosophy" or overall goal for your effort. (This section has been dropped in later proposal format.)

3. APPROACH

   A. Plan of Action: Besides a clear statement of your activities, this section might include the theoretic considerations/conceptual base (literature, etc.)
   B. Time Frame or Time Projections
   C. Data to be Collected. Evaluation Process/Design
   D. Organizations, Cooperators, Consultants

4. GEOGRAPHIC LOCATION (Attach a map or maps)

5. OTHER

   A. Director (Résumé)
   B. Other Key Personnel
   C. References

CERTIFICATIONS, APPENDIXES, ATTACHMENTS FOLLOW THE NARRATIVE

*Usually, if there are no page limits, it is suggested that you make introduction and key points (1-5) as center headings (capitalized). The other dividers shown here (A, B, etc.) are freestanding side headings, and each starts a new page during proposal-writing time so that it is easy to make changes as you review the work or get feedback from others. In later application packets, there is a request for a 25-page (double-spaced) limit. Starting each section on a separate page may be a lost luxury.

---

general needs (even those used to argue for the legislation at congressional hearings) to specific needs (at your local site). Where possible, use recognized sources such as census data, standard test scores, etc. Consider needs at several levels, e.g.:

General Needs to Specific Needs

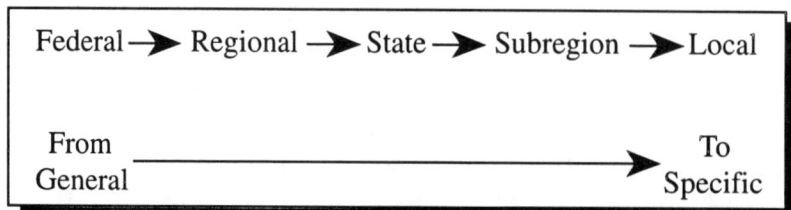

Federal ➤ Regional ➤ State ➤ Subregion ➤ Local

From General ————————————————➤ To Specific

The *Needs* section, although emphasizing conditions that your project will address, should show that these *needs* relate to a *class* or *group* of people deserving help or assistance. Although you are seeking support for *your* clientele, the agency will want to support a worthy, innovative effort that can be generalized to others like your clients—a model that may be "transportable" and provide a cost-effective stable solution to a fairly common problem that has been clearly documented by the needs you have carefully compiled.

Besides being important in their own right, thoroughly documented needs are important to other aspects of the proposal and, ultimately, to the project. The needs become

- Baseline data to assist in the evaluation plan or design.
- A "target" giving substance to each objective.
- An organizing element around which you will structure key activities.

The objectives provide an organizing framework for the proposal and for the activities you will do to achieve the objectives. Objectives should be specific; as much as possible, they should be stated in "measurable terms." Unless the project is extremely complex, 4-8 objectives will be adequate. You need an objective to guide each major concern but not for minor efforts; each objective will be the focus of several enabling activities.

Results or Benefits Expected

The *Results or Benefits Expected* section (seldom used in Department of Education applications now) provides you an opportunity to state a general view of the project's potential. The brief comments here may take the form of philosophical statements or goals. These points need not be "measurable" in the sense that objectives are, but they should tie things together, provide a view of how successes with this project may lead to a model or generalized solution, and express how this project may contribute to a stream of research or project development. (In recent applications for grants, this section, per se, has been dropped and points usually sought here may be addressed in such sections as Meeting the Purposes of the Authorizing Statute or How Well the Objectives of the Project Relate to the Purposes of the Program.)

—— **Grant Tip** ——

The objectives provide an organizing framework for the proposal; as much as possible, they should be stated in "measurable terms."

Approach

This section delineates the proposer's unique way of addressing the needs and purposes of the authorizing statutes. In this section the proposer explains clearly a "plan of action" that includes such things as

- Theoretic considerations/conceptual base.
- A literature review showing how this project will "fit" with current thinking and extend the state-of-the-art.
- Explanations of how each activity of note will contribute to project success.
- A plan showing how personnel will be deployed to perform the activities and to achieve the objectives.
- A management plan to show how the proposer will organize and operate the project in an efficient and effective manner.
- A plan to guide formative and summative (process and product) evaluation.
- A clear picture of ideas for disseminating project results to important audiences.

The *Approach* section will include a timeline, time frame or projections of approximately when things will be completed. The timeline may be in graphic form and will relate to the management plan. Figure 5.3 shows one format for a timeline that relates major

Figure 5.3. Major Activities Planning Form

Major Activities	Dates (By month or quarter)											
	Q 1			Q 2			Q 3			Q 4		
	Jan	Feb	Mar	Apr	May	Jun	Jul	Aug	Sep	Oct	Nov	Dec

activities to completion times (by months and/or quarters of the project year). You do not need to specify *exact dates*—in fact, you may not be able to control these anyway. Use months or two-week intervals to show your checkpoints for progress.

An *Evaluation Plan* or design is also part of the approach. The evaluation plan will specify the data to be collected to assess the project's processes and products. The needs data, carefully developed, will be part of evaluation in that they serve as the *baseline* information. (A project is successful if its activities reduce the need that generated the project in the first place.) It is not enough to state that you will employ an external agency to do your evaluation. Your proposal must contain enough good evaluation information so the proposal readers can assess the rigor and utility of your evaluation plan. One simple plan to organize project evaluation is shown in Figure 5.4. Each point should be addressed in the evaluation narrative. This includes the evaluation purpose or focus, types of data, and perspective or locus of the evaluator(s).

──── **Grant Tip** ────

Your proposal must contain enough good evaluation information so the proposal readers can assess the rigor and utility of your plan.

Figure 5.4. A Simple Model to Structure Project Evaluation Efforts

Evaluation & Data Type	Evaluator Perspective	PURPOSE OR FOCUS OF EVALUATION		
		Formative (Process)	Summative (Product)	Project Management
Quantitative	External Internal			
Qualitative	External Internal			

Seldom does a single agency accomplish all of a project's outcomes by itself. A successful project has persons/agencies that *cooperate* in the project's efforts. Be sure to describe the cooperating entities and specify the particulars of the cooperation. Include any special contributions of each "cooperator." (The proposal may contain an appendix with letters or sample letters that describe a cooperator's involvement and contributions.) Commitments of specifics (time, money, space, etc.) are much more valuable than general support.

In the *Geographic Location* section you should specify why the funding agency can benefit from locating the project *here.* Explain ease of travel, special resources, unusual geographic characteristics or demographic influences, etc. One or two good maps will help the reader visualize the location. This brief section should not only be convincing, but the location should support project activities.

The *Other* section of the narrative will contain information about project personnel—the director and staff. If the project requires activities that staff do not have specific and particular skills to deliver, list by name and areas of special expertise consultants who will fill in the gaps. End this section with a listing of the references cited in the theoretic framework/conceptual basis for the project and other sources that *strongly* support what you anticipate doing. Try to have no references over 5-7 years old *unless* the reference is considered a "classic."

A later section in this chapter outlines some recent variations on the "standard" proposal format. The newer structures build on *EDGAR* and remove some repetition and extra materials that the original format seemed to engender. "General" and philosophic "stuff" has been removed, leaving only the "scientific." The normative, ethical, and moral elements of the proposal seem to have been removed for a more "businesslike" approach.

The Project: Planning and Design

The standard format, proceeding as it does from Objectives/Needs to Other (including personnel), seems to suggest a chronology and linear approach following that design. Indeed, some proposal-writing seminars and writing guides also suggest a flow of activity from *needs* to *objectives* to *activities,* etc. Figure 5.5 shows the *usual* "flow" of project-development and proposal-writing efforts, including the theoretical or usual approach, as espoused in these training seminars. (Realistically, however, most successful grantwriters do not follow the model taught in these seminars and workshops.)

Perhaps this model would work easily if people started from "ground zero" and if there were no time limits or deadlines. (Remember: *There is no such thing as a late proposal!)* This idealized model, useful for instructional purposes and not revealing the actual approach of successful grantwriters, suggests a seeking out of needs (a "shotgun" approach), followed by a refining and shaping of needs to (1) reflect your agency's clientele and (2) to meet the funding agency's priorities.

Figure 5.5. Flowchart of Project-Development/Proposal-Writing Efforts

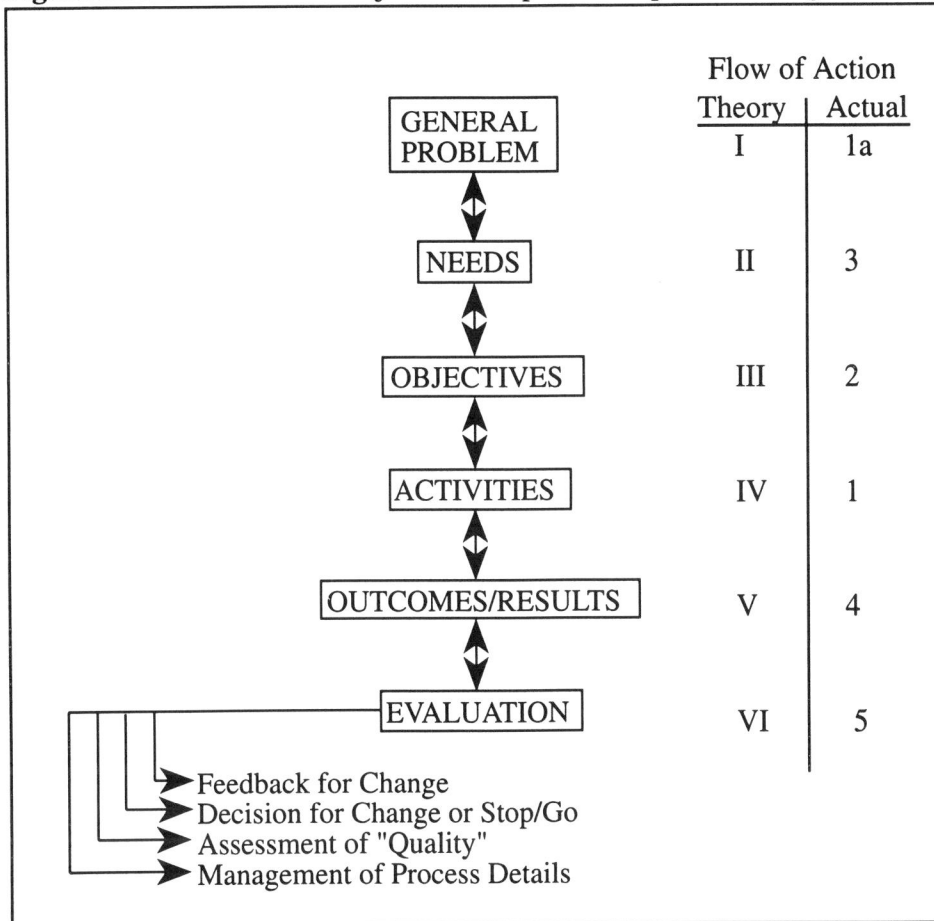

In actuality, the applying agency usually has existed for some time and agency personnel have analyzed what *really* needs to be done—and what local customs and mores will allow to be done. They have used their Informed Professional Judgment (IPJ) to identify the activities needed to get the job done. Thus, the applying agency personnel know the *general problem* and the *activities* that make sense *given* the certainties and expectations of persons in the service areas. They know what they want to do and what they can do. Logically, then, they start their project/proposal planning and development there (problem and activities). They use what they already have concluded from their IPJ. Thus, in the real realm of the proposal-development process, the set of events goes something as follows:

1. **Activities** (IV on Figure 5.5). Activities are already known to the writer by IPJ of the agency staff or clients. The proposal writer then asks a logical question. . .

   Why do we want to do these activities? The answers, often beginning with "to" or "because," offer the outline of the. . .

2. **Objectives** (III on Figure 5.5). Several activities are likely to cluster under one objective. Then, for each rough objective, ask a logical question. . .

   Why are these objectives important (or what generated these objectives)? The answers, often beginning with "because," offer the outline of the. . .

3. **Needs** (II on Figure 5.5). Now, rather than *searching out* needs (a "shotgun" approach), your task is to *document* the needs (a "rifle" approach). Assign someone to find compelling evidence and proof for needs. Next, return to each objective (III on Figure 5.5) and ask a logical question. . .

   What will happen if we fulfill the objectives? The answers, usually stated as a benefit or improved condition, offer the working outline for the. . .

4. **Outcomes and Results** (V on Figure 5.5). The next logical questions stem from the projected outcomes and are. . .

   How will we recognize our success in obtaining the outcomes? What evidence will show that the outcomes have been attained? The answers to these questions will help in framing the plan or design for. . .

5. **Evaluation** (VI on Figure 5.5). The evaluation will then be refined to fulfill at least the four purposes shown at the bottom of Figure 5.5.

These steps, fairly easily and quickly done by agency staff and perhaps a consultant or two in a "brainstorming session," provide a working outline or structure for a proposal. Each major section needs careful review, revision, and refinement, but this outline, in the "real world" sequence, will offer a guideline to get the proposal development process underway without the bickering that often slows down the process. This process asks and seeks resolution to the *What* questions and the *How* questions that avoid philosophy and values (the *Why* questions). This is *really* how grantwriting is done *successfully.*

- •How will we measure the results?
- •How will we do it?
- •What shall we do?
- •What can we do?

The Evolving Federal Standard "Proposal" Format

The OBM Circular A-102 got the standardization process for grants and applications off to a start (see Figure 5.6). The evolution of the standard definitions, rules and regulations, criteria for judging applications, etc., led to *EDGAR.* As program personnel became comfortable with *EDGAR,* the program's implementing rules and regulations (from the *Federal Register*) began to reflect *EDGAR's* criteria rather than promulgating program-specific implementing rules and regulations. Nevertheless, you should always review each program's specific rules and regulations to be sure you cover *all* requirements. Use of the process established in 9/77 by A-102 led to certain changes, such as usually dropping the original Part II (Project Approval Form—see Figure 5.1), and relying instead upon state

Figure 5.6. The Evolving Federal Grant Application Format

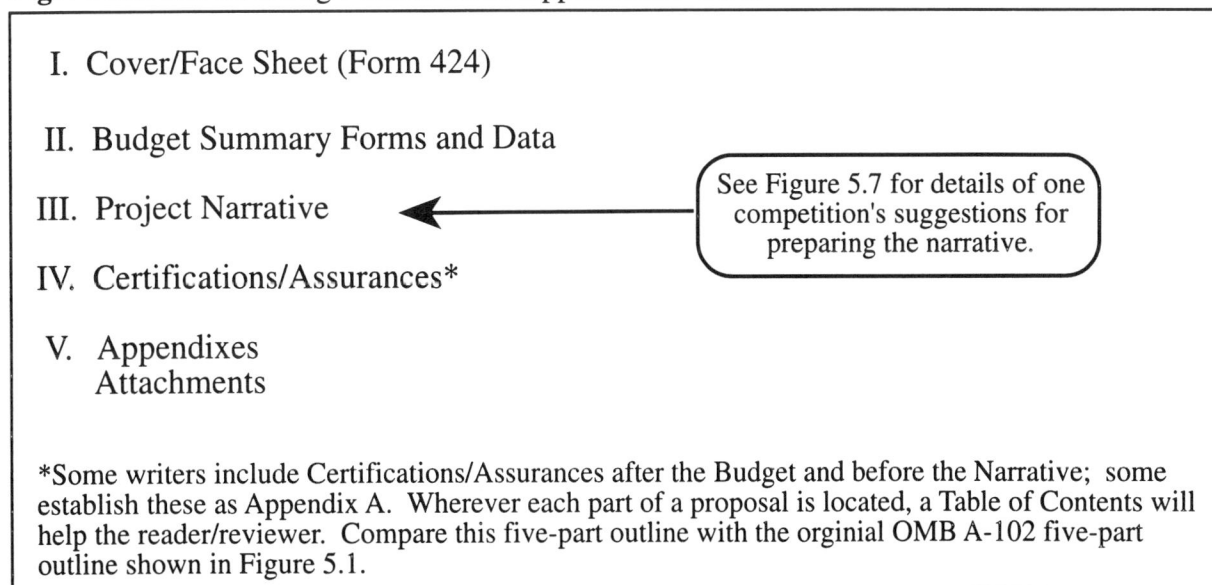

I. Cover/Face Sheet (Form 424)

II. Budget Summary Forms and Data

III. Project Narrative ◄—————— See Figure 5.7 for details of one competition's suggestions for preparing the narrative.

IV. Certifications/Assurances*

V. Appendixes
Attachments

*Some writers include Certifications/Assurances after the Budget and before the Narrative; some establish these as Appendix A. Wherever each part of a proposal is located, a Table of Contents will help the reader/reviewer. Compare this five-part outline with the orginial OMB A-102 five-part outline shown in Figure 5.1.

clearinghouses or Single Points of Contact (SPOC) in each state to determine if the project proposal requires review by the SPOC to meet the mandate of Federal Executive Order 12372.

Recent federal grant applications substitute the SPOC for the former Part II and result in a three-part proposal rather than a four-part proposal (see Figure 5.6). Form 424, the Standard Cover Sheet, has been simplified and the new Narrative section is no longer usually restricted to the general headings (see Figure 5.2); the narrative format is now tailored to *EDGAR* criteria and the specific idiosyncrasies of the particular competition (see Figure 5.7 for an example). Note that the instructions in the sample (Figure 5.7) ask the proposer to describe the proposed project following the selection criteria in the order in which the criteria are listed. Figure 5.8 shows the *EDGAR* selection criteria as used and weighted for this particular grant competition (Secretary's Fund for Innovation in Education Program). Note that the criteria as listed total 85 points with an additional 15 points that can be distributed as the agency (Secretary) decides; for this competition

Figure 5.7. Details of Suggestions for Preparing the Narrative for the Department of Education Grant Competition.[1]

PART III — NARRATIVE

Before preparing the Narrative, an applicant should read carefully the Application Notice describing the priorities and selection criteria used to evelute applications.

The Narrative should encompass each function or activity for which funds are being requested and should

    1. Begin with one-page Abstract; include statements about
        (i) the need for the project
        (ii) the proposed plan of operation
        (iii) the project's significance/intended outcomes.

    2. Describe the proposed project in light of each of the selection criteria (see Figure 5.8) in the order in which the criteria are listed in the Application Notice.

    3. Include any other pertinent information that might be useful in reviewing the application.

The Secretary strongly requests the applicant to limit the Application Narrative to no more than 25 double-spaced, typed pages (on one side only), including appendixes, although the Secretary will consider applications of greater length. The Department has found that successful applications under this program meet this page limit.

---

[1]The requirement for an abstract and the strong suggestion for page limitations.

the "floating" 15 points will be added to the Plan of Operation, making this section now worth 30 points. Thus the outline for this proposal (for Part III or the Narrative—see Figures 5.6 and 5.7) is the *EDGAR* outline as provided in Figure 5.8.

Figure 5.8. *EDGAR* Selection Criteria as Used and Weighted for the 1992 Secretary's Fund for Innovation in Education Program

EDGAR Selection Criteria

(a) How This Section Works

(1) If a discretionary grant program does not have implementing regulations, the Secretary uses the criteria in this section to evaluate applications for new grants under the program.
(2) The maximum score for all of these criteria is 100 points.
(3) The maximum score for each criterion is indicated in parentheses.

(b) The Criteria

(1) *Meeting the purposes of the authorizing statute.* (30 points) The Secretary reviews each application to determine how well the project will meet the purpose of the stature that authorizes the program including consideration of—
 (i) The objectives of the project; and
 (ii) How the objectives of the project further the purposes of th authorizing statute.
(2) *Extent of need for the project.* (20 points) The Secretary reviews each application to determine the extent to which the project meets specific needs recognized in the statute that authorizes the program, including consideration of—
 (i) The needs addressed by the project;
 (ii) How the applicant identified those needs;
 (iii) How those needs will be met by the project; and
 (iv) The benefits to be gained by meeting those needs.
(3) *Plan of operation.**(15 points) The Secretary reviews each application to determine the quality of the plan of operation for the project, including—
 (i) The quality of the design of the project;
 (ii) The extent to which the plan of man agement is effective and ensures proper and efficient administration of the project;
 (iii) How well the objectives of the project relate to the purpose of the program;

 (iv) The quality of the applicant's plan to use its resources and personnel to achieve each objective;
 (v) How the applicant will ensure that project participants who are other wise eligible to participate are se lected without regard to race, color, national origin, gender, age, or handi capping condition; and
 (vi) For grants under a program that re quires the applicant to provide an opportunity to participation of stu dents enrolled in private schools, the quality of the applicant's plan to pro vide that opportunity.
(4) *Quality of key personnel.* (7 points)
 (i) The Secretary reviews each application to determine the quality of key personnel the applicant plans to use on the project, including —
  (A) The qualifications of the project director (if one is to be used);
  (B) The qualifications of each of the other key personnel to be used in the project;
  (C) The time that each person re ferred to in paragraph (b)(4)(i) (A) and (B) will commit to the project; and
  (D) How the applicant, as part of its nondiscriminatory employment practices, will ensure that its per sonnel are selected for employ ment without regard to race, color, national origin, gender, age, or handicapping condition.
 (ii) To determine personnel qualifica tion under paragraphs (b)(4)(i)(A) and (B), the Secretary considers —
  (A) Experience and training in fields related to the objectives of the project; and
  (B) Any other qualifications that pertain to the quality of the project.

(5) *Budget and cost effectiveness.* (5 points) The Secretary reviews each application to determine the extent to which —
 (i) The budget is adequate to support the project; and
 (ii) Costs are reasonable in relation to the objectives of the project.
(6) *Evaluation plan.* (5 points) The Secre tary reviews each application to determine the quality of the evaluation plan for the project, including the extent to which the applicant's methods of evaluation —
 (i) Are appropriate to the project; and
 (ii) To the extent possible, are objec tive and produce data that are quan tifiable.

(Cross-reference: See 34 CFR 75.59 Evaluation by the grantee.)

(7) *Adequacy of resources.* (3 points) The Secretary reviews each application to determine the adequacy of the resources that the applicant plans to devote to the project, including facilities, equipment, and supplies.

(c) Weighting the Criteria*

(15 points) The Secretary distributes an additional 15 points among the criteria listed in paragraph (b) of this section. The Secretary indicates in the applica tion for the program how these 15 points are distributed.

*For purposes of this competition, the 15 additional points will be added to the Plan of Operation for a possible total of 30 points.

Table of Contents

The Table of Contents serves mutiple purposes. It shows the location of the key ingredients of the proposal but—and perhaps more importantly—it shows the proposal reader/evaluator where to locate the specific elements that constitute the criteria (for points) that guide the rating of the proposal. If the proposal should receive points, the Table of Contents should make extremely clear where that section is located.

——**Grant Tip**——

Every required section that gets points in the proposal evaluation process should have an entry in the Table of Contents.

The Table of Contents should be the page immediately behind the cover sheet, Part I (Form 424). It is convenient and greets the reader as soon as the reader turns the cover page. If you have remarks related to an entry on Form 424, those should be on the reverse (back) of Form 424 so the Contents are on the first right-hand page after the cover sheet.

A sample Table of Contents conforming to the 25-page request is shown in Figure 5.9. This Contents section corresponds to the grant application shown in Figures 5.7 and 5.8. Note that because the Narrative (Part III) is supposed to be approximately 25 pages, the Assurances/Certifications are put ahead of the Narrative and designated with lower-case Roman numerals. Another proposal writer might have made the Assurances/Certifications into an Appendix. Note the cross-referenced sections (Budget Summary and Detail, pp. v-vii and the Narrative on Budget and Cost-Effectiveness, p. 19). Some proposals will not need a references section. In the Appendix with Letters of support and participation, you can list the letters as "on file," because including 10-20 letters here will add unneeded bulk.

The Cover or Face Sheet

Part I of the proposal is usually a standard form that is used as the cover for the proposal. This is Form 424 or something similar. Take time to complete this carefully. You will identify the Federal Program. (This will be the *CFDA* number; it may be preprinted or you may need to fill in the numbers.) Use a good descriptive title. Include, where asked, the name of the person who knows the most about the project and proposal. This is the person the funding agency will contact for budget negotiations or if there are questions. Here you do not want the proposal submitting agency's Chief Executive Officer who may know the project only by name—you want a person who can handle detailed questions. Follow instructions closely. This form is

Figure 5.9. Example of a Table of Contents

SAMPLE TABLE OF CONTENTS (for the program described in Figures 5.7 and 5.8 with an entry for each item that is eligible for POINTS as described in Figure 5.8).

the agency's and the reader's first contact with your project. *First impressions count!*

Appendixes and Attachments

The Appendixes and Attachments are for supporting data. The program may call for a copy of your catalog or your IRS tax-exempt data. You may want to send along important letters or data to strengthen your application. Use the Appendixes wisely. Include only important and related materials. Refer to all Appendixes in the narrative.

Abstract

Now that you are finished, review the proposal carefully. Then develop a clear, concise, and cogent *Abstract* that will "sell" your idea in 200-250 words. You are now done, except for mailing or delivering the proposal *on time.*

In Conclusion

Write the proposal carefully. Treat it as if it were an article going to a good publishing outlet with tough editors. The readers will be thorough in reading and evaluating your work. Try to make the agency's work easier by attending carefully to all elements of the proposal.

6

Writing a Proposal

Introduction

The first five chapters have introduced you to the preliminaries of grant proposal writing and the concepts of grants. This chapter will further assist you in understanding the process of writing a grant proposal—giving you the anatomy of a successful application. Chapter 7, "Reviewing a Funded Proposal," reviews in detail a successful grant application that was funded.

Application Procedures for Federal Grants

Before beginning your proposal, review *EDGAR* so that you are particularly familiar with the following subparts:

> Subpart C • How to Apply for a Grant.
> Subpart D • How Grants Are Made.
> Subpart E • What Conditions Must Be Met by a Grantee?
> Subpart F • What Are the Administrative Responsibilities of a Grantee?

After reading these sections, if you still have questions, call the contact person listed in the request for proposal (RFP) and request further clarification or information.

Prior to beginning your needs assessment, you should have written to the appropriate office of the U.S. Department of Education to request the application packet for the proposal you want to write.

Although technically called a "request for proposal" packet (RFP) if you are writing a contract, and an "application" packet if you are applying for a grant, both packets are referred to as RFPs by most proposal writers. The RFP contains all forms and application information for your proposal. Review the RFP in detail. Ensure that persons connected with the proposed project are aware of their roles and what will be expected of them in the project. Seek commitments from the decision makers at your institution regarding office space and furnishings, teaching space, and adequate time for implementation, among other things. Their prior commitments will avoid problems, and possible failure, later.

After you receive the RFP and determine that you have sufficient time and resources to develop a proposal, establish a time frame. Consider federal deadlines along with adequate time for your institution's procedures and the mechanics of preparing the physical document. Do not procrastinate. List your institution's procedures for submitting an application proposal. (For example, at one institution, a pre-application form must be completed that notifies certain officers and personnel of the grantwriter's intent to submit a proposal. This procedure allows the institution's leaders to decide if the proposed project is in harmony with the institution's mission statement, philosophy, and projected plans.) Determine which officers or persons at your institution need to review and/or approve your proposal. Then ensure that the appropriate people will be available for review and approval. (For example, one of the authors painstakingly developed a very difficult proposal, only to meet with failure when the approving officer was absent and no other official of the institution would accept the responsibility for approving the document.) These seem like small details, but such slip-ups due to lack of communication or advance planning can result in disappointment and lost time and energy.

Allow ample time for typing or word processing your document. *Most proposals will be subjected to three or four rewrites.* Allow sufficient time for duplication. Always assume that the copy machine will break down as your document is being printed. Allow enough time for such emergencies and unexpected obstacles. Notify your duplication service a day or two in advance that you will soon bring them a sizeable document for duplication. This will allow them to plan their work schedule to accommodate your work.

—— **Grant Tip** ——

After you receive the RFP and determine that you have sufficient time and resources to develop a proposal, establish a time frame. Consider federal deadlines along with adequate time for your institution's procedures and the mechanics of preparing the physical document. Do not procrastinate.

Features of a Proposal

Your proposal is the document by which your proposed project will be evaluated and a decision made as to whether or not you will receive funding. It is the only vehicle the panel of readers can use to judge your ideas; everything you say in your proposal will make an impact on the readers. You want that impact to be positive and impressive. Let's look at some features that proposal writing experts and the U.S. Department of Education personnel have identified as characteristic of a good proposal, a proposal that is likely to be funded.

1. Proposals that demonstrate strong institutional, local, and/or private sector commitments to the project seem to be favored. This sometimes takes the form of in-kind or cash contributions that increase the likelihood for project success.

2. Good proposals always have the total commitment and support of the sponsoring institution and any other institution that serves the same target population, purposes, or both. For example, if you are writing a proposal to serve migrant and seasonal farmworkers, as does the sample proposal in Chapter 7, seek the commitment and support of the State Migrant Council, the migrant education coordinator at your state education agency, the migrant directors of appropriate local school districts, and directors or consultants at other local agencies that serve migrants, such as employment centers, training projects, health organizations, and law enforcement units.

3. A component that describes continuous monitoring of the project and participants' performance is essential. The monitoring mechanism needs to allow for ongoing modifications of troublesome areas. Often personnel do not monitor or evaluate until near the end of the cycle or project year. This precludes adjustments that could have improved performance, and hence, outcomes.

4. Good proposals are so well-defined and clear that any responsible staff person can effectively operate the project according to the instructions contained in it. Readers who review the narrative should feel that they could operate the project successfully by basing their management upon the instructions and descriptions.

5. An important feature of the proposal is its physical appearance. Narrow margins, small type (elite rather than pica), charts that have been reduced or are third or fourth generation copies, or dot matrix printing may result in the reader tiring quickly and exerting little effort to understand your project. Leave white space—that is, allow ample margins, use space-and-one-half or double-spaced text, and double-space between paragraphs (unless there are page limits or special instructions to the contrary). Make sure your copier prints clear, dark-print copies. Write in plain English. Avoid professional, academic, or technical jargon when possible.

——**Grant Tip**——
Make your document "reader friendly" by making it physically attractive and easy to read.

6. Check to see if the RFP forbids binders; if not, use one. If you put your document in a binder, ensure that the binder does not obscure any of the text. If you punch holes for a three-ring binder, be certain the text is not so close to the margin that you punch holes in it.

7. Most grants require the *Standard Face Sheet* (Form 424) as the proposal cover. This should be completed with care.

8. Begin each major section with an overview explaining what the reader will find in that section. End each section with a summary emphasizing major points. Include a comprehensive table of contents. Detail each criterion in the table. That way, the reader may refer to the *Table of Contents* and look up specific items. An attractive cover on your proposal should bear the name of the program in large letters, the sponsoring institution and its address, the *CFDA* number of the program, and the dates of the project.

9. If the project is to help participants improve their education or obtain employment, include specific sections to describe how the project will accommodate them. The following three are examples:

    a. U.S. Department of Education personnel prefer that project directors conduct follow-up on their participants. Thus, you should survey those who have completed your project to ascertain its effect on them and their careers, especially if they have continued their postsecondary education.

    b. A quality proposal provides incentives for academic achievement. This does not mean gifts or additional money, but, rather, support systems such as a mentoring program, peer tutoring, individualized assistance in job placement or obtaining financial aid to continue postsecondary studies. Other incentives might include individual or small-group tutoring, special skill-building classes, and frequent seminars and workshops designed specifically to meet student needs.

    c. Proposals that emphasize and strengthen the basic and higher-level skills of project participants are well-received. Such emphasis and strengthening lead to the participants' becoming independent of the project. When a project fosters participant dependency, participants find it very difficult to continue their pursuit of project goals. Strive to build independence and confidence among participants.

Review your rough draft to ensure that it reflects these characteristics of a good proposal.

Understanding a Request for Proposal (RFP)

A needs assessment is required by most but not all federal programs. Outline your project and convert your outline into a narrative that details what you propose to do. The RFP tells you how to focus your needs assessment. Some programs request specific information, whereas others do not. (For example, for the proposal presented in Chapter 7, the program requests specific information regarding the number of migrant and seasonal farmworkers in the target area.) The application packet often contains suggestions indicating where you can obtain the information requested and in what format it should be presented.

The next few pages describe the information contained in one application for grants packet provided by the U.S. Department of Education. The packet used for this discussion is the *Application for Grants Under the College Assistance Migrant Program (CAMP)*, provided by the Office of Elementary and Secondary Education.

Cover Letter of Application Package

Many packets begin with a "Dear Colleague" letter. This letter officially announces that applications for funding for a grants competition are being accepted. The letter generally indicates which rules apply to the program and in which *Federal Register* they were published. A critical part of the letter is the due or closing date for proposals. Be sure you meet the deadline criterion: *There is no such thing as a late proposal.* The closing date is also printed on the cover of the application packet.The letter usually contains the name and address of a person you may contact if you need further information.

——Grant Tip——
The "Dear Colleague" letter is your source of important dates and information.

Focusing on Purpose

The application packet contains a variety of valuable information. It lists the purpose for which grants are awarded. Write the purpose on a card and keep it in front of you as you write your proposal. As you consider objectives, ask yourself often, "How does an objective of this project relate to the program sponsoring the grant competition?" This will help keep the grant focused, eliminate extraneous material, and ensure that you fulfill not only local need but also the needs of the sponsoring office. For example, the purpose of the College Assistance Migrant Program (CAMP) is

> *To provide grants to institutions of higher education for projects that address the educational needs of migrant and seasonal farmworker students at the postsecondary level.*

Everything in a CAMP proposal must relate to this purpose.

Review by State Education Agency (SEA)

Some federal programs require state review. The review may be by the state agency (e.g., education) or by the Single Point of Contact (SPOC). The application package provides the deadline for intergovernmental review comments, if such review and comments are required. Executive Order 12372—Intergovernmental Review— requires contact with the SPOC to find out about, and to comply with, the state's process under the Executive Order. If you plan a project to serve a population in states other than your own, notify the SPOC for each state and follow the procedures established in those states under the Executive Order. Most packets include a list of the SPOC for each state. If your state does not have a SPOC, send a copy for review to the appropriate office or person in your State Education Agency. Someone at the state level must have an opportunity to review and comment on your application proposal.

What is the SPOC? Basically, Executive Order 12372 provides a vehicle by which different agencies and departments of state are advised that you plan to submit a proposal, enabling them to coordinate other similar projects with yours. They may feel that your project will contribute major services to the proposed population or that it will duplicate or conflict with existing projects. Contact someone in your SPOC and discuss your proposal prior to writing it. This may provide you with valuable information to include in the proposal and it may save you negative comments from the SPOC reviewers.

You do not need to submit your completed proposal to the SPOC office prior to submitting it to the funding agency, although some

——Grant Tip——
Relate each area of your proposal to the purpose of the program.

agencies appreciate seeing an abstract of your proposal. After you have completed your proposal, send a copy to the SPOC. Write a *Letter of Transmittal* and include a copy of this letter in the copies of your proposals submitted to Washington, D.C., as well as in the copy you send to the SPOC. Indicate in this letter the date by which comments from the Single Point of Contact must be received in Washington, D.C., and the address where the comments must be sent. *This address is different from the address to which you will send your proposal.*

Remember, if *Executive Order 12372—Intergovernmental Review*—is in effect for the program you wish to establish, *you must submit your proposal to the Single Point of Contact for review.* Failure to do so may disqualify your application proposal. Even if there is no requirement for review, it may benefit you if you send copies of your proposal to state officials interested in your project.

Facts About Funding

The "Dear Colleague" letter also indicates the amount of funding Congress has appropriated for the fiscal year of the program, the estimated range of awards, the estimated average size of awards, and the estimated number of awards. Study this information carefully. For example, the appropriation for the CAMP program was only $1,200,000. The *Estimated Range of Awards* for the CAMP program represented in Chapter 7 was $150,000-$350,000. You can be sure that, with only $1,200,000 available, if your proposal significantly exceeds the Estimated Range of Awards, your chances of being funded will be reduced. The *Estimated Average Size of Awards* for the CAMP program is $250,000. You will stand a better chance of being funded if you submit a budget near this figure.

Pay particular attention to the *Estimated Number of Awards.* For the CAMP program, the U.S. Office of Education estimated that only five awards would be made. The competition would be extremely keen for this program. You need to write a nearly perfect proposal in order for it to be funded. A perfect CAMP proposal receives a total of 300 points from the review panel (100 points per reader). The proposal that appears in Chapter 7 received all 300 points. In contrast, other programs such as the Student Support Services, a part of the TRIO Programs, estimated that approximately 700 awards would be made. Competition, therefore, for a Student Support Services Program may not be nearly as keen as for the CAMP program.

——— **Grant Tip** ———
Pay particular attention to the Estimated Number of Awards.

The "Dear Colleague" letter also indicates the *Project Period,* or number of months for which a grant may be awarded. For example, the CAMP program is funded for up to 36 months. You probably will always request funding for the maximum number of months allowable (and you must provide objectives and an estimated budget for that duration).

The last part of the letter lists the various regulations governing the program. Review these regulations. If your proposal is funded, you will be held accountable for following them even if you do not read them. Ignorance is not an excuse. Time spent studying the regulations will pay dividends later.

Use Care in Mailing

———**Grant Tip**———

Include a self-addressed label for federal personnel to mail the application package back to you.

The application packet usually contains an entire page of mailing instructions. *Read them carefully.* Do not send your proposal to the wrong address. Obtain proof of mailing, and mail early enough in the day to ensure that your package does not receive the next day's postmark.

The mailing instructions provide the correct address for mailing your proposal. Use a colored highlighter and mark this address. Be sure to type it or write it clearly on the package containing your proposal.

Carefully review the acceptable proof of mailing. A private metered postmark or a mail receipt not dated by the U.S. Postal Service is usually not acceptable. This section of the packet also contains detailed information regarding applications that are hand delivered or delivered by courier service. Study these instructions carefully if you choose to send your proposal any way except through the mail. *Make sure the postmark the post office places on your package contains the current date.* Always send your proposal by registered mail or by an official courier mail service.

Rules and Regulations

Chapter 3 discussed the *Federal Register* and the *Code of Federal Regulations.* Review carefully the *Federal Register* that contains the rules and regulations governing your application. These Rules and Regulations are usually included in the application packet. These Rules and Regulations are your "bible." They contain all criteria the Secretary of Education uses to evaluate your proposal. If you do not address the criteria, your application will not be considered. *It is as simple as that.*

The Rules and Regulations may contain a section of Supplementary Information. Study this section with care. It sometimes offers valuable insights, such as the Department of Education's (or Congress's) rationale for including certain Rules and Regulations. The Rules and Regulations list the authority under which the program is funded and additional guidelines that apply. They provide special definitions of terms that apply to the program. A key section is entitled *What Types of Services May Be Provided.* List the items that appear in this section and address each service listed in this section. For example, services that may or must be provided in a CAMP project include:

- Outreach and recruitment services.
- Supportive and instructional services such as
  —personal, academic, and career counseling
  —tutoring and academic skill-building instruction and
   assistance
  —assistance with special admissions
  —health services
  —other services as necessary to complete program.
- Assistance in obtaining student financial aid such as
  —stipends; scholarships; student travel; career-oriented
   work-study; books and supplies; tuition and fees;
   room and board; and other assistance.
- Housing support for on-campus living.
- Exposure to cultural events; academic programs; and
   other activities not usually available to migrant youth.
- Other support services as necessary.

This section tells you what the Department of Education expects a CAMP project to include. The review panel looks for references to these items. As you read Chapter 7 and the *Sample Proposal,* you will find each of the above services addressed in various ways.

Some Rules and Regulations also include services that *may not be included* in the application. Avoid including any expressly excluded services.

The section *What Must Be Included in an Application?* specifies items that, if omitted, may disqualify your proposal. For example, in the CAMP program, your application will be disqualified if you do not include a budget of at least $150,000 or a management plan that contains certain specified assurances and provisions.

Evaluation of Proposal by the Secretary of Education

—— **Grant Tip** ——
The most important part of the rules and regulations describes how the Secretary evaluates your application.

The most important part of the Rules and Regulations describes how the Secretary evaluates your application. It generally specifies exactly what the Secretary (i.e., the panel of readers) looks for and how many points each criterion is worth.

Usually an application is read and evaluated by three or more panel members. The makeup and duties of this panel are discussed in greater detail in Chapter 8, "Understanding How Grants Are Awarded." Each panel member studies the application and awards points for each section of the entire application. These points are averaged and your final score is between 1 and 100. If three readers evaluate the proposal and each gives your proposal the maximum score (100 points), the total would be 300 points.

Additional points may be awarded for the successful operation of a previously funded project. These points are designated as *prior experience points* or *points for prior performance*. Usually such points are not awarded by the panel of readers but rather by personnel in the U.S. Department of Education. For example, Congress mandated that CAMP projects be awarded up to 15 additional points for having operated a successful project. Specific criteria are usually provided to guide the Department in awarding these additional points. Prior experience points enable a successful existing project's application to earn up to 115 points, whereas the proposal from an institution that has never operated a CAMP project can earn only a maximum of 100 points. This serves to provide continuity; it also gives an advantage to existing projects and encourages administrators to operate high quality, successful projects.

An institution in Texas had operated a federally funded project for 12 years. This project was funded through yearly competitions, which means that a complete proposal had to be submitted each year. For 12 years the institution's application was successful. However, no prior experience points were awarded; all applications were awarded between 0 and 100 points. Unfortunately, even though the institution in Texas had operated its project successfully for 12 years, its last proposal was not of the highest quality. In the 13th year, an institution that had never operated this particular project submitted a well-written proposal and was funded. In spite of its history of a well-operated project, the Texas institution lost its funding because of a carelessly written application.

This example demonstrates the importance of prior experience points and the need to operate a successful project. Had prior experience points been part of the criteria, the Texas institution could have earned up to 15 points more than the other institution. These points might have been sufficient to qualify the Texas institution for funding.

If the program from which you seek funds provides prior experience points, be sure to study the criteria for those points carefully. As you write, include those criteria in your plan of operation and objectives.

Many programs do not award prior performance points. In this case, all proposals compete equally. Thus, a person with a good idea has the same chance as a person who has operated a successful project. An equal start helps assure that there can be no favoritism or friendship factors involved in the choice; each proposal is judged on its own merit. Prior experience points do make sense when continuity is a goal. They do not seem useful when innovation, efficiency, or short-term work is the goal.

Sections of an Application

The Rules and Regulations contain the actual criteria for evaluating your application. These criteria, in effect, constitute the outline you use in writing your proposal. The sections of an application vary from program to program. Below are the sections and points of the College Assistance Migrant Program (CAMP) proposal.

1. Plan of Operation (25 points)
2. Objectives and Activities (20 points)
3. Evaluation Plan (15 points)
4. Quality of Key Personnel (10 points)
5. Budget and Cost-Effectiveness (10 points)
6. Interagency Consultation and Coordination (10 points)
7. Adequacy of Resources (5 points)
8. Recruitment (5 points)

Other programs may have additional or slightly different sections such as Impact, Dissemination, or Program Factors. Each section represents a major criterion that may be divided into several more detailed criteria. The more detailed criteria of section *(a) Plan of Operation for CAMP* are reprinted in Figure 6.1. Unless otherwise instructed, address each criterion in the same order it is presented in the *Rules and Regulations*. This is important because the readers'

Technical Review Form is organized in this order. The task of reading and evaluating your document is easier if readers do not have to turn from page to page, section to section, to complete their evaluations. Some programs, such as TRIO (Upward Bound, Educational Talent Search, Student Support Services, etc.), provide specific instructions in the application packet for you to arrange the criteria in a different order. If such instructions are provided, follow them carefully. The readers' Technical Review Form is probably organized according to the order requested.

Figure 6.1. Criteria for Conducting a Plan of Operation for Project CAMP

---

§206.31 What selection criteria does the Secretary use to evaluate an application?

(a)   Plan of operation [25 points]
   (1)   The Secretary reviews each application for information that shows the quality of the plan of operation for the project.
   (2)   The Secretary looks for information that shows the following:
      (i)   High quality in the design of the project.
      (ii)   An effective plan of management that assures proper and efficient administration of the project.
      (iii)   A clear description of how the objectives of the project relate to the purpose of the program.
      (iv)   A clear description of the way that the applicant plans to use its resources and personnel to achieve each objective of the project.
      (v)   A clear description of how the applicant will provide equal access and treatment for eligible participants who are members of groups that have been traditionally underrepresented, such as
         (A)   Members of racial or ethnic minority groups
         (B)   Women
         (C)   Handicapped persons
         (D)   The elderly

**From Here to the End of Chapter 6
the Reader May Wish to Follow the Examples
in the Sample Proposal in Chapter 7.**

Notice that the sample proposal in the following chapter contains the face page (Standard Form 424). Most proposals must have this page. Detailed instructions for completing this and other required forms are part of the application packet. Complete Form 424 with care and ensure that it is signed in ink. A copy of this form bearing an original signature must be included with one copy of your proposal.

Include a complete Table of Contents. Often readers must refer to a previous section. A good Table of Contents will facilitate the reading process. A short Abstract will assist the readers in capturing an overview of the entire proposal. It helps them to know what to look for in the document, briefly describes the needs, and explains what the project hopes to accomplish.

Plan of Operation

The Plan of Operation provides detailed information explaining how you plan to operate the project. This section usually carries the highest number of points of any proposal section. Develop it carefully; address each individual criterion listed in the *Federal Register*. Figure 6.1 is a reprint of the criteria for the CAMP proposal (see Chapter 7) as they appear in the Rules and Regulations.

As you address each criterion, draw the reader's attention to that criterion by putting it in **bold type,** underlining it, placing it in a box, or using some other way to guide the reader. Try not to make the readers search for information they need to evaluate your proposal. Notice how the author of the proposal in Chapter 7 has carefully set apart each criterion in the order in which it appears in the *Federal Register*. The criterion, in bold type, is centered on the page with the first letter of each major word capitalized. Under each criterion, the author has cited the exact reference and the number of possible points awarded that criterion. As the readers proceed through the document, they find each criterion highlighted in this way. The readers gain confidence in your proposal and in your ability to organize as they see how carefully you follow the required criterion. Help your readers by paraphrasing each criterion and citing the numerical reference: e.g.,

Plan of Operation (206.31(a) - 25 points)

You may want to preface the first section, Plan of Operation, with some background material such as why the program is needed and what special conditions exist that merit a project. Refer to the first part of the proposal in Chapter 7 for a sample of Background Information.

The background material begins with a map depicting the geographic area to be served by the proposed project. Another map appears a couple of pages later showing other areas of the country that are presently served by CAMP projects. A complete description of the need for a CAMP project is offered, including published statistics and a list of specific areas in which the target population is lacking, i.e., effective motivation, financial resource information on the part of the student and the parents, and the poor self-concepts of the farmworker students. The proposal also points out verifiable factors identified as causes for students dropping out of postsecondary programs. You are the person most familiar with your target area and institution. Tell the readers what they need to know.

A major mistake committed by many proposal writers is to assume that the reader is familiar with the conditions of the target area. Generally, readers are assigned to evaluate proposals from geographical locations other than their own. Therefore, they know little about conditions that exist in your target area. In a very succinct way, provide specific and compelling reasons why a project should be established in the proposed target area.

In addressing the criteria in the *Plan of Operation*, notice how the author draws the readers' attention to the purpose of the CAMP program. The first paragraph of the Plan of Operation reviews for the reader those things that will be contained in the remainder of the document. Keep the readers' attention on the purposes for which funds are awarded. Demonstrate that the document addresses those purposes.

Notice that frequent reference is made to the *Federal Register*. This assures readers that you know the specific elements of the program as outlined. It assures them that you are trying to serve the needs of the targeted population, not trying to develop a project that centers on your needs and only peripherally on the needs of the students. Each service identified in the *Federal Register* is carefully detailed. A description and a well-planned chart are provided, indicating how the staff plans to accomplish the services.

The proposal points out that the project will be an integral part of the university structure (one major feature of a quality proposal) and that project administrators have full responsibility for its operation. This is a firm foundation for a solid plan of management. Projects whose administrators do not have full control of the implementation often do not achieve the desired results. The plan of management in this proposal places total responsibility—from submitting the application, administering the project, training and supervising its staff, overseeing the curriculum, managing the budget, to evaluating the results—upon the project administrators.

Study the remainder of the Plan of Operation, noting how each criterion is addressed. The completeness of this section helps to assure that the readers will award the full 25 points. Note the flow of the narration, the transition from one criterion to the next, and the physical appearance of the document. The author has left sufficient white space and has not crowded too much information onto one page. The author uses lists and numbers items that are of most importance, using boldface type, italics, and indenting to delineate various information. The author leaves space between each paragraph and between each numbered item. All of these details contribute to the rapid and easy reading of the proposal. The reader does not have to search for information. Because the material on each page is not crowded, the reader can create a visual image of the important aspects of each page and process that information comfortably. Readers will be more inclined to award a greater number of points for this type of writing than if they have to labor over the narration, search for obscure information, and read between the lines.

————**Grant Tip**————
Use lists, numbered items, boldface type, italics, and the like, to catch the reader's eye.

Objectives and Activities

Operationally, the Objectives and Activities section is probably the most important section. It describes to the reader, the U.S. Office of Education personnel, your institution, and the employees of the project (including the Director) how the project is to be operated. It is the project's road map. The proposal in Chapter 7 employs an effective format.

There is no magic number of objectives appropriate for a proposal. Do not create more objectives than necessary, but include sufficient objectives to demonstrate that all aspects of the purpose of the program are covered.

The objectives used in the sample proposal have the following components:

1. Component Title—identifies the objective topic.
2. Goal—states the broad intention for the objective.
3. Objective—tells what the author is going to do and defines it in measurable outcomes (the product).
4. Activities—instructs the staff as to the specific procedures or ways the objective is to be met.
5. Timeline—specifies when the activities of the objective will be met.
6. Evaluation—determines if, and to what degree, the objective was met.

7. Staff Responsibility—shows the staff member responsible for activities.

Component Title—This title should be descriptive and immediately indicate to the reader the content of the objective. Any reader should be able to review a list of the objectives and have a good idea of the of the scope and depth of the project.

Goal—This is a statement of the overall outcome of the objective. It is board and does not generally specify a procedure, but rather what one might expect of the objective.

Objective—The ultimate purpose of the progam to which you are writing the proposal should be reflected in every objective. An objective describes what the program will accomplish. Some objectives may relate to intermediate aspects of the ultimate purpose. For example, the purpose of the CAMP program is *"to assist students...who are enrolled...on a full-time basis in the first academic year at an IHE."* Each objective should relate to this ultimate purpose. Some objectives will deal with financial matters, some with areas of curriculum, some with recruitment and retention, and others with social aspects of the project. Whatever the intermediate aspect of the objective is, the overall importance of the objectives is to contribute to the completion of the ultimate purpose of the program.

—— **Grant Tip** ——

Objectives and activities are your road map to a successful proposal. Use the active when writing objectives and make them measurable.

The objectives are among the most important elements of your proposal, particularly if the program to which you are writing awards points for prior performance. Generally, in the points for prior performance section, you will need to provide an accounting of accomplishments for each objective. Therefore, write objectives that are narrow in scope, that are not difficult to evaluate, and that are measurable. If possible, include a percentage or numerical outcome in your objective. Measurable objectives are extremely important. Whether they are called program objectives, outcome objectives, performance, or behavioral objectives is not important; they tell the readers what you hope to accomplish by the end of the project.

Notice the first objective of the sample proposal in Chapter 7. The objective is:

To review and evaluate collected data on 100% of the CAMP participants and develop an Individual Educational Plan (IEP) showing special academic help and tutorial assistance needed by each student by the second week they are accepted into the program.

This objective has three major components: review, evaluate, and develop. This specific outcome objective tells what you hope to accomplish, with what number of participants, and how it will be measured. The objective is reasonable. It is attainable given the resources and level of effort described in the proposal, and it is challenging. It is not so easy that little effort will be required to attain it. Data must be collected on 100% of the participants. This may be readily demonstrated by listing all participants and identifying the data collected, i.e., Self Report Questionnaires, High School Transcripts or GED Score Reports, ACT Score Reports, and the results of California Achievement Tests if administered. All of these items are mentioned in the activities section of the objective. A review and evaluation of this material will render a profile of the participant, from which an Individual Educational Plan (IEP) will be developed. In other words, elaboration of the IEP is proof of the review and evaluation of the data. The IEP can be included either in an evaluation or in a summary of IEPs, and the IEPs themselves can remain on file.

The purpose of this process is to develop an objective that is important, contributes significantly to the success of your participants, and produces an outcome that can be readily determined. Avoid, if possible, developing objectives that cannot be evaluated quantitatively or that describe a process only. Your objective should not depend on your opinion or on the opinion of a member of your staff in order to determine if it was successful. Of 17 objectives in the model proposal, only objective 12 does not include a specific numerical or percentage citation that can be quantitatively measured. The success or failure of the other objectives can be measured statistically.

Activities—The activities describe what the staff will do in order to accomplish the goals and have successful outcomes for the objectives. Don't outline *every* step, but do list the major steps in the order in which they will occur. Some writers list the activities numerically; others provide the activities in narrative or chart form. Several ways can be used to accomplish the purpose effectively.

Timeline—The reader wants to know when during the project the activities will occur. This also provides an excellent mechanism to pace the staff in implementing and operating the project. Be realistic with timelines; avoid too many activities at any given time. When the project is funded, make a master list of your timelines, or, using a large wall calendar, list the date of each activity. At a glance, you can survey your needs and have ample time to plan for each activity, secure the necessary supplies or materials, and have your personnel prepared.

Evaluation—The evaluation part of your objective need not be exhaustive. One criterion requires an in-depth evaluation of your complete project. The evaluation included in each objective should simply state how you will know when you have accomplished the objective and to what degree it was successful. Often the documents necessary to show this are listed in the evaluation description. For example, the evaluation could state that the IEPs, questionnaires, transcripts, test results, etc., will be on file, or it could state that this objective will be successfully completed when an IEP is completed on 100% of the program participants.

Staff Responsibility—This clearly defines who is responsible for what. In the sample proposal, responsibility for each objective is assigned to one or more staff persons. Some writers refine it more by stating that one person has the major responsibility and is assisted by others. For example, the sample proposal states that the Associate Director, Counselor, and Recruiter/Counselor are responsible for the successful completion of the first objective, Student Assessment. It could have been stated as follows: Responsibility: Associate Director, assisted by Counselor and Recruiter/Counselor.

——**Grant Tip**——
Make sure your objectives and activities are clear enough so a person unfamiliar with your project could successfully implement them.

Study the objectives and all of their components as they appear in Chapter 7. Use them as patterns for creating the objectives in your application. Plan to spend considerable time on the objective section. After you have completed it, ask someone unfamiliar with the program and its purposes to read your objectives. The objectives and activities should be clear to this person, who should feel that, given very little direction, they could implement and carry them out in a timely and effective manner.

Evaluation Plan

The evaluation section can present difficulties for proposal writers. The evaluation plan need not be elaborate and steeped with strategies. *EDGAR (CFR 75.590)* requires you to evaluate the following three areas:

1. The progress of the project in achieving its objectives.

2. The effectiveness of the project in meeting the stated purpose of the program.
3. The effect of the project on the persons being served, including any persons who are members of groups that have been traditionally underrepresented.

The evaluation section of the sample proposal in Chapter 7 provides a built-in ongoing evaluation plan. It permits the administrative staff to collect and analyze data continuously, thus allowing them to detect problems and improve strategies. An important flow chart is included to outline the evaluation plan.

The evaluation section provides a short but informative plan for assessing the effectiveness of the project in meeting the purpose of the CAMP program. The author reviews for the reader the stated purpose of the CAMP program according to the *Federal Register* and proposes to conduct a "procedural assessment" to compare the data collected with the goals and objectives as stated in the proposal. This is one of the most prevalent and useful evaluation models (or designs) used in social action programs. It essentially uses the program as its own comparison. It does not attempt to generalize to the degree of most quasi-experimental or experimental designs, but attempts to demonstrate success or lack of success of the project within agreed-upon (and thus in one sense *validated*) parameters. It gives control to project management over variables to be measured, because these are defined by project goals and objectives.

Near the end of the year, project goals and student objectives are evaluated for purposes of *summative assessment*. This overall process uses the project records, student activities, credits attempted and grades earned, student questionnaires, etc., as the basis of the evaluation.

The sample proposal includes an elaborate chart outlining the *management by objective* plan for the project. This type of evaluation instrument provides an impressive amount of valuable information in a very small amount of space. It allows the reader to follow through the process quickly to ensure that the evaluation is meaningful and produces information that can be used for project improvement.

Quality of Key Personnel

Even though this proposal section is time consuming, develop it with care. Demonstrate that you have the personnel resources necessary to operate the project effectively. Be realistic in expectations of future project staff. Often, in an effort to impress readers, proposal developers include qualifications that are not necessary in order to carry out the project goals. Insist on well-qualified personnel and describe these qualifications in your document. However, do not require degrees and certificates that look good but do not add to the employee's expertise or ability to carry out the assigned duties.

If you require a doctorate, for example, have specific reasons in mind rather than requiring the degree for *window dressing*. Persons with doctoral degrees are often difficult to find for employment in grant-funded projects where a position carries no academic rank or tenure-track option. *Soft money* positions will last for only the project's duration with no guarantees that other positions will be available when the grant terminates. Often persons who have invested time and effort on advanced degrees prefer to seek employment that leads to academic stability. Highly-trained persons demand higher salaries, which may cause a personnel budget to appear excessive. If the position can be filled just as well with a person with a bachelor's or master's degree, so be it. These persons often are interested in soft-money positions as a means of acquiring valuable experience.

Build into this section a strong affirmative action plan—one that goes well beyond your institution's affirmative action plan. Indicate how you will develop your positions to attract persons or groups of persons traditionally underrepresented in this type of employment. Describe how you will advertise such positions, even to the extent of naming the regional or statewide newspapers in which you will place advertisements. Describe how you will seek referrals from other universities or agencies, and how you will seek out and recruit such individuals. Explain how you will treat a situation in which you find that two applicants for a particular position are equally qualified in every way, except that one is a member of a group traditionally underrepresented.

Indicate how all applicants will be given equal treatment before and after they are employed. In other words, once persons are on the payroll, how will you ensure that they will not become a token person of an underrepresented population? Explain the promotion policy, how all employees share in a benefits package, and how all have equal access to the institution's various services and perks.

Describe the special qualifications and characteristics of persons already on staff who will become associated with the new project when it is funded. Explain how their preparation and experience will contribute to project success.

Develop a position description for each position in your project. Include items such as the following:

1. *Classification*—Will they be professional; exempt, nonexempt; termed employees; full- or part-time employees?
2. *Employed by*—Who has the authority to review and judge the persons' qualifications for the position?
3. *Responsible to*—To whom will the people occupying the positions report? Who will supervise their activities
4. *Purpose of the position*—A one- or two-line job description.
5. *Major responsibilities*—List the major areas of responsibility for each position. Be specific.
6. *Qualifications*—Define the training and experience you want these persons to have. Include both formal and informal training or experience.

This section requires thorough planning and preparation. In developing the next section, Budget and Cost Effectiveness, you will realize that one of the largest budget line items will be personnel. Each position in the organization chart adds thousands of dollars to the budget. Plan well to ensure that all positions are necessary, well-defined, and will contribute significantly to the project's success. On the other hand, take care not to overlook an important position.

As an example, in developing the project budget for a CAMP project, one author carelessly omitted the position of Associate Director. Inasmuch as the author served only as a one-quarter time Director, the Associate Director's position was essential for the smooth and efficient operation of the project. During budget negotiations the error became apparent. By then it was too late. The Department declined a petition to add the position, and the Director was forced to operate for a year without it. This severely limited the project's effectiveness. Costly errors of this nature can spell failure for a project.

You cannot revise your project and add a position without prior approval from the sponsoring office. If you do, you put yourself in jeopardy of an audit exception and may be required to repay any salary, fringe, and other related expenses. Therefore, carefully review your document, creating both an organization chart and a chart that outlines all responsibilities involved in your proposed project. Cross-check them carefully. This will ensure that adequate personnel are listed in your budget.

Budget and Cost Effectiveness

The line-item budget for the sample proposal in Chapter 7 is at the beginning of the application. Some proposal writers include it in the body of the proposal in the Budget and Cost Effectiveness section. If the instructions do not indicate where in the proposal you should locate the budget, you may choose to place it either at the front or in the Budget and Cost Effectiveness section. The Table of Contents should show where the budget is placed. In either location, you must carefully plan each budget expenditure.

The CAMP application packet's *"Dear Colleague" letter* gave hints as to an acceptable *cost per student.* Try to create a budget that is close to the national *cost per student* average. If the budget is significantly under the national average, provide ample explanation. Is it because the institution is contributing personnel, supplies, scholarships, etc., for the project? Explain any such contributions. Although these contributions can be beneficial, they must be carefully explained.

If costs greatly exceed the national average, provide a thorough explanation. For example, one of the authors' projects requires considerable travel for recruitment. As a result, the travel budget is necessarily large, significantly increasing the overall cost per student average. Without a clear explanation, the readers may think that the budget is inflated and unrealistic and may withhold points.

A good rule of thumb is to dream a little, and ask for what you need. What about the "dream a little" statement? Do not hesitate to ask for legitimate items that may not be absolutely necessary but which, if granted, would certainly enhance the project. For example, several CAMP projects have found that a summer orientation enrichment session just before the beginning of each fall term enables participants to be ready to hit the ground running. During this orientation, participants are administered a variety of tests; attend intensive workshops or seminars on study skills; become acquainted with the campus, its administration, policies, and rules; learn where the laundry facilities are located; and complete other such necessary but time-consuming tasks. Having done this, they are prepared to begin the term without distractions. This orientation is not absolutely necessary, but it certainly helps students and staff get off to a great start. If such a preliminary orientation would be helpful, include it in the objectives and budget. If it is accepted and funded, participants will have a head start. If it is not funded, the project will still be intact and operable.

———**Grant Tip**———
Dream a bit, but not too wildly; be creative, but realistic. Estimate costs slightly on the high side to account for inflation.

After elaborating your line-item budget, create a narrative to explain any unclear or unusual budget requests. Don't include items that do not directly relate to the purpose of the program or to objectives outlined in the *Objectives* section. A common error is to include items in the budget, such as computers, typewriters, additional travel, etc., that are not mentioned in the body of the proposal. When the readers review the body of your proposal, if they find no reference to such items that appear in the budget, they may believe you are attempting to use the grant not to serve the target population, but to buy equipment or allow for extra travel. If you need computers for the successful accomplishment of a specific objective, the objective itself should cite the need and provide an explanation.

For example, one of the authors designed a curriculum that used many tutorial assistants, computer-assisted instruction, and supplementary video cassette tapes. Each tutor was assigned four participants. As the tutor worked one-on-one with two participants, the other two were using computers and/or video cassette tapes to reinforce previously-learned material. The curriculum was well-defined, time tables were developed, and a schedule of instruction was presented. All of this was explained in the objective itself. The request for 15 computers and three video cassette recorders and monitors was well-supported within the application narrative. During budget negotiations, the negotiator questioned the need for so much equipment. After reviewing the objective that documented the need for the equipment, the negotiator granted the request. It was obvious that the project would not be as effective without the necessary equipment.

The line-item budget presented in the sample proposal in Chapter 7 is an example of a conservative budget. After you have completed your budget, divide the total cost by the number of persons you plan to serve to determine the cost per participant.

If your application is recommended for funding, an officer of the U.S. Department of Education, Grants and Contracts Office, will telephone you to negotiate the budget. The two of you will discuss each budget line item and modify it according to the amount of funds available for your project. Usually this means a reduction in the amount requested. Discuss each item, and if the negotiator recommends reductions, explain the reasons behind your original request and advocate for the full amount requested. However, experience will teach any person who negotiates grant budgets that there is not a significant amount of room to negotiate. Be willing to effect a quick revision of your project and amend it according to the allocation. Remember the *Time-Cost-Performance* balance that was addressed in Chapter 1. Chapter 8, "Understanding How Grants Are Awarded," discusses budget negotiations more fully.

Interagency Consultation and Coordination

Earlier in this chapter, we discussed Executive Order 12372— *Intergovernmental Review.* Do not confuse that requirement with the criterion of this section. The two are not related.

——**Grant Tip**——
Gain the support of your target community by including its members in the planning of your proposal.

This section is designed to ensure that in planning and developing the project you have consulted and coordinated with other agencies that serve similar populations, and that you will continue to consult and coordinate with them. Begin this part of your application very early in the proposal writing process. Identify the agencies or offices that serve your target population. These may include (among others):

- School districts
- Welfare agencies
- Law enforcement agencies
- Other federal and state-funded programs or projects
- Centers for employment training
- Private and nonprofit training agencies
- Councils that deal with your target population
- Community centers
- Junior colleges and other postsecondary institutions in your target area
- Employment centers
- State agencies

Prior to contacting each agency, prepare a fact sheet containing an outline of the project you propose. Include a map of the target service area. Personalize each fact sheet with a few questions for the specific agency you are about to visit, or with a few suggestions of ways agency personnel can assist in serving the target population.

For example, when developing the CAMP project, one author visited high schools in the target area. He had prepared a referral form on the back of a self-addressed, postage-paid postcard. The school counselor or principal could easily complete it and drop it into the mail. Persons at each school agreed to assist in recruitment by mailing these referral cards to the Project Director.

Together with the fact sheet, the author also prepared a list of services the school or agency could provide the CAMP program. The list included items such as the following with space for a check:

[ ]   We will provide space for posters and advertising of the
        CAMP program.
[ ]   We will distribute brochures and application forms for
        CAMP to interested persons.
[ ]   We will provide space for CAMP counselors to interview
        potential participants.
[ ]   We will invite CAMP personnel to Parents Night and
        provide time on the program to disseminate information.
[ ]   We will provide duplicating services and limited supplies
        for use in the CAMP program.
[ ]   We will dedicate 1   2   3   4   5 (circle the correct
        number) school-sponsored scholarships to students who
        enroll in CAMP.
[ ]   We will permit authorized CAMP personnel to review
        nonprivate school records in an effort to locate previous
        students who may qualify for CAMP.
[ ]   The school newspaper and parent newsletters will print
        articles and information regarding enrollment in and the
        benefits of CAMP.

Ask personnel at each agency visited to submit a letter regarding
your visit. The letter should include three important items: (a) a
statement indicating that you discussed the project with them, (b) a
statement indicating that you invited their comments and suggestions,
and (c) a statement indicating their support and the contributions they
will make to the project. The letter must indicate support and not just
an endorsement. A letter of endorsement might simply state that
agency personnel are aware of the program, consider it worthy, and
extend blessings to you. A letter of support, on the other hand, includes items (a), (b), and (c) above. You may want to take a sample
letter that another agency has provided or draft a sample letter to use
as a model. Keep each letter on file. Create an appendix that contains
these letters or representative samples. In the Interagency Consulta-
tion/Coordination section of the proposal, summarize each letter
received. An example of such summaries is in the sample proposal.

Adequacy of Resources

Often, excellent proposals are developed that describe quality
projects designed to meet the purpose of the program as described in
the *Federal Register* and to meet the needs of the proposed target
population. It is one thing to have a good project and project design.
It is another to be able to implement the project if it is selected for

funding. In the *Adequacy of Resources* section, describe the resources your institution has available that it is willing to commit to successful implementation and operation of the proposed project.

As you design and develop the project, list the resources the project will need in order to be successful. Then list resources currently available. Identify the persons who can supply or provide the resources you lack. For example, one of the authors proposed to establish a Student Support Services Program at his institution. A major needed resource was adequate office, counseling, and tutorial space. None being available in the building where most of the federal grants were housed, he and his dean approached the president of the university. The president determined that the Student Support Services Program would be of value to the university and set aside adequate space. He confirmed this in a letter that was included in the proposal. The proposal was successful, and the project was implemented in the newly remodelled space.

Provide a sentence or two explaining how each resource will contribute to project success. Notice that the sample proposal contains a list of 19 resources that directly contribute to project success. If you are applying for a service-oriented project, provide floor plans of housing, office, tutorial, and classroom space, menus from the food services facilities, a list of resources and services available at the library, the student union, the media and materials center, the counseling center, the student financial aid and career planning centers, etc., in an appendix. Include a brochure of extracurricular activities, such as theaters, cultural centers, athletic events, special events center, forums, lecture series, and social events.

Indicate also how this project will interface with other federally funded projects; explain why they do not overlap or duplicate services. Networking among projects is impressive and demonstrates that sound student services are available. For example, at one university, students are first contacted by either the Educational Talent Search or Upward Bound counselor. They receive special help to complete high school and, upon graduation, they can get help in enrolling in postsecondary school. These projects work closely with public school personnel to identify students who may leave high school prior to graduation. If a student qualifies for Educational Talent Search or High School Equivalency Program services, the appropriate referral is made. The university also operates a variety of service-oriented projects. It is not uncommon for a student to be contacted by an educational specialist from the Talent Search Program and, after assessment, to be referred to Upward Bound. If students complete high school through Upward Bound and meet project eligibility requirements, they may be referred to the College Assistance Migrant Program. Administrators of this project may determine that the student is interested in elementary education and needs tutorial assistance in order to be successful. Students may eventually be referred to the Bilingual Teacher Training Program to begin coursework on an elementary bilingual degree while receiving special tutoring from the Student Support Services Program.

Networking seems to contribute to positive funding decisions. A special caution is in order. Ensure that your project services do not overlap or duplicate each other, and ensure that, when prohibited, students do not receive services from two projects simultaneously. For example, a student cannot receive services from both Talent Search and Upward Bound at the same time. This is prohibited in the regulations. But a student may receive simultaneous services from Student Support Services and Bilingual Education or CAMP.

Recruitment

Inasmuch as grant programs designed to help migrant target populations often cover wide geographic areas, readers need to know how recruitment will be accomplished. When target populations are migrant, recruitment is difficult.

Build a recruitment program that will reach sufficient participants to fill all of the *slots* in your project as well as generating a *waiting list*. Often projects recruit only sufficient students to fill the vacancies. Then when a participant must leave the project unexpectedly, there is no one to fill the vacancy.

Notice in the sample proposal how the author built in a networking system of 14 agencies to receive referrals. This helps make recruiting successful. Chances of participants succeeding are greatly enhanced if they are referred by someone else. This shows they are interested in self-improvement, have initiative, and are willing to follow through. Build a network of schools, agencies, institutions, community organizations, and individuals to supply your program with potential participants. Use the list generated in the Interagency Consultation/Coordination section, for example.

Summary

This chapter has presented the meat and potatoes of proposal development and referred to a sample proposal (Chapter 7). Application procedures for federal grants were reviewed. You were encouraged to request an RFP early, study it thoroughly, and conduct your needs assessment using the RFP as a guide.

Important features of a proposal were outlined. As you develop your document, continually ask yourself, *"Does this part contribute to one of the important characteristics of a successful proposal?"*

Each aspect of one RFP was discussed. You were advised to study the RFP in detail, make notes, highlight important parts, make a list of timelines and important items to include. Make a checkoff list to ensure that you have met all requirements.

Study the system for awarding points. Determine before you begin if points for prior performance will be awarded. If so, ensure that your entire document addresses these criteria in general and that your objectives address them in particular. Never take the attitude that a particular section is difficult and that if you can earn 12 or 13 of the 15 points, you will be satisfied. Never be satisfied until you have polished your proposal to the point that you are confident you will earn all of the points. Every single point counts. Dozens of proposals fail to be recommended for funding by a point or two! One of the authors scored an average of 96 out of 100 points and still failed to make the funding cut. Never take the point system for granted. Earn every possible point available. Expend that extra hour or two to earn one additional point.

When you are ready to mail your proposal, place a note on the outside cover indicating which copy contains the original plus four copies, as well as a courtesy copy under separate cover to the program director if the application is for a previously funded grant. This assures that in addition to the "original signature" or file copy, each of the three readers on the panel will have a dark clear copy. Feedback from U.S. Department of Education personnel has been positive in this regard. It makes their work easier.

Chapter 7, "Reviewing a Funded Proposal," provides one example of an application. This proposal scored 100 points, thus receiving the highest possible score. A careful study of its components will assist you in formulating a quality application proposal worthy of funding.

7

Reviewing a Funded Proposal

Introduction

This chapter contains an example of a federally funded grant proposal in its entirety except for the appendixes. It was submitted by one of the authors and funded by the U.S. Department of Education for a three-year period. This project was one of four funded in the United States during competition in response to an *Application for Grants under the College Assistance Migrant Program.* The main purpose of this project was to provide academic and support services and financial assistance to students who were engaged in or who were from families engaged in migrant and other seasonal farmwork. The program must have met other eligible guidelines that are outlined in the regulations..

Chapter 4, "Using the *Catalog of Federal Domestic Assistance (CFDA),*" uses this program as an example for discussing parts of the *CFDA.* "What Are the Components of a Proposal?" and "Writing a Proposal," Chapters 5 and 6, respectively, use various sections of this proposal in describing the aspects of writing grant proposals. The *Application Technical Review Form,* which is addressed in Chapter 8, "Understanding How Grants Are Awarded," shows how field readers review and evaluate a grant application such as the one presented in this chapter against selected criteria that are established by the Secretary.

Selection Criteria

The funding agency—in this example, the U.S. Department of Education—instructs potential applicants as to what must be included in an application and how the Secretary reviews and evaluates the proposal against the stated criteria. In this particular example, the Secretary indicated that the application would be evaluated on the following selection criteria. The maximum number of points possible for each criterion are listed.

——Grant Tip——
Selection criteria are weighted with a point value and each one must be addressed by an applicant when responding to a grant proposal.

Selection Criteria	Maximum Number of Points Awarded
Plan of Operation	25
Objectives and Activities	20
Evaluation Plan	15
Quality of Key Personnel	10
Budget and Cost-Effectiveness	10
Interagency Consultation and Coordination	10
Adequacy of Resources	5
Recruitment	5

Plan of Operation

This section provides information to show the quality of an effective plan of management that ensures proper and efficient administration of the project. The plan of operation presents a clear description of the way the applicant (university) plans to use its resources and personnel to achieve project objectives. In this section, the applicant describes how it will provide equal access and treatment for eligible participants who are members of groups that have been traditionally underrepresented, such as members of racial or ethnic minority groups, women, handicapped persons, and the elderly.

Objectives and Activities

The *Objectives and Activities* section of this sample proposal demonstrates how the applicant provided information that shows the quality in the design of objectives and activities for project participants. Because the main purpose of this proposal is to provide academic and support services and financial assistance to students engaged in migrant and other seasonal farmwork, the project's objectives and activities respond to the academic, support, and financial needs of the participating students. The applicant also addressed the size, scope, and quality of the project activities and how they contribute successfully to meeting the project objectives and program purposes.

Evaluation Plan

This section includes information that shows the quality of the evaluation plan for the proposed project. Specifically, the applicant addressed evaluation methods appropriate for the project and to the extent possible, that are objective and produce quantifiable data. Note how the applicant assesses the progress in achieving the objectives, the effectiveness of the project in meeting the purposes of the federal program, and the effect on persons being served by the project.

Quality of Key Personnel

When dealing with the *Quality of Key Personnel* section, the applicant provides information that shows adequate qualifications for the key personnel the applicant plans to use in this project. Typically in the appendixes you would provide a full résumé and job description for each person you plan to use in the project. If you have not identified a person for a specific position, include a job description. The narrative of this section includes the qualifications of the project director and each other key person in the project—this includes experience and training in fields related to the objectives of the project, the time each person will commit to the project, and the extent to which the *applicant* encourages applications for employment from persons who are members of disadvantaged backgrounds.

Budget and Cost-Effectiveness

In this section the applicant provides information showing that the project has an adequate budget and is cost-effective. Information shows how the budget will support project activities and indicates that costs are reasonable in relation to proposed objectives.

Interagency Consultation and Coordination

This section demonstrates that the applicant conducted adequate consultation and coordination with other agencies in planning and developing the proposal. In addition, the applicant describes how it consults and coordinates with appropriate agencies in implementing and evaluating the project.

Adequacy of Resources

This section shows how the applicant plans to devote adequate resources to the project. This section provides information relating to project office facilities, academic facilities, and residential facilities that will be utilized by the project. The *Adequacy of Resources* section describes resources and support activities available to the project.

Recruitment

In this section note how the applicant provides information that shows the quality of the recruitment plan. The applicant outlined how the plan will identify, inform, and recruit eligible participants who are most in need of the academic and support services and financial assistance provided by the project.

Appendixes

The authors did not include any appendixes in the following example because of limited space. Appendixes are important in some proposals but may be prohibited in others. This particular proposal had five appendixes:

APPENDIX	CONTENT
A	Letters of Support
B	Résumés
C	Job Descriptions
D	Program Forms
E	Program Materials

If appendixes are prohibited in the proposal you wish to write, you should still seek the same kinds of support and commitments you would normally include in the appendixes. Paraphrase and condense such letters and commitments into your narrative and indicate that the documents are on file and available upon request. In this manner you can often accomplish nearly the same effect you would if you were able to include appendixes.

Sample Proposal

The sample proposal included on the following pages was initially written and submitted by Ernest W. Brewer, The University of Tennessee, Knoxville, in 1985 and rewritten for continued funding in 1987. This was one of four proposals what were funded by the U.S. Department of Education for three years in response to the grant competition of *CFDA* 84.149.

OMB Approval No. 0348 0043

APPLICATION FOR FEDERAL ASSISTANCE

2. DATE SUBMITTED *12-11-89*	Applicant Identifier

1. TYPE OF SUBMISSION:	
Application ☐ Construction	Preapplication ☐ Construction
☒ Non-Construction	☐ Non-Construction

3. DATE RECEIVED BY STATE	State Application Identifier
4. DATE RECEIVED BY FEDERAL AGENCY	Federal Identifier

5. APPLICANT INFORMATION

Legal Name: *The University of Tennessee*	Organizational Unit:

Address (give city, county, state, and zip code)	Name and telephone number of the person to be contacted on matters involving this application (give area code)
404 Andy Holt Tower *Knoxville, Tennessee 37996*	*Dr. Ernest W. Brewer, Principal Investigator* *(615-974-4466)*

6. EMPLOYER IDENTIFICATION NUMBER (EIN):

☐☐ - ☐☐☐☐☐☐

7. TYPE OF APPLICANT: (enter appropriate letter in box) **[I]**

A. State	H. Independent School Dist.
B. County	I. State Controlled Institution of High Learning
C. Municipal	J. Private University
D. Township	K. Indian Tribe
E. Interstate	L. Individual
F. Intermunicipal	M. Profit Organization
G. Special District	N. Other (Specify): _____

8. TYPE OF APPLICATION:

☒ New   ☐ Continuation   ☐ Revision

If Revision, enter appropriate letter(s) in box(es):

A. Increase Award   B. Decrease Award   C. Increase Duration

D. Decrease Duration   Other (specify)

_____

9. NAME OF FEDERAL AGENCY:

U.S. DEPARTMENT OF EDUCATION

10. CATALOG OF FEDERAL DOMESTIC ASSISTANCE NUMBER: [8][4] • [1][4][9]

TITLE: *Southeastern College Assistance Migrant Program*

11. DESCRIPTIVE TITLE OF APPLICANT'S PROJECT:

The University of Tennessee's Southeastern College Assistance Migrant Program

12. AREAS AFFECTED BY PROJECT (cities, counties, states, etc.)

Alabama, Florida, Georgia, Kentucky, North Carolina, South Carolina, Tennessee, and Virgiinia

13. PROPOSED PROJECT:		14. CONGRESSIONAL DISTRICT OF:	
Start Date	Ending Date	a. Applicant	b. Project
09 01 90	*08 31 91*	*Second*	*All of AL, FL, GA, KY, NC, SC, TN, and VA*

15. ESTIMATED FUNDING:

a. Federal	$	*402,930* .00
b. Applicant	$	*83,757* .00
c. State	$	.00
d. Local	$	.00
e. Other	$	.00
f. Program Income	$	.00
g. TOTAL	$	*486,687* .00

16. IS APPLICATION SUBJECT TO REVIEW BY STATE EXECUTIVE ORDER 12372 PROCESS?

a. YES, THIS PREAPPLICATION/APPLICATION WAS MADE AVAILABLE TO THE STATE EXECUTIVE ORDER 12372 PROCESS FOR REVIEW ON:

DATE: *12 1 89* _____

b. NO ☒ PROGRAM IS NOT COVERED BY E O 12372

☐ OR PROGRAM HAS NOT BEEN SELECTED BY STATE FOR REVIEW

17 IS THE APPLICANT DELINQUENT ON ANY FEDERAL DEBT?

☐ Yes   If "Yes" attach an explanation.   ☒ No

18. TO THE BEST OF MY KNOWLEDGE AND BELIEF, ALL DATA IN THIS APPLICATION/PREAPPLICATION ARE TRUE AND CORRECT. THE DOCUMENT HAS BEEN DULY AUTHORIZED BY THE GOVERNING BODY OF THE APPLICANT AND THE APPLICANT WILL COMPLY WITH THE ATTACHED ASSURANCES IF THE ASSISTANCE IS AWARDED.

a. Typed Name of Authorized Representative	b. Title *Vice-Provost for Research*	c. Telephone number *615/974-4466*
d. Signature of Authorized Representative		e. Date Signed

Previous Editions Not Usable

Standard Form 424 REV 4 88
Prescribed by OMB Circular A-102

Authorized for Local Reproduction

i

Table of Contents
College Assistance Migrant Program
The University of Tennessee
1990-93 Program Year

II.   Table of Contents ii

III.   Budget Information... iii

IV.   Background Information.. 1

        Narrative (206.31 a-h - 100 points)

        Plan of Operation (206.31a - 25 points) 3
            Recognition of the Legislative Intent of the Project....................... 3
            High Quality in the Design of the Project 4
            Effective Plan of Management 6
            Relationship of Objectives to the Purposes of the Project............... 7
            Use of Resources and Personnel... 7
            Equal Access and Treatment for Eligible Participants 8
        Objectives and Activities (206.31b - 20 points) 8
        Evaluation Plan (206.31c - 15 points) 12
        Quality of Key Personnel (206.31d - 10 points)................................. 15
        Budget/Cost Effectiveness (206.31e - 10 points) 18
        Interagency Consultation/Coordination (206.31f - 10 points)............... 19
        Adequacy of Resources (206.31g - 5 points) 21
        Recruitment (206.31h - 5 points).. 22

V.   Certifications and Assurances 23

VI.   Appendixes

        Appendix A - Letters of Support ....
        Appendix B - Résumés ....
        Appendix C - Job Descriptions..
        Appendix D - Program Forms ....
        Appendix E - Program Materials...

ii

PART III--BUDGET INFORMATION

FOR THE

COLLEGE ASSISTANCE MIGRANT PROGRAM

SECTION: A BUDGET SUMMARY

OBJECT CLASS CATEGORIES	FEDERAL FUNDING AMOUNTS
a. Personnel	$ 132,563.00
b. Fringe Benefits	$ 29,810.00
c. Travel	$ 10,300.00
d. Equipment	$ 980.00
e. Supplies	$ 1,600.00
f. Contractual	$ 00.00
g. Other	$ 197,830.00
h. Total Direct Charges (a-h)	$ 373,083.00
i. Indirect Charges	$ 29,847.00
j. Total (lines h + i)	$ 402,930.00

iii

College Assistance Migrant Program
Base Budget 1990-93
{Raises and adjustments will be computed annually}

DIRECT COST

A. Personnel {Example — list and price each}
    1.   Director (25% time for 12 mos.) $15,600.00
    2.   Associate Director (100% time for 12 mos.) $39,200.00
    3.   Counselor (100% time for 12 mos.) $18,500.00
    4.   Recruiter/Counselor (100% time for 12 mos.) $18,500.00
    5.   Principal Secretary (100% time for 12 mos.) $14,663.00
    6.   *Part-time Tutors (4-5 @ 20/30 hrs/wk for 10 mos.) $26,100.00

                        Sub-Total for Personnel $132,563.00

B. Fringe Benefits $29,810.00

    (The University of Tennessee's employee benefits are calculated at
    28%. *Graduate assistants and part-time employees do not receive
    fringe benefits.) (28% x $106,463.00 = $29,810.00)

                        Sub-Total for Fringe Benefits $29,810.00

C. Staff Travel {list and describe each — e.g.}

    1.   Local Travel (pick up students at bus station, $10,300.00
        take students to service agencies, etc.)

                        Sub-Total for Staff Travel $10,300.00

D. Equipment (Two typewriters @ $490/each) $980.00

                        Sub-Total for Equipment $980.00

E. Consumable Supplies {supplies, copies, etc. — add details} $1,600.00

                        Sub-Total for Supplies $1,600.00

F. Contractual $00.00

                        Sub-Total for Contractual $00.00

iv

G. Other

1.	Tuition and Fees (30 in-state students @ $468/ Qtr. x 1 Qtr. = $14,040 + 30 out-of-state students @ $1,186/Qtr. x 1 Qtr. = $35,580)	$49,620.00
2.	Stipends (60 students x $40/mo. x 9 mos.)	$21,600.00
3.	Student Travel (60 students x $80 = $4,800)	$4,800.00
4.	Student Dorm (60 students x $425/Qtr. x 2 Qtrs.)	$51,000.00
5.	Student Meals (60 students x $430/Qtr. x 2 Qtrs.)	$51,600.00
6.	Testing Materials	$300.00
7.	Duplication (forms, classroom handouts, etc.)	$700.00
8.	Postage	$800.00
9.	Communication (telephone service charges)	$5,200.00
10.	HEP/CAMP Dues	$350.00
11.	HEP/CAMP Scholarships (10 x $1,186)	$11,860.00

Sub-Total for Other $197,830.00

H. Total Direct Cost $373,083.00

I. *Total Indirect Costs {explain details} $29,847.00

J. Total Cost $402,930.00

*The University is contributing indirect costs of $83,757.00 based on Modified Total Direct Costs (MTDC). MTDC are total costs less capital outlay items. 38.9% and 22.0% are the officially audited Indirect Costs rates by DHHS Audit Agency under OMB A-88 Negotiation Agreement, dated January 27, 1989 for UT-Knoxville on-campus and off-campus other sponsored activities.

v

Background Information

Institution and Region

The University of Tennessee (UT) is a multi-campus, multi-purpose system of higher education with branches throughout Tennessee. As Tennessee's state university and federal land-grant institution, it is regarded as the "capstone of the state's educational system." *The College Money Book* calls UT the **"best buy"** for students, based on "high quality education at an economical cost." In carrying out its unique public service responsibilities, UT has a statewide mission beyond that of any other institution of higher learning in the Southeastern region of the United States. The University offers more than one hundred fields of study and sponsors a full program of student services and activities.

As the major institution in the state, UT has a RESPONSIBILITY to develop and administer programs to meet the needs of special populations. Currently, there is an overwhelming need to re-establish a College Assistance Migrant Program (CAMP) in the southeastern region of the United States. At present, UT's CAMP program was the only one that existed in this region. UT remains an IDEAL GEOGRAPHIC LOCATION to serve migrant/seasonal farmworkers and their dependents from the southeast because NINE (9) STATES BORDER TENNESSEE, and the Migrant Education Program office in Washington, D.C. furnished a report indicating that there were over 107,362 migrant students of 0-21 years of age in the eight (8) state (Alabama, Florida, Georgia, Kentucky, North Carolina, South Carolina, Tennessee, and Virginia) targeted area of the southeastern region. The reason that a large geographical area will be served is due to the fact that there are only five (5) CAMP projects in the U.S. and those are in Texas and on the West Coast. The service area, consisting of the eight states mentioned, is shown in the map below.

Map of Targeted States
Southeastern College Assistance Migrant Program

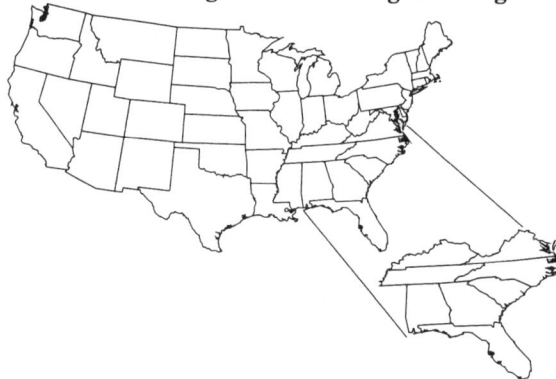

The statistical data cited in the paragraph above indicates that there are significant populations of migrant/ seasonal farmworkers in the region, many of whom benefitted from the operation of Southeastern HEP/ CAMP at UT. The University is aware of the educational and socioeconomic problems of disadvantaged students including the migrant/seasonal farmworker student. The University currently operates the High School Equivalency Program (HEP), an Upward Bound program, an Educational Talent Search program, and a Student Support Services program which have benefitted migrant/seasonal farmworker youth at the secondary and postsecondary level. The southeastern region of the United States, recognized as a major home-base area for migrant/seasonal farmworkers, is an ideal location for funding a CAMP program.

1

Program Need

Migrant/seasonal farmworkers have a unique background and possess UNIQUE educational needs that only the CAMP program can address. These students have the lowest rate of college admission, the lowest rate of college completion, and the highest rate of under- and unemployment. The University has developed and implemented programs designed to correct academic skill deficiencies, promote student self-worth, and create an environment in which students feel welcome and non-threatened by its institutional structure and academic environment. These programs, along with the specialized tutoring and counseling, enable farmworker students to have the necessary support to adjust successfully to college life and maximize their learning potentials while enrolled.

The Need for CAMP in the Targeted Area

The Southeastern CAMP Program will be the only CAMP program available in the southeastern region of the country, in spite of the fact that a very large number of youth from migrant/seasonal farmworker families have been identified in our target area. The Association of Farmworker Opportunity Programs (AFOP) has stated that its member organizations in the eight (8) target states served 40,916 farmworkers during the 1983-84 program year. The Association estimates that TOTAL farmworker population from the eight (8) state area is over 801,500 of which 267,000 were identified as migrants (according to the Department of Labor's Farmworker Farm and Rural Employment and Training Office). Furthermore, this need is supported by the USDA's ranking of the states as to the number of farms over 400 acres. Of the targeted states that we currently serve and propose to serve within this proposal, three (3) of the eight (8) states ranked as follows: Kentucky is ranked Number 4 with 101,000 farms; Tennessee is ranked Number 7 with 95,000 farms; and North Carolina is ranked Number 11 with 79,000 farms (*U.S. News and World Report*, October 22, 1984).

In addition, very low numbers of students from migrant/seasonal backgrounds attend any kind of postsecondary program. The reasons for this can be identified by examining the barriers typically present for this type of student:

1. There is a *lack of effective motivation among farmworker youth.* It is difficult to stimulate migrant/ seasonal farmworker youth to attend college. Parents discourage them from attending either because they need them to work the fields with them or because they are doubtful that they can be successful.
2. *Farmworker students often lack financial resources* to pay for a college education and are often unfamiliar with Federal aid programs designed to assist low-income students.
3. *Families of farmworker students lack financial resources* to pay for a college education and are often unfamiliar with Federal aid programs.
4. *Farmworker students have poor self-concepts and fear the unknown* situation and experiences of college life.

Our experience in administering programs for disadvantaged students has led us to identify factors which contribute to students' dropping out of postsecondary programs. These factors, which relate to problems encountered by students from migrant farmworker backgrounds, are:

1. *Lack of financial means* for school. Students have difficulty getting summer jobs and are usually unable to rely on resources from the family.

2

2. *Poor academic progress* and an *insufficient number of earned credits.* The results of inappropriately "declared majors" or change of majors cause students to lose credit for nonrelevant classes.
3. *Lack of career goals* which affect a student's sense of purpose and commitment.
4. *Feelings of alienation, fear of failure, lack of acceptance,* and *disbelief in one's ability* to succeed.

These issues and barriers are especially painful and real to students from migrant/seasonal farmworker backgrounds and will not be conquered without such programs as UT's Southeastern CAMP Program which has been designed to ENCOURAGE these students to enroll in college and receive ACADEMIC SUPPORT, FINANCIAL ASSISTANCE, and COUNSELING to help them believe in themselves and overcome those barriers which exist.

The map of the United States shown below indicates where the five (5) 1989-90 CAMP programs are located and shows the lack of program support for the migrant/seasonal farmworker population in the southeastern region of the United States.

Map of 1989-90 CAMP Programs

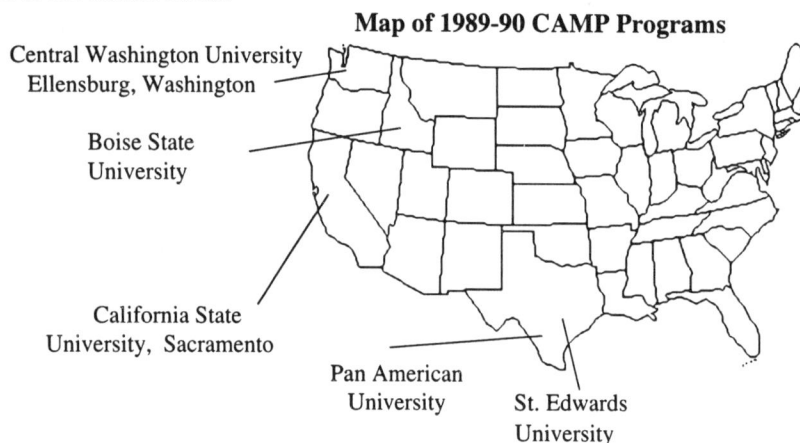

Central Washington University
Ellensburg, Washington

Boise State
University

California State
University, Sacramento

Pan American
University

St. Edwards
University

In summary, the need exists to provide CAMP services to the migrant/seasonal farmworker of the Southeastern United States and to coordinate the identification and recruitment of the migrant/seasonal farmworker population. Programs which are designed to enhance student academic performance and retention must be provided. Efforts must be made to diagnose and remediate academic difficulties so that appropriate learning programs may be prescribed. Students must be provided with tutorial services and counseling so that appropriate career objectives can be identified. And finally, efforts must be made to ensure the positive growth and development which focuses on generating pride in one's cultural and ethnic heritage. These needs provide the basis for the program design narrative which follows.

Plan of Operation
(206.31(a) - 25 Points)

Recognition of the Legislative Intent of the Project
(206.31(a)(2)(iii))

As is stated in the *Federal Register*, Volume 52, Number 126, July 1, 1987, CAMP will provide assistance to help migratory and seasonal farmworker students in:

3

1. Making the transition from secondary school to postsecondary school;
2. Generating the motivation necessary to succeed in postsecondary school; and
3. Developing the skills necessary to succeed in postsecondary school.

Furthermore, those eligible migrant and seasonal farmworkers will be identified in accordance with the regulations described on page 24918 of the *Federal Register*, dated July 1, 1987.

This new college experience provides a genuine opportunity for many of these individuals to leave a lifestyle of failure and poverty, an option not readily available to this population. The proposed CAMP project will combine University resources with program resources to provide assistance in all areas of student need. This project will provide students with total financial assistance for their freshman year through a combination of grants, work study, loans, and scholarships to cover tuition, fees, and other college expenses. Following their freshman year, the Financial Aid Office at UT will continue to assist students by providing financial aid awards to the full extent of the demonstrated financial need for years two, three, and four of the student's college experience.

High Quality in the Design of the Project
(206.31(a)(2)(i))

The overall project is designed in accordance with the guidelines stated in the *Federal Register*. Most importantly, in preplanning the design, assurances were made to incorporate all of the services listed in the *Register*. As is shown on page 24921, seven (7) services areas are outlined "to assist the participants in meeting the project objectives and in succeeding in an academic program of study at the IHE." Those services are as follows: (1) recruitment; (2) special counseling; (3) housing support; (4) career exploration services; (5) exposure to academic institutions, programs, cultural events; (6) inservice training for staff; and (7) tutoring and supplementary instruction including basic skills, subject areas needed by the student, related areas such as study skills, and other essential supportive services.

In addition, page 24918 of the *Register* states that the purpose of CAMP is to provide services in three major areas: (1) academic; (2) supporting; and (3) financial. These service areas as well as the services indicated in the previous paragraph have all been integrated and coordinated in the overall project design. Services to be provided are as follows (see Flowchart the following page):

1. **Student Assessment:** The CAMP staff will use information gathered from forms which the students completed during the recruitment process. ACT scores and the student's high school record or GED scores will be used to identify student's academic needs, strengths and weaknesses. In those cases where additional academic data is necessary, the California Achievement Test (CAT) and the Test for Adult Basic Education (TABE) will be utilized. From this data an Individual Educational Plan (IEP) will be established for each student. Also included in the student assessment will be an evaluation of the psychological and emotional needs of the student. Each student will have an individual interview to determine attitudinal problems which may interfere with optimal academic achievement. The CAMP staff will identify students' academic motivation and self-concept to determine the degree to which students feel secure about their educational pursuits. Students will complete a Self-Report Questionnaire to assist counselors with identification of the above mentioned concerns. Those students feeling insecure about themselves or their academic ability will participate in peer support groups to encourage the development of self-confidence and acceptance.

4

2. **Study Skill Development:** Special classes will be established for study skills development. Such skills as time-management, effective notetaking, planning, organizing and other basic academic techniques will be taught.

3. **Academic Instructional Support:** Special sections of university courses will be arranged by CAMP in the areas of English, math, and science so that regular university faculty can instruct CAMP students in a manner appropriate to their learning style and academic preparation.

4. **Tutoring:** Part of the IEP for each student will include a tentative tutoring schedule. CAMP staff will coordinate the tutoring schedule and will document all tutoring received. The Basic Skills Specialist will maintain contact with academic faculty and CAMP staff to assess student progress and determine the need for additional tutoring. CAMP students experiencing high academic success in certain subjects will be encouraged to participate as tutors in a peer tutoring program.

5. **Staff Training:** The majority of the CAMP staff members have been previously trained in working with migrant and seasonal farmworkers and additional training will continue. It is necessary for each staff member to receive information and training to help develop greater awareness and sensitivity to the needs of this particular population. In order to provide this information and training a series of preservice sessions will be planned and conducted, and each staff member will be required to attend. Those sessions will be held early in the program year and prior to the arrival of students.

> **Similar detail is provided for all additional entries (student recruitment, student orientation, counseling, career exploration, social/cultural enrichment, housing/meals, health care, transition, follow-up, financial aid, stipends, and CAMP scholarships.**

The University of Tennessee's
Southeastern College Assistance Migrant Program (CAMP)

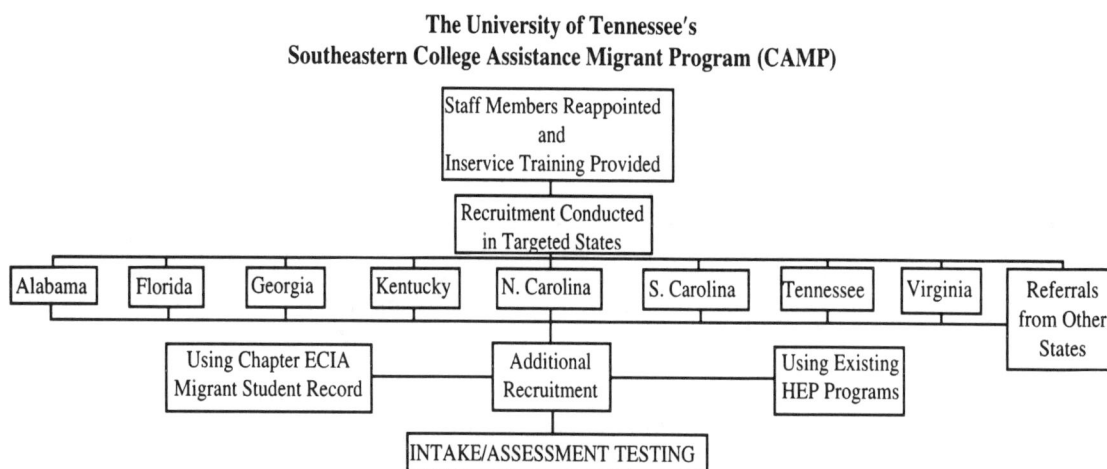

Partial flowchart showing CAMP details.

The *Flowchart of Services and Activities* shows the overall design layout and the interrelationship of each service component.   *5*

Effective Plan of Management
(206.31(a)(2)(ii))

The university is an equal opportunity, affirmative action employer and does not discriminate on the basis of race, sex, color, religion, nationality, age, handicap, or veteran status in providing employment of educational opportunities and benefits.

The program will be an integral part of the university structure within the College of Education's Technological and Adult Education Department. This university (grantee) designates the CAMP Director and Associate Director as the University Administrators responsible for program grant compliance and management. Within this context, the CAMP Director and Associate Director are responsible for:

(Three samples of nine shown.)

1. Preparing, submitting, and negotiating the College Assistance Migrant Program (CAMP) proposal and other reports required by the U.S. Department of Education (DE);
2. Administration of the program and coordination with the DE's Migrant Education Program, the University, State Farmworker agencies, and Referral/Placement Services;
3. Assuring that the coordination between the CAMP staff and students and the university administration and faculty is accomplished on a timely basis;

The CAMP staff members are employees of the univerisity, governed by university personnel and employment policies and have all rights, privileges, and benefits afforded university employees.

The Director reports to the College of Education's Technological and Adult Education Department, provides reports as necessary, and meets weekly with the CAMP staff. These meetings are augmented by progress reports and frequent communications. The organizational chart for the project and its relationship to the university administrative structure is shown below. The QUALITY OF KEY PERSONNEL Section of this proposal is located on pages 15-17 and shows the personnel which the University currently has employed in the last project and their qualifications. Resumes and Job Descriptions are located in Appendixes B and C, respectively, of this proposal.

(Partial organizational chart)

Project Organization of Personnel

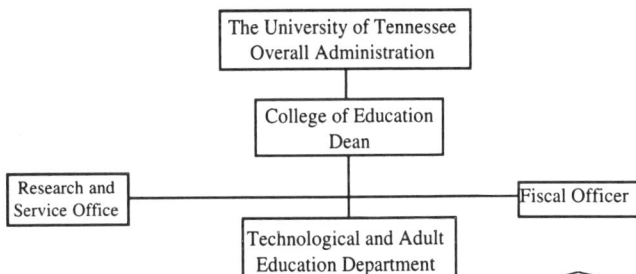

6

Relationship of Objectives to the Purposes of the Project
(206.31(a)(2)(iii))

As was stated in the design section of the plan (operation), Page 24921 of the *Federal Register* states that the purpose of CAMP is to provide academic services, supporting services, and financial assistance. All of the components of the objectives section as shown on pages 8-11 are designed to address these three (3) major service areas. The outline below demonstrates how each objective component relates to the three (3) service areas of the overall purpose of the project:

1. Academic Service Area Objectives:
   a. Student Assessment
   b. Study Skills Development
   c. Academic Instructional Support
   d. Tutoring
2. Supportive Service Area Objectives:
   a. Staff Training
   b. Student Recruitment
   c. Student Orientation
   d. Adjustment Workshops
   e. Counseling
   f. Career Exploration
   g. Social/Cultural Activities
   h. Housing/Meals
   i. Health Care
   j. Freshman-Sophomore Transition Assistance
   k. Follow-Up
3. Financial Assistance Area Objectives:
   a. Financial Aid
   b. Student Stipend
   c. CAMP Scholarship

In summary, four (4) objectives focus on academic service areas, eleven (11) objectives focus on supportive service areas, and three (3) focus on financial assistance service areas.

Use of Resources and Personnel
(206.31(a)(2)(iv))

We value greatly the high degree of University support and the numerous University resources that are available to the CAMP project and its participants. These resources serve to supplement and enhance the learning and social environment for CAMP students. Examples of those resources which are available include:

(Three of original 12 examples appear here.)

1. An Office of Finance which provides complete fiscal services (accounting, budgeting, purchasing, payrolls, etc.) and other financial records necessary for fiscal compliance.
2. An Office of Personnel which ensures equal employment opportunities for all staff and provides the personnel services necessary for hiring staff and processing grievance and due process hearings.
3. A Maintenance Department which provides OFFICE SPACE and equipment, other necessary space for activities, maintenance of buildings and grounds, and also performs custodial service.

7

These are representative of the resources which the university offers to enrich and enhance the academic program and to help make the students' stay at the University more fulfilling as well as enlightening. A more detailed description of the Project's resources can be found in the ADEQUACY OF RESOURCES Section of this proposal. LETTERS OF SUPPORT showing University personnel and significant others as resources are located in APPENDIX A.

Equal Access and Treatment for Eligible Participant
(206.3(a)(2)(v))

The University is in full compliance with all Federal and equal access regulations and will provide equal access and treatment for eligible participants and staff members who are members of groups that have been traditionally underrepresented such as members of racial or ethnic minority groups, women, and handicapped persons. This is outlined more explicitly in the OBJECTIVES and ACTIVITIES Sections of this proposal.

In employing CAMP staff these same Federal and equal access compliance guidelines will be adhered to. Careful consideration will be given to the experience and training of all applicants to assure that those hired have a background which is appropriately related to the objectives of the project.

Other Sections Supportive to the Plan of Operation

The following sections do NOT APPEAR in the PLAN OF OPERATION but are presented in their respective areas according to Subpart D 206.31 of the Request for Proposal (RFP) on "What selection criteria does the Secretary use to evaluate the application?" These sections are an integral part of the overall operation of the project and are presented in detail in this proposal as indicated as follows. The OBJECTIVES AND ACTIVITIES Section of this proposal, pages 8-11, has the various COMPONENTS of the project. These objectives and activities of the project are designed to respond to the academic, supportive, and financial needs of the participating CAMP students. The EVALUATION Section of this proposal is located on pages 12-15 which shows the comprehensive evaluation plan for the project. The QUALITY OF KEY PERSONNEL Section of this proposal, pages 15-18, identifies the qualifications of the project director and other key personnel, the time that each person plans to commit to the project, and the extent to which the University, as part of its nondiscriminatory employment practices, encourages applications from members of groups that have been traditionally underrepresented. The BUDGET and COST-EFFECTIVENESS Section, located on pages 18-19, documents that the budget for the project is adequate to support the project activities, and costs are reasonable in relation to the objectives of the project. On pages 21-22 the ADEQUACY OF RESOURCES Section is presented, which identifies the facilities, equipment, and supplies that the applicant plans to use. The last section of this proposal is RECRUITMENT (pages 22-23) which addresses the recruitment services of this project.

Objectives and Activities
(206.31(b) - 20 points)

(**Four done in detail; others listed.**)

8

Quality of the Design of Objectives and Activities for Participants
(206.31(b)(1))

Page one of the Plan of Operation, lists the three broad service areas which were cited in the *Federal Register* on page 24922. These are academic services, supporting services, and financial services. Within these broad service areas, seventeen (17) specific services were identified as necessary in order to meet the needs of project participants. For each of these services an objective with appropriate supportive activities has been written, and these are presented in the following format:

1. Component title - identifies the objective topic.
2. Goal - states the broad intention for this objective.
3. Objectives - defines the measurable outcome (the product).
4. Activities - lists the specific procedures or ways the objective is to be met (the process).
5. Timeline - specifies when the activities of the objective will be met.
6. Evaluation - determines if, and to what degree, the objective was met.
7. Staff responsibility - shows the staff member responsible for activities.

Objectives and Activities Designed to Respond to Academic, Supporting, and Financial Needs of Participants
(206.31(b)(2)(i))

This section consists of the Project's seventeen (17) objectives and activities and are presented according to the design format shown above. They respond to the academic, supportive, and financial needs of the participants.

1.   Student Assessment

Goal: To create an individual profile of each participant which identifies strengths and weaknesses.

Objective: To review and evaluate collected data on 100% of the CAMP participants and develop an Individual Educational Plan (IEP) showing special academic help and tutorial assistance needed by each student by the second week they are accepted into the program.

Activities: 1.   Review data on initial intake form.
                      a.   Self Report questionnaires;
                      b.   High School Transcript (GED Score Report); and
                      c.   ACT Score Report
                  2.   Administer additional assessment data, such as the California Achievement Test (CAT), as necessary.
                  3.   Determine study skill needs of each participant.
                  4.   Determine special class instruction needs of each participant.
                  5.   Determine tutoring needs of each participant.
                  6.   Evaluate any special psychological, emotional, or motivational needs which exist for each student.

9

7. Develop an IEP for each participant.
8. Conduct conferences to review IEP with the each participant.

Timeline: September 12, 19XX - Collect and Review all student data.
September 28, 19XX - Complete IEP on each student.

Evaluation: Place all data collected in student folder. Have copy of IEP in folder with a list of special academic help and tutorial assistance the project will provide each participant.

Staff Responsibility: Associate Director, Counselor, Recruiter/Counselor

2.   Study Skills Development

Goal: To conduct an effective study skills development program.

Objective: To provide a minimum of three hours of study skills training and instruction to 90% of the CAMP participants.

Activities:
1. Administer study skills pretest at beginning of first study skills class.
2. All students attend a study skills development class for three weeks.
3. Instruct students in study techniques, note taking, time management, and other fundamental study skills designed to improve college class performance.
4. Administer and score study skills posttest.
5. Record results of posttest gains in students' IEP.

Timeline: September 30, 19XX - Administer pretest; Students attend first session
October 7, 19XX   - Second session
October 17, 19XX   - Administer posttest

Evaluation: Maintain an attendance log recording the hours each student attended the tutoring classes. Attach copies of class outlines or syllabus to demonstrate the topic discussed.

Staff Responsibility: Basic Skills Specialist

3.   Tutoring

Goal: To conduct a tutorial program which will focus on the individual academic course needs of each student.

Objective: To provide an individualized tutorial program consisting of a minimum of ten tutorial sessions per quarter to at least 95% of those CAMP participants who demonstrate this service.

Activities:
1. Review student assessment data including: high school record, GED scores, ACT scores, and the results of the California Achievement Test (CAT) and the Test of Adult Basic Education (TABE).

10

2. Develop a list of tutorial needs from this data.
3. Include this list of tutorial needs with each student's IEP.
4. Assign tutors to each student needing this assistance.
5. Monitor student tutorial progress throughout each quarter and periodically reassess tutoring needs.

Timeline: September 30, 19XX - Assess data and develop individual needs list for each IEP.
                       September 30, 19XX to June 13, 19XX - Provide tutoring to students.

Evaluation: Maintain a copy of each student's individual tutorial program including an attendance sheet that demonstrates attendance at a minimum of 10 sessions.

Staff Responsibility: Associate Director, Basic Skills Specialist, Tutors

4.   Staff Training

Goal: To conduct a job training program which is especially relevant to areas of recruiting, teaching, and counseling migrant/seasonal farmworker students.

Objective: To provide a minimum of five job training sessions for one hour each to 100% of the CAMP staff during the academic year.

Activities: 1. Plan and develop a training manual and a training program for CAMP staff consisting of five sessions which are designed to increase awareness of the needs of the migrant/seasonal farmworker student.
                       2. Conduct four (4) training sessions of one hour each.
                       3. Provide training on material and techniques gathered by those staff members who attended the National CAMP Technical Conference.

Timelines: July 1, 19XX — Plan and develop training program for CAMP staff
                       July 11, 19XX — Conduct preservice session #1
                       July 12, 19XX — Conduct preservice session #2 and session #3
                       July 13-14, 19XX — Conduct preservice session #4 and session #5

Evaluation: Maintain a log indicating attendance of staff at each session. Maintain copies of the content taught in each session. Have the Training Manual and Training Program available for inspection.

Staff Responsibility: Project Director

> **Additional objectives in the same format related to student recruitment, student orientation, college life adjustment, counseling, career exploration, social/cultural enrichment, housing/meals, health care, freshman/sophomore transition assistance, follow-up, financial aid, and student stipends.**

11

The Size, Scope, and Quality of Activities
(206.31(b)(2)(ii))

A total of eighty-four (84) activities has been presented in the section of the proposal. Each of these activities is specifically stated so it can be implemented effectively. However, the activities on the whole are broad in scope so as to include all of the aspects necessary to implement the objective properly. Quality implementation of the activities is assured through the evaluation procedure established for each component.

Evaluation Plan
(206.31(c) - 15 points)

This section of the proposal shows methods of evaluation that are appropriate for the project, and to the extent possible, are OBJECTIVE and PRODUCE QUANTIFIABLE data. The university will meet the requirements of EDGAR (CFR 75.590) and the funding agency in providing an annual evaluation covering the following three (3) areas:

1. the progress of the project in achieving its objectives;
2. the effectiveness of the project in meeting the stated purpose of the CAMP program; and
3. the effect of the project on persons being served, including any persons who are members of groups that have been traditionally underrepresented.

PROGRESS IN ACHIEVING FUNDED OBJECTIVES

The University of Tennessee's CAMP Program views the evaluation process as an essential factor contributing to its success in the quality of service. The program's multi-faceted nature requires continuous critical self-evaluation in all phases of program operation. Effective management and quality services depend on frequent feedback to document progress and detect problems. Our evaluation plan (see Flowchart below) is an integral

EVALUATION PLAN FLOWCHART

The University of Tennessee's CAMP Program

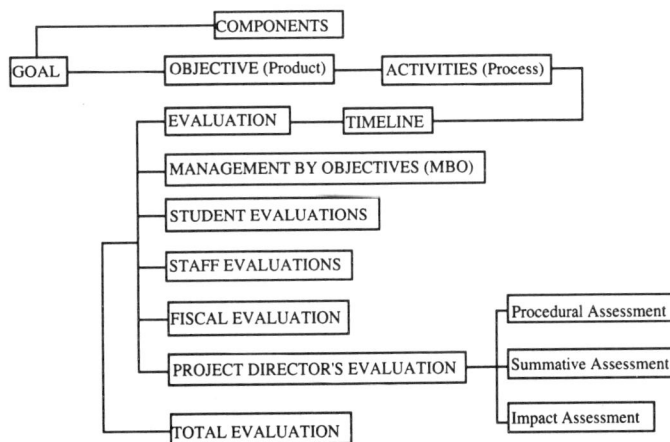

12

resource enabling the CAMP staff to plan, monitor, and refine project processes and to collect and analyze empirical information that can be used to improve strategies and control costs. The proposed CAMP Program's performance evaluation will be based on meeting the objectives (PRODUCTS) of each component as outlined in the OBJECTIVES AND ACTIVITIES Section of this proposal. Each "COMPONENT" is composed of a clearly stated NEED, GOAL, OBJECTIVE (product), ACTIVITY (process), TIMELINE, EVALUATION, and STAFF RESPONSIBILITY. Additionally, by using a Management by Objectives (MBO) approach each component is evaluated in measurable criteria. (See Management by Objectives in this section of the proposal).

PROJECT EFFECTIVENESS IN MEETING THE PURPOSE OF THE PROGRAM

The degree to which this project meets the purpose of the programs will be assessed by the CAMP staff. According to the *Federal Register*, "CAMP provides assistance to help migratory and seasonal farmworker students in - (1) Making the transition from secondary school to postsecondary school; (2) generating the motivation necessary to succeed in postsecondary school; and (3) developing the skills necessary to succeed in postsecondary school."

The design of the project, the objectives, and the activities are all constructed in a manner that will bring about the overall purposes of the CAMP program (i.e., transition from secondary schools; generating motivation, developing skills). A series of checks, balances, and evaluations have been designed to determine if, in fact, the design, objectives, and activities accomplish the stated goal.

The CAMP staff will include these criteria in its evaluation which determine whether the overall purpose has been achieved. Staff members will be required to prepare a self-evaluation showing their projected work objectives, duties, and performance indicators. This activity demands a high level of accountability and self-evaluation on the part of each staff member. Questionnaires will be submitted to the administrative office, analyzed, and the findings discussed with all staff members. Also, the Project Director will be conducting an ongoing internal evaluation for program management, modification, and improvement by including the following three elements of evaluation. Particularly important is the element of *PROCEDURAL ASSESS-MENT* whereby program activities and management procedures may be assessed and compared to the design intents expressed in the original proposal. Program goals and student objectives must also be evaluated at or near the year's end for purposes of *SUMMATIVE ASSESSMENT*. Inasmuch as many of the desired effects of a CAMP project are fairly far-reaching into the second, third, and fourth years of students' educational development, it would be appropriate to pay at least some attention to the matter of longitudinal assessments of *PROGRAM IMPACT*. These three elements are reflected in our evaluation design.

PROCEDURAL ASSESSMENT. Particularly during the new funding period, the Director should function as a special resource person to the staff. During this period, concepts and intentions for program operations, as reflected in the application proposal, are translated into specific structures and practices. Some evaluators refer to this as a *FORMATIVE EVALUATION* process.

In this assessment, the Director will determine to what degree the actual project activities and management compare with the planned activities and management. These comparative data will be analyzed, and a determination will be made by the Director as to which activities should continue, which should be changed in some way, and which should be discontinued altogether.

13

SUMMATIVE ASSESSMENT. Each of the program goals and student objectives identified in the objectives and activities section of this proposal will be evaluated according to accepted techniques of summative assessment. Project records of enrollments, student activities, credits attempted and earned, and grades awarded will constitute the basis of this assessment. A specially prepared student questionnaire will also be administered at year's end for the purpose of obtaining feedback regarding strengths and weaknesses of the program implemented, self-reported attitudinal changes that have taken place, and an assessment of the overall value of the program.

IMPACT ASSESSMENT. To the extent possible, given the uncertainty of future funding, it would be a valuable experience to conduct a longitudinal evaluation of the CAMP student population. Follow-up studies tend to be rather expensive, for as subjects leave an area the costs of pursuit frequently become prohibitive. However, to the extent that CAMP students remain on The University of Tennessee campus, academic records are easily and inexpensively obtained.

Finally, at the end of the year, the Director will analyze the demographic characteristics of the CAMP participants. The data compiled would be used to make sure that groups which have traditionally been underrepresented are represented adequately as participants. The Director will also evaluate the extent to which the program has performed and functioned as stated in the proposal.

EFFECT OF THE PROJECT ON THOSE BEING SERVED

The CAMP participants will also evaluate the program by responding to ongoing questionnaires assessing the benefits which they have derived from the program, the quality of services received, and their impressions of the program. In addition to student evaluations, the staff will evaluate the program at the end of each quarter. All data compiled on the project activities will be available to U.S. Department of Education personnel and other interested agencies. This report will be sent to U.S. Department of Education, network agencies, educational institutions, and appropriate human services organizations which are involved with migrant and seasonal farmworkers.

SOUTHEASTERN COLLEGE ASSISTANCE MIGRANT PROGRAM
MANAGEMENT BY OBJECTIVES (MBO) FOR 1990-1993 PROGRAM YEARS

KEY ACTIVITY AREA	INDICATOR	STAFF	TOTAL PROPOSED GOAL	ACTUAL NO. OBTAINED	% OF PLAN ACCOMPLISHED
Student Assessment	a. No. of students receiving diagnostic achievement test	RC	225		
	b. No. of students receiving Individual Educational Plan (IEP)	RC	180		
	c. No. of Individual IEP Conferences conducted	RC	180		
Study Skills	a. No. of students attending Study Skills Instructional Program	BSS	180		
	b. No. of students completing pre-post test	BSS	180		

14

Tutoring			
	a.	No. of tutors available for CAMP program year	D	5
	b.	No. of students having access to tutoring services when needed	AD	180
	c.	No. of tutorial hours per student during CAMP program	T	30
	d.	No. of students receiving night tutoring services	T	20
	e.	No. of students receiving Saturday tutoring services	T	20

Three of 17 are shown as examples.

Quality of Key Personnel
(206.31(d) - 10 points)

This section of the application proposal provides information that shows adequate qualifications for those key personnel that the university plans to continue to use in the Southeastern CAMP Project. Qualifications of key personnel, the duration which staff will be appointed to the project, and the university's nondiscriminatory employment practices are also presented here.

Nondiscriminatory Employment Practices
(206.31(d)(2)(iv))

The University will adhere to the Affirmative Action Plan as an equal opportunity employer. The procedures used in implementing an affirmative action plan are as follows:

1. Advertising copy prepared to announce available positions at UTK shall comply in all regards with Federal, state, and local regulations for faculty and staff-exempt positions; copies of advertisements placed will be maintained on file by the unit advertising the vacancy. The UT Personnel Office will place all advertisements for staff-nonexempt position vacancies and will maintain on file copies of all such advertisements.
2. Sources of referral utilized by UT units are to be informed in writing of this policy and of UT's intention to SEEK OUT and to employ qualified applicants without regard to race, color, religion, sex, age, national origin, handicap, or veteran status. A copy of such notification shall be maintained on file by the head of the unit contacting the source of referral, in the case of faculty and staff-exempt positions. The UT Personnel Office will notify sources of referral for staff-nonexempt positions and will maintain on file copies of the notification.
3. Employment decisions shall be based solely upon individuals' qualifications for the position for which they are being considered.
4. Promotions shall be made in accordance with the principles of equal employment opportunity. Only valid, job-related requirements for advancement will be established.
5. No employee shall be excluded from participation in any university-sponsored activity or denied the benefits of any University program on the grounds of race, color, religion, sex, age, national origin, or veteran status. The university is prepared to make reasonable accommodations to allow participation by the handicapped in its programs, activities, and benefits.

15

Members of traditionally underrepresented groups will have equal opportunity for employment (i.e., members of racial or ethnic minority groups, women, handicapped persons, and/or the elderly). Full-time vacant positions will be advertised through the University Personnel Office. Due to the nature of the project, its intended participants, and the requirements in the Federal regulations, special efforts will be made to attract and employ members of groups traditionally underrepresented. For example, if two persons, both equally qualified, apply for a given position, and one is a member of a group traditionally underrepresented, that person will be given preference for the position. The Director will interview applicants and make the final decision in the selection process after consulting with the Dean of the College of Education. Upon notification of the grant award, current staff members would be retained from the current CAMP Program. An organizational chart is presented in this section of the proposal which depicts the structure of project personnel. Although the proposed CAMP Program will utilize the services of numerous University offices and programs within the academic and student affairs divisions of the campus, it will staff only those positions that provide exclusive service to CAMP students (refer to EMPLOYMENT DURATION CHART).

These positions include the following: project director, associate project director, counselor, recruiter/counselor, basic/skills specialist (graduate student, 50% time), residential counselor (graduate assistant, 25% time), secretary, and five (5) tutors (graduate students and upperclass students, hired hourly on an as-needed basis). Volunteers from the College of Education who are majoring in education, counseling, community service, and/or certain related areas will also be recruited for the project.

Employment Duration Chart
Southeastern College Assistance Migrant Program
(206.31(d)(2)(iii))

POSITION	% TIME	DURATION	S	O	N	D	J	F	M	A	M	J	J	A
Director	25%	12/mos	X	X	X	X	X	X	X	X	X	X	X	X
Associate Director	100%	12/mos	X	X	X	X	X	X	X	X	X	X	X	X
Counselor	100%	12/mos	X	X	X	X	X	X	X	X	X	X	X	X
Recruiter/Counselor	100%	12/mos	X	X	X	X	X	X	X	X	X	X	X	X
Secretary	100%	12/mos	X	X	X	X	X	X	X	X	X	X	X	X
*Basic Skills Specialist	50%	9/mos		X	X	X	X	X	X	X	X			
*Residential Counselor	25%	9/mos		X	X	X	X	X	X	X	X			
*Tutors (5)	hrly	9/mos		X	X	X	X	X	X	X	X			

*The Basic Skills Specialist and Residential Counselor will be master's or doctorate degree candidates (graduate assistants).

Qualifications of the Project Director
(206.31 (d) (2) (i))

The Project Director will be responsible for the CAMP as proposed and will report directly to the College of Education's TAE Department Head. The specific responsibilities of the Director, employed 25% time with the CAMP program for twelve (12) months, would include staffing, public relations, program planning, writing and negotiating the proposal, conducting inservice, conferring with key project personnel, evaluating the project, expending the budget, and overseeing the general operation of the CAMP participants (see Job Description, Appendix C).

(Name), who is currently Executive Director of the University of Tennessee's High School Equivalency Program (HEP), Upward Bound, Veterans Program, Educational Opportunity Center, Talented Minority

16

Research Fellowship Program, Math and Science Regional Center, and Educational Talent Search, has a doctorate degree in education with an emphasis in administration and a master's degree in rehabilitation counseling education. He has directed CAMP and HEP projects at the University and has many years' working experience with migrant/seasonal farmworkers, economically deprived youth, drop-outs, and potential drop-outs. Prior to (Name) current position, he was the Project Director and Associate Director of other University Federally funded programs. He is a professional educator with over twelve years of experience in education with several national counseling certifications. Before coming to the University, he served as Executive Director of a comprehensive rehabilitation facility and has served on numerous human service advisory committees.

(Name) appointment as Director for the College Assistance Migrant Program project is convenient to his current employment with the University (see Resume, Appendix B).

Qualifications of Other Key Personnel
(206.31(d)(2)(i))

Associate Director

The Associate Director's primary responsibility will be to be in charge of the daily running of CAMP. The Associate Director will report directly to the Director. Specific responsibilities of the Associate Director, employed 100% time, 12 months, would include supervising the day-to-day operations of the project, assisting in in-service, recommending budget expenditures, supervising CAMP staff, and assisting in evaluation (see Job Description, Appendix C).

(Name), who is currently Project Director for the HEP program, has a master's degree in Adult Education. Prior to (Name) appointment to the HEP project, she served as a personnel administrator/trainer for the National Farmworkers Association, where she had responsibility for all staffing and training. She also worked as a Job Placement Coordinator and was responsible for operating a Federally funded program (see Resume, Appendix B).

> **Follow similar format for each position that you include in your application.**

Additional Staff (Tutors)

Additional information on all the staff personnel is shown on the RESUMES in Appendix B of this proposal. JOB DESCRIPTIONS for each of the staff positions are located in Appendix C.

As indicated on the RESUMES in Appendix B, most of the CAMP staff members have worked previously with the CAMP/HEP project. This past working experience with migrant and seasonal farmworker participants, years of academic and Federal program experience among the staff members, master's and doctoral degree graduates/candidates who have been available for two to three years, along with the staff's participation in a comprehensive in-service training program, serve as key factors of a knowledgeable, motivated, and involved staff.

17

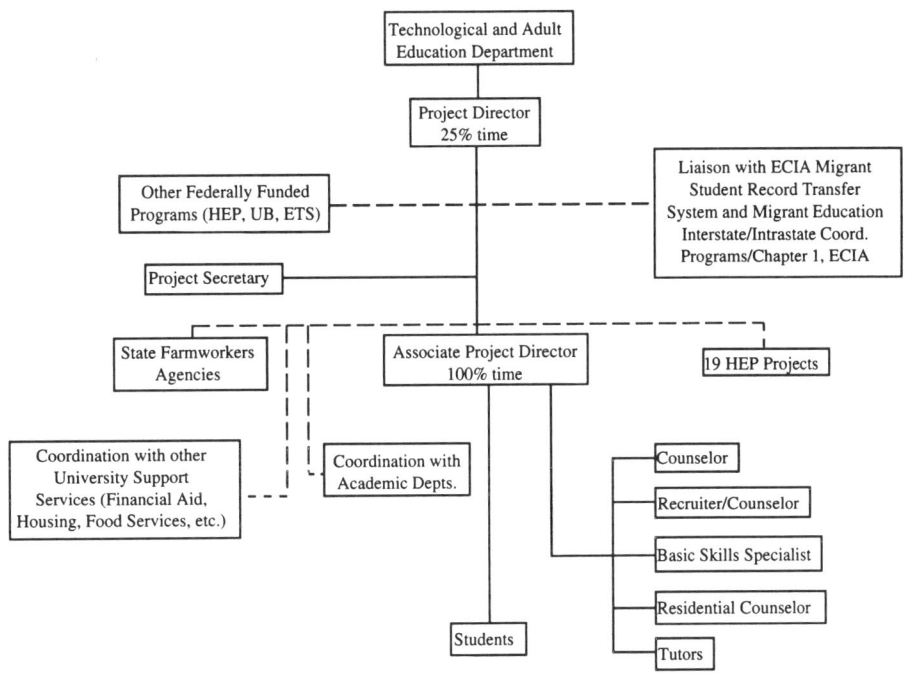

```
                          ┌─────────────────────────┐
                          │ Technological and Adult │
                          │  Education Department   │
                          └─────────────────────────┘
                                      │
                          ┌─────────────────────────┐
                          │     Project Director    │
                          │       25% time          │
                          └─────────────────────────┘
                                                          ┌──────────────────────────┐
  ┌────────────────────────┐                              │  Liaison with ECIA Migrant │
  │  Other Federally Funded │- - - - - - - - - - - - - - -│  Student Record Transfer   │
  │  Programs (HEP, UB, ETS)│                             │  System and Migrant Education│
  └────────────────────────┘                             │  Interstate/Intrastate Coord.│
                                                          │  Programs/Chapter 1, ECIA  │
       ┌──────────────────┐                               └──────────────────────────┘
       │ Project Secretary│
       └──────────────────┘

  ┌──────────────────┐    ┌──────────────────────┐   ┌──────────────┐
  │ State Farmworkers │    │Associate Project Director│ │ 19 HEP Projects│
  │    Agencies       │    │       100% time       │   └──────────────┘
  └──────────────────┘    └──────────────────────┘
                                                          ┌──────────────┐
  ┌────────────────────────┐   ┌──────────────────┐       │  Counselor   │
  │ Coordination with other │   │ Coordination with │       └──────────────┘
  │  University Support     │   │  Academic Depts.  │       ┌──────────────────┐
  │ Services (Financial Aid,│   └──────────────────┘       │Recruiter/Counselor│
  │ Housing, Food Services, etc.)│                          └──────────────────┘
  └────────────────────────┘                               ┌──────────────────┐
                                                           │Basic Skills Specialist│
                                                           └──────────────────┘
                                 ┌──────────┐              ┌──────────────────┐
                                 │ Students │              │Residential Counselor│
                                 └──────────┘              └──────────────────┘
                                                           ┌────────┐
                                                           │ Tutors │
                                                           └────────┘
```

Budget/Cost-Effectiveness

(206.31(e)(1) and (2)(i) - 10 points)

COST-EFFECTIVENESS

This section of the proposal elucidates the project budget's adequacy and cost-effectiveness. In addition, it describes how the budget is adequate to support the project activities and how the costs are reasonable in relation to the objectives of the project.

The project proposes to serve 180 students on a low-cost basis due to the fact that numerous university resources are available and will be utilized by the current proposed CAMP program at NO COST to the program itself. According to the Department of Education's Migrant Education Program Office, the current average cost per student in all existing CAMP programs runs up to $6,784.00 per student. Our budgeted cost per student is $6,710.

The proposed budget is highly cost-effective in relationship to services provided because, of the total CAMP staff, only the Director, Associate Director, Secretary, Counselor, Basic/Skills Specialist, and Recruiter/Counselor are twelve (12) month appointments (see Employment Duration Chart in the Personnel Section of this proposal). In addition, upperclassmen and graduate students will be serving as tutors, counselors, and dorm staff in the project. By utilizing these students as tutors, lower cost wages can be paid and will be expended only on an hourly, as-needed basis. Although part-time employment is cost effective, it does NOT compromise service delivery or neglect the quality herein proposed. In addition, the university does not pay part-time staff

18

fringe benefits, thereby eliminating these extra costs. Efficient utilization of part-time employment seems to be an appropriate vehicle for maintaining high quality services in a cost-effective manner.

It should be noted that, in addition to the services directly provided to CAMP participants, students will continue to receive benefits of University and other specially funded programs. Moreover, the cost per participant ($6,710) reflected in the budget does not include university contributions of OFFICE SPACE, UTILITIES, EQUIPMENT, and other "direct cost" items that are considered "in kind." Free speech and hearing exams, eye exams, community donations, etc., keep the cost very reasonable. Self-instruction materials and standardized test materials previously purchased by other projects are currently available and would not have to be purchased for this project.

Costs Are Reasonable in Relation to the Objectives of the Project
(206.31(e)(2)(ii))

This program will provide the following types of services to assist CAMP participants in completing their first academic year of college successfully: recruitment services for enrolling project participants; instructional services in academic subject areas; special academic, career, and personal guidance, counseling, and testing services; residential program services; stipends and transportation; and services designed to expose participants to academic institutions and programs, cultural events, and other activities not usually available to the participants yet important to their intellectual, cultural, social, and personal development.

Interagency Consultation/Coordination
(206.31(f) - 10 points)

This section describes how the project will continue to coordinate with other agencies within the eight (8) state targeted area. In addition, this section addresses the coordination and consultation with agencies which serve migrant/seasonally employed farmworkers and their dependents.

Information That Shows Adequate Consultation
and Coordination With Other Agencies
(206.31(f)(1))

While responding to CAMP/HEP proposals and receiving funds since 1981, the Director of this program has continually involved institutional and migrant/seasonal state farmworker officials in requesting input from respective states with respect to the overall purpose of this Federally funded program. He has consulted and coordinated with appropriate agencies in planning, developing, implementing, and evaluating the initial project in 1982-83, as well as subsequent years. At present, about fifty (50) agencies are actively participating through referral, consultation, services, transportation, etc. Many officials have already sent letters of COMMITMENT AND ENDORSEMENT showing their support for the program (see Appendix A). Upon receiving notice of the award, the university will continue to consult other community agencies to elicit their cooperation and support to be used to implement this project.

The CAMP program will continue the development and expansion of interagency consultation and coordination for the purpose of augmenting and improving the quality of services to our CAMP participants. Innovative suggestions and recommendations will be implemented whenever possible. The project will actively contact existing linkages and establish new ones with appropriate agencies which provide consultation, coordination,

19

and other free services. Also, the project plans to release public service announcements to targeted state newspapers and radio stations, distribute program brochures and posters, and speak to other agency staff about the proposed services. Local institution and community resources will be used to motivate and provide skills to participants which are necessary for success in college. The university's commitment of $83,757 (see budget breakdown) as an "in-kind" contribution will provide the necessary office space, classrooms, recreational and cultural facilities necessary for the project's operation. Speech and hearing services will provide the necessary evaluations at NO COST to the project. Local businesses have donated supplies to the project and certain individuals have donated money and clothing (see Letters of Commitment and Support in Appendix A).

Information That Shows the Project Will Consult and Coordinate Adequately With Other Agencies in Implementing the Project
(206.31(f)(2))

The project plans to continue to inform the targeted state farmworker organizations and the educational communities of the goals and objectives of the Southeastern CAMP Project at the university and the selection criteria for acceptance into the CAMP program.

As program needs dictate, there has been a focus on developing and maintaining linkages with agencies that provide services to migrant and other seasonally employed farmworkers and their dependents (see Flowchart below). This interagency consultation and coordination has permitted the staff to plan, develop, and implement programs which can interface with PEEM to meet the educational needs of farmworker youth. Additional contact has been established in linkages with 303 Programs, Dept. of Agriculture Farmworker Organizations, and DOL. These linkages demonstrate the benefits that can accrue from extensive program interfacing and coordination.

Institutional and Community Support

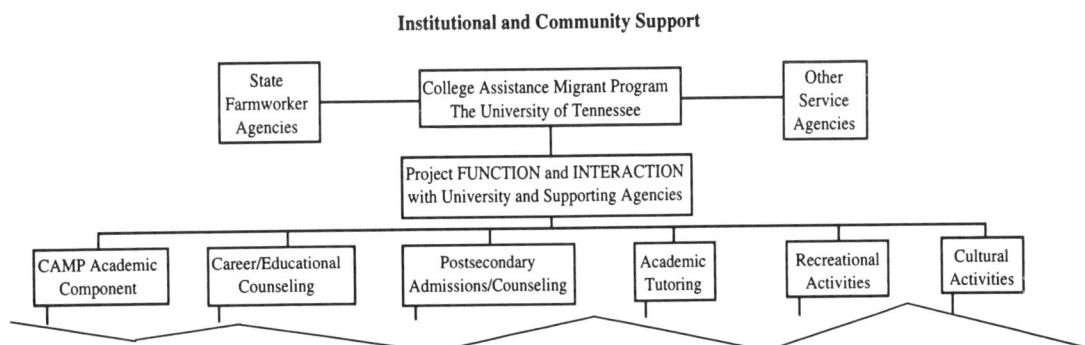

The staff will apprise all significant agencies and institutions in the targeted areas of the goals and objectives of the CAMP program. Regular contacts will be made with state farmworker professionals, school administrators, counselors, teachers, community agencies, parents, and students to provide updated information concerning the program goals and activities and to explain information concerning the program goals and activities and to explain changes in the program. The orientation of the targeted states will be more readily accomplished because the university is service oriented, well-known, and well-respected in the targeted states.

20

Moreover, upon the initiation of recruiting activities in the fall, the CAMP Recruiter/Counselor will work with project participants to establish a liaison relationship and publicize project goals, purposes, and activities. Other liaison relationships will be developed with postsecondary institutions in the vicinity for the provision of information to CAMP participants regarding various educational options.

In summary, the project has strong institutional and community support (see Flowchart below) which will enhance the opportunities available to the CAMP students at the University. In addition, the LETTERS OF COMMITMENT and ENDORSEMENT indicate that the project will have a close and cooperative working relationship with targeted states. And finally, the extensive interagency linkage developed during the operation of our HEP Program will greatly assist our staff in the initial stages of program publicity, participant identification, and student recruitment.

The following are samples of interagency consultation and cooperation currently in place:

Seven in orginal—two shown.

1. The Telamon corporation, which assists migrant and seasonal farmworkers in four (4) states within our targeted area, has been very supportive of our migrant program. Telamon involves itself with every facet of the program allowable to an outside agency including offering financial support/ incentives when possible. The agency has a solid network established within itself as well as with the community (and its agencies) it serves. Telamon provides for personal, as well as educational needs and tries to eliminate as many obstacles as possible for those clients choosing to continue their education. For example, Marguerite Brown, Regional Manager of the Aiken, South Carolina office, has referred several students and has provided continuous support for the program. Mrs. Brown enthusiastically proclaims her patronage of our program and is a strong source of encouragement to those clients qualifying along with providing placement assistance.
2. Genesco Migrant Center's Project Trainer, Mr. Bob Lynch, states that the program provides opportunities and alternatives to migrants who have few advantages available to them. Not only has Mr. Lynch referred candidates to the program, he has also provided additional sources of agency contacts throughout the service area and letters of encouragement and support to those students who were enrolled. The Genesco organization also offers the Mattera Educational Scholarship for migrants as an incentive for secondary and post-secondary education. In addition, the job development component has provided another avenue of service which assists HEP with placement. Mr. Lynch has also expressed his readiness to continue his working relationship with our migrant program.

Adequacy of Resources
(206.31(g) - 5 points)

The university has a wide variety of resources and support to the College Assistance Migrant Program. As a land-grant institution and major graduate and research center in Tennessee, the University has excellent staff and facilities to support the CAMP Program. As the major university in the state, UT has tremendous resources (laboratories, libraries, cultural enrichment, and recreational activities and facilities) available at no cost to the project. The CAMP Program will be able to use campus resources including media equipment and materials, learning centers, laboratories, recreational facilities, educational films and libraries, in addition to the University Center with its programs. These facilities are modern and exceptionally well-equipped. The

21

College of Education has a large and fully-equipped media center and support units such as the Bureau of Educational Research and Service (BERS) through which the CAMP Program would be administered as a restricted account.

The University also conducts other compensatory educational programs from which the project could seek professional in-service training, consultation, and to a certain degree, services, at NO COST to the project. The special services for disadvantaged students include the Upward Bound, the Educational Talent Search, the Educational Advancement, and the High School Equivalency (HEP) Programs.

Some of the resources and support activities that will be available to this program include:

(Four samples of 19 listed items appear as an example.)

1. An OFFICE OF FINANCE which provides complete fiscal services such as accounting, budgeting, purchasing, payrolls, etc. and other financial records necessary for fiscal compliance.
2. An OFFICE OF PERSONNEL which ensures equal employment opportunities for all staff and provides the personnel services necessary for hiring staff and processing grievance and due process hearings.
3. A MAINTENANCE DEPARTMENT which provides the office space and equipment and other necessary program space for activities, maintenance of buildings, grounds, and custodial service.
4. A fully-equipped MEDIA CENTER offering a wide variety of audio-visual equipment, student learning carrels and television studio facilities.

Additionally, the University's College of Education has been awarded a number of other human service programs because of its strategic location and large target population. Through continuous application for these human service awards, the University's commitment to assist the poor and educationally disadvantaged with their academic, social, cultural and personal development is well-demonstrated.

SUMMARY

In summary, extensive resources of the University more than adequately meet the needs of the participants in the proposed College Assistance Migrant Program. In addition to providing adequate classroom and office space, the proposed project has access to the University Center for students' social activities, ACT testing facilities, Career Planning and Placement Center, Media Center, Teacher Materials Center, Learning Resource Center and school libraries, and many university recreational and educational support facilities. The project also has access to dorm rooms and vans and buses for field trips at low-cost rates.

Recruitment
(206.31(h) - 5 points)

At the beginning of the program year, recruitment services will be performed by a Recruiter/Recruiter Counselor, along with other staff members, who will identify, inform, and recruit eligible participants who are in need of the academic and supporting services and financial assistance provided by the project. The linkages already developed between the University's migrant programs and the farmworker organizations in the Southeast will provide a high degree of accessibility to farmworker populations in the eight (8) state targeted

22

areas (see Recruitment Flowchart). The recruiters will contact these farmworker organizations and other community agencies in each target state to inform them of the program and seek referral of potentially eligible candidates. Besides telephone and face-to-face contacts made by the recruiter, public service announcements and previously developed brochures and posters will be placed in establishments visited by farmworkers to alert potentially eligible candidates of the program's existence. Special emphasis will be placed on the recruitment of women, social and ethnic minorities, and the handicapped.

Recruitment Flowchart

The University of Tennessee
College Assistance Migrant Program

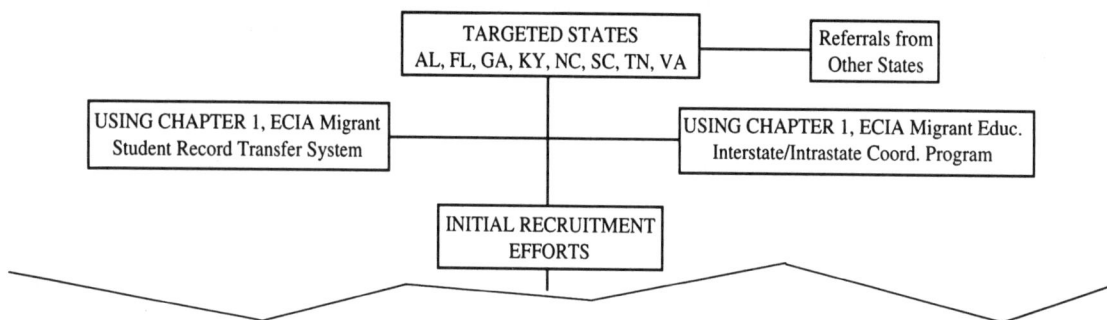

The recruiter will visit each target state and individually interview potential candidates to determine eligibility, discuss the program, and enroll participants. A pre-assessment, using the Test of Adult Basic Education (TABE) and the Wide Range Achievement Test (WRAT), will be performed on all applicants. The recruiter and other project staff who are participating in recruitment will explain the three basic components of the admission process to CAMP applicants. These components are: (1) the UT Application; (2) the ACT Test; and (3) the Financial Aid Form (FAF).

The Recruiter/Counselor will be employed for a twelve (12) month period. Initially, the recruiter's full-time responsibility will be recruitment. When all CAMP students have been recruited, the recruiter's responsibility will then shift to counseling and other on-campus student support duties.

The need for a Recruiter/Counselor was identified due to the large geographical area to be covered, namely eight (8) Southeastern states. The Recruiter/Counselor, along with the Counselor and the Associate Director, will be assigned specific geographical areas in which to recruit. It is anticipated that the recruiting staff will be on the road three (3) nights per week initially in order to perform these duties. The recruitment staff will be working toward assigned goals, and recruitment productivity will be monitored by the Associate Director. At the end of the program, a questionnaire will be sent to farmworker agencies and other community organizations to determine the effectiveness of the recruitment campaign. Throughout the operation of the CAMP Program, a system of linkages and coordination will continue to be established with government agencies, private institutions, schools, private citizens and businesses for the purpose of identifying the target population to be served by this project and to initiate the application and verification process of each potential candidate. At this time, the University's CAMP program plans to work with the following:

22

1.	State Farmworker Organizations	8.	Office of Voc. Rehab.
2.	HEP Programs	9.	Agric. Extensions
3.	State Dept. of Labor	10.	Schools/Churches
4.	Employment Security	11.	PEEM
5.	Dept. of Human Services	12.	Farmwork Unions
6.	State Migrant Educ. Offices	13.	Farm Owners
7.	State Dept. of Education	14.	Food Stamp Offices

Other possible contact locations such as rural gathering places, country stores, tobacco barns, produce markets, and feed distributors will also be explored and utilized as appropriate.

V. CERTIFICATIONS AND ASSURANCES

Required certifications are appended. The total Law was included.
For this *handbook*, only the names are provided.
•Certification Regarding Drug-Free Workplace Requirements
Grantees Other Than Individuals
•Certification Regarding Debarment, Suspension,
Ineligibility and Voluntary Exclusion
Lower Tier Covered Transactions
•Civil Rights Certificate

VI. APPENDIXES

APPENDIX A - Letters of Support
APPENDIX B - Résumés
APPENDIX C - Job Descriptions
APPENDIX D - Program Forms
APPENDIX E - Program Materials

23

8

Understanding How Grants Are Awarded

Introduction

An important aspect of proposal writing is understanding what happens to your document once it gets to the funding source. This chapter discusses common procedures used to evaluate your proposal by personnel of the agency to which it is sent. Each agency has its own procedure, so this chapter deals in general terms.

Funding agency staff assign a control number to the proposal and subject it to a preliminary review to ensure that it addresses the purpose of the program. Usually panels of readers thoroughly read, evaluate, and score the proposal. From the reading process, the proposals are often rank ordered, and the budget is reviewed. Funding agency personnel estimate the number of awards that the appropriated dollars will support and establish a *cutoff* point. Proposals scoring above the *cutoff* point are then *negotiated*. Usually unsuccessful applicants are not notified until all successful proposals have been negotiated. An award document is issued, at which time the grant award becomes official. The following provides additional details for each step.

Agency Review and Approval

Given the large number of applications that may be submitted in a competition, funding agency personnel endeavor to ensure that only those addressing the purposes of the program or statute are evaluated by the readers. Some competitions are very small. As few as 25 or 30 applications may be submitted, whereas other competitions may receive 1,500 or more applications.

Staff persons usually review the proposal abstract, table of contents, and perhaps the objectives. They look for indications that the proposal includes all necessary information such as original signatures, standard face page, required assurances, etc. They also ensure that the proposal addresses the criteria outlined in the application, that it is within the scope of the authorizing legislation, and that the expected outcomes are in accord with overall program goals. Proposals missing vital information are judged inappropriate and may be returned to the institution without further review.

Each agency or program may have its own specific criteria for evaluating proposal applications. For example, the Fund for the Improvement of Postsecondary Education (FIPSE) utilizes three outside readers, but there is no group discussion of the proposals among the three. The Office of Special Education and Rehabilitation Services (OSERS) uses three readers in addition to an evaluation by an ad hoc panel. The Office of Postsecondary Education (OPSE) submits proposals to three readers who then meet and discuss their evaluation to arrive at a group score. Other agencies may have still different review procedures.

In the abstract, you should clearly state the purpose of the proposal, such as *"The purpose of this proposal is to establish an international studies project for 30 students to study one academic year in the People's Republic of China."* Use bold face type, under-line, or in some other way highlight this important statement. As you begin various sections of the document, restate the purpose. For example, as you elaborate the objectives, preface the section with a statement such as, *"The following section contains the objectives of our international studies project that will support an academic year of study for 30 students in the People's Republic of China."*

Both the preliminary reviewers and review panel will be reading or will have read many similar proposals. After reading 12 to 14 proposals discussing the same general topic, a reader could confuse the contents of one proposal with others previously read. By re-stating your purpose several times throughout the document, you will reduce the possibility of error and confusion and keep the reviewers' attention focused on *your* application.

Panel Reading, Review, and Scoring

The most important phase of the proposal review process is the work of the reader panel. If the readers understand and like your proposal, they will score it high and it will go on to be considered by the department or agency. If your proposal doesn't make it past the readers, the department or agency will never see it. The review process may take from a few days to two or more weeks to complete. In an effort to make the selection process as fair as possible and to eliminate bias, the funding agency implements its specific review process described previously.

――― **Grant Tip** ―――
Restate the purpose of your proposal in a variety of different ways. Each panel of readers may review 15 to 20 proposals. Make yours stand out.

Try to learn how your proposal will be evaluated. This may help you in terms of how you present your material. If your reviewers will be persons highly specialized in your grant area, they may be more critical of your plan of operation, facilities, and how you will evaluate your efforts. You may want to seek the advice of experts to help you write these sections. If your reviewers come from broader, less specialized backgrounds, you may want to be less technical and emphasize the importance and need of the services you propose to provide and how those services will benefit the target population.

One researcher in the area of proposal development and writing suggests that there tends to be a *cumulative effect* among readers. This suggests that if the readers find excellence in the proposal in the first few areas, their perception of the remainder of the document will be positively influenced (Cavin, 1984). On the other hand, if the first areas of the proposal are weak or inadequate, the readers will tend to perceive the remainder of the document as being weak and inadequate.

Persons interested in serving as reviewers may submit a letter of application and their resume to the agency. After a review of these documents, readers are selected and invited to Washington, D.C. (or another designated site) to receive orientation for reviewing and scoring the applications. Readers are selected from all walks of life. They may not be educators and thus may be unfamiliar with educational programs funded by the U.S. Department of Education. They may not fully understand the application and funding process employed by the Department. They may represent the group(s) to be served by the proposed projects.

——**Grant Tip**——
The readers are your first audience. Write in terms they understand.

Sometimes employees of various other divisions within the Department serve as reviewers. For example, a Department employee who works in programs for the physically impaired may review proposals for vocational education programs. In such cases, the panels are generally composed of one federal reviewer and two nonfederal reviewers.

In selecting reviewers, care is taken to avoid persons who may have a conflict of interest. A conflict of interest exists if the reviewer reviews an application that involves (a) him/herself, (b) a spouse, (c) an organization for which the reviewer serves as an officer, director, trustee, partner, or employee, (d) a person or organization that employs the reviewer or from which the reviewer derives financial interest, and (e) an agency with which the reviewer has any personal ties (such as the university the reviewer attended). If reviewers think they have a conflict of interest, they must report it to the program staff immediately.

Those selected to review applications must agree to maintain confidentiality. Confidentiality means that (a) the reviewer may not discuss the application with others who are not members of the review team, and (b) the reviewer may not remove the application from the review location.

Because of the varied backgrounds of the reviewers, their orientation is of enormous importance. The Department of Education issued a document entitled *Reviewing Applications for Discretionary Grants and Cooperative Agreements: Orientation Trainer's Manual* (Horace Mann Learning Center, 1988). It describes in detail the orientation received by members of the review panels prior to reading and scoring the application. The process is designed to ensure that projects are worthwhile and that awards are fair and impartial.

Figure 8.1 outlines the funding and decision framework for discretionary funds and the review process that involves 15 distinct steps *(Reviewing Applications . . .)*. Understanding these steps will give you a better sense of how the review panels fit into the process. Steps one through seven are preparatory to the review process. Step eight is the actual review and scoring of the application. Steps 9 through 15 describe what happens after the review is completed.

Figure 8.1. Steps in the Funding and Decision Framework for Discretionary Funds

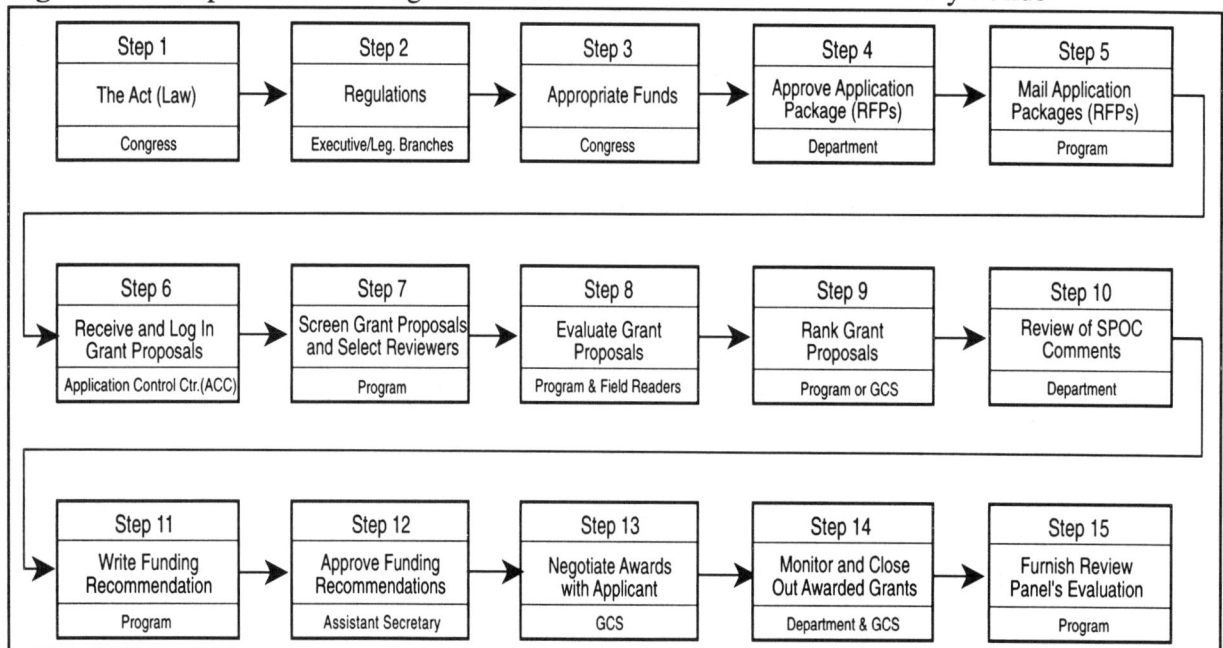

Step 1 • Congress passes an education *act (law)*. This becomes the enabling legislation to fund a specific program. It lists the authorized funding.

Step 2 • Department *establishes regulations* governing how the act's objectives are to be carried out.

Step 3 • After Congress *appropriates funds,* the Department conducts a process designed to award those funds.

Step 4 • Department establishes a schedule of awards and approves an *application package* (RFP) for each funding program.

Step 5 • Department *mails out application packages* (RFPs) as requested.

Step 6 • Department's Application Control Center (ACC) receives and *logs in applications.* These are date-stamped on receipt and assigned an application control number.

Step 7 • Program office personnel *screen applications* for eligibility and conformity to general administrative regulations, select reviewers, and assign applications to panel. Applications that do not conform to some basic administrative requirements do not enter the review process.

Step 8 • The review panel *reviews the application.* This review is the foundation for funding recommendations made at later stages in the cycle. Program officers verify accuracy and sufficiency of written evaluations.

Step 9 • *Applications are ranked* according to scores assigned by the review panel. Staff members at the control centers review, check, record, and enter raw scores or normalized scores in computer.

Step 10 • *Review SPOC comments.* Those applications requiring the Executive Order 12372 process will go through the SPOC and are reviewed as part of the funding and award process.

Step 11 • Department prepares a summary of *funding re-commendations* using the evaluations of the re-view panel, SPOC comments, and other factors such as equitable geographical distribution of awards and unnecessary duplication of effect and/ or services.

Step 12 • Department reviews and approves or disapproves the funding recommendations, and *a recommended slate is forwarded for approval.* Congress is noti-fied of results and receives a list of awards.

Step 13 • Funding levels are negotiated for approved appli-cations. The Grants and Contracts Services (GCS) *negotiates the final funding of each project.*

Step 14 • *Monitoring and closing out* of awarded grants. Typically, those applicants who were not selected are notified by letter.

Step 15 • Distribution of the *review panel's evaluation* to applicants, as requested.

Technical Review Form

During orientation, panel members receive instructions for reviewing and scoring the application according to the Technical Review Form the Department provides. The summary page of the *Technical Review Form* of the CAMP of the Office of Elementary and Secondary Education is presented in Figure 8.2. It contains most of the information that the application package guidelines include. There is a detailed page for each criterion and readers summerize the details on this summary page.

This emphasizes the importance of organizing an application in the same order and sequence suggested in the application packet. The panel of readers will find your document easier to read and score if the order and sequence are carefully followed. Chapter 6, "Writing a Proposal," deals with this in more detail.

After receiving the orientation, the reviewers are assigned to panels usually consisting of three members each. A team leader is responsible for coordinating team efforts. Generally the team will receive three to six or more proposals to read each day. Sometimes the teams read as a group, and sometimes members read separately and then convene to review and discuss each proposal.

Figure 8.2. Example of a Technical Review Form Cover Page

Application Technical Review Form

Special Educational Programs for Students Whose Families are Engaged in Migrant and Other Seasonal Farmwork-High School Equivalency Program (HEP) and College Assistance Migrant Program (CAMP)

FY 90 PR No. _____

Type of Application: [   ] High School Equivalency Program (HEP) (CFDA 84.141)
(Check one)   [   ] College Assistance Migrant Program (CAMP) (CFDA 84.149)

Name of Applicant: _____

Address of Applicant: _____

Name of Project Director: _____

Title of Application: _____

Instructions: This Application Technical Review Form contains eight criteria published in the *Federal Register* (December 30, 1980 and July 6, 1981) which must be used in reviewing the attached application. After reading the application and completing the identification information on this page of the Review Form, begin recording your assessment of the application. On the following pages, please write specific review comments in the space provided with regard to the strengths and weaknesses of the application as judged against the specified criterion. Circle the descriptor on the scale for each criterion which describes the adequacy of the application. Finally, for each criterion, assign a score consistent with the descriptor which denotes your rating. Complete pages 2 through 9 in that order and rate each criterion independently. The maximum score per application cannot exceed 100 points. After completing pages 2-9, return to this page and complete the bottom. Sign your full legal name and date your review.

		Individual Rating	Post-Panel Rating
1. Plan of Operation	(25)		
2. Objectives and Activities	(20)		
3. Evaluation Plan	(15)		
4. Quality of Key Personnel	(10)		
5. Budget and Cost-Effectiveness	(10)		
6. Interagency Consultation and Coordination	(10)		
7. Adequacy of Resources	(5)		
8. Recruitment	(5)		
Total	(100)		

Complete This Section After Pages 2 Through 9

Total points given application: _____
(Maximum is 100)

Summarized Strengths:

Summarized Weaknesses:

_____   _____
Reviewer's Signature   Date

——Grant Tip——

*Always request a
copy of your readers'
comments.*

As an example, assume that the individual readers receive the proposal from the team leader and retire to their hotel rooms or other designated areas to evaluate it. Using the *Technical Review Form* which contains the criteria for each section, the reviewers carefully study each section of the proposal according to the instructions provided in the orientation. The reviewers provide written comments on the strengths as well as on the weaknesses found in each section. The comments may eventually be made available to the author of the application for use in future proposal writing. *If you desire a panel's comments on your proposal, submit in writing a request to the agency or department that administers the program.*

The maximum number of points possible appears at the top of each section of the technical review form. The reviewer assigns a score within the range of possible scores for that section. After each reviewer has studied and scored each section of the proposal, the three reviewers reconvene as a panel to discuss the proposal and their scores. Through discussion with other panel members, concepts are often clarified. During this discussion, a reviewer may choose to adjust a score. The reviewer may find an important item that was overlooked or misunderstood. Generally during the discussion process, the reviewers arrive at an agreement of the quality of the application, and their scores do not differ greatly. (If there is great disparity in scores, another panel may read the proposal.)

The panel leader usually collects the completed review forms containing the written comments and scores and submits the forms to the Department supervisor. This completes the review process as performed by the panel of reviewers. The responsibilities of the reviewer can be summarized as follows:

1. Report any conflict of interest (which will remove a reader from the panel reviewing the proposal for which there is a conflict).

2. Provide a specific and well-documented critique of each application including constructive written comments.

3. Evaluate applications independently of personal feelings.

4. Participate in panel discussions.

5. Maintain confidentiality.

Rank Ordering of Reviewed Proposals

The review panel's forms are checked to ensure that each section was carefully reviewed, written comments describing the strengths and weaknesses were included, and that a score was assigned. The Department representative then proceeds to rank order the applications according to the total score assigned. Figure 8.3 provides an example of how the rankings may appear for a specific program. Sometimes the scores of the reviewers are averaged; sometimes they are adjusted by a formula that assigns a numerical value to theraw scores. At any rate, the Department organizes a slate of proposals recommended to be funded arranged in rank order.

Figure 8.3. Example of a Technical Review Summary

PR NUMBER/FILE KEY APPLICATION NAME		PANEL NUMBER SCORES			MEAN SCORE	FUNDS REQUESTED	FUNDS RECOMMENDED
842AH2663 X University	173365	98	21 99	93	96.67	368,983.	323,358.
842AH2113 Y Universtiy	163432	93	18 100	97	96.67	398,368.	356,322.
842AH0021 University Z	153342	97	25 94	96	95.67	402,930.	365,334.
842AH3225 X State University	165332	93	19 99	89	93.67	297,006.	292,338.
842AH3326 Y Central Washington	163325	96	22 93	89	92.67	433,226.	00.
842AH2263 X Institute of Human Resources	163323	89	21 91	93	91.00	532,335.	00.
842AH1221 W University	153223	88	18 89	92	89.68	493,335.	00.
842AH9531 XY University	151091	85	25 79	83	82.33	491,219.	00.
842AH8335 XYZ, Inc.	162322	79	15 83	86	80.28	168,000.	00.

Note: Partial listing of proposals considered under this competition (names changed for practical reasons).

Cutoff Point

After the proposals have been rank ordered by score, the Department uses the slated cutoff score that is usually established in the regulations. The Department personnel again review each proposal with particular attention to the proposed budget. Usually during the Departmental review of the budget, reductions and modifications are suggested. The Department then recalculates the anticipated total budget of each proposal and subtracts that amount from the total appropriated by Congress or assigned by the Department for the program. An operational cutoff is established at the point where the totals of the budgets of the highest ranked proposals equal the funds appropriated or assigned by the Department.

In competitions with many applications, several proposals may receive the same score. It is not uncommon for the cutoff to fall at a point where two or more proposals are tied with the same score. In such cases the Department often reviews the *Needs* or other comparable section of the tied proposals. The scores on that section are rank ordered, and the two scoring the most points on that particular section will be recommended for funding. Sometimes, the competitions have requirements for regional distribution of monies and/or projects. That may be another factor taken into consideration.

In recent years competition for federal grants has become extremely keen. The operational cutoff point may include scores only in the middle to high nineties. Frequently only a half point or less may separate a funded proposal from an unfunded proposal. This emphasizes the necessity for careful elaboration of each part of every section of the proposal.

─── **Grant Tip** ───
Write to the review panel, your first and most important audience.

The readers on the review panel are your first and most important audience. Often proposal writers direct their writing to agency or Department personnel, assuming that they are familiar with the program requirements, target population, acceptable activities, etc. Writers have a tendency to omit detail, clarification, and *obvious* information. Remember, the review panel scores your proposal, not the agency personnel. If the review panel does not score your proposal high enough, the agency and/or Department personnel will never see it. Therefore, write to the review panel, which is your first and most important audience.

Negotiations

After the slate of proposals to be funded has been completed and the budgets reviewed and revisions recommended by the Department program staff, a negotiator from the grants/contracts office will telephone the contact person designated in the application. The purpose of the first telephone call is generally to set a time and day to *negotiate* the budget. At times during this initial call, the negotiator will indicate the recommended *bottom line* figure for the budget. This gives you an idea of the amount of money available or set aside for your project.

Negotiation simply means that you (or another designated person) will, through a telephone conversation with a grants officer, negotiate the line items of the budget of your application. The total amount of your budget is seldom open to negotiation. After you have received the call to set a date and time to negotiate, prepare yourself. Re-read your document several times. Make sure you are completely familiar with each part of the proposal and how each particular part is supported through the budget. Review your budget carefully. Assuredly, the Department will negotiate your budget downward.

The program officer assigned to your project will carefully review your proposed program and the supporting budget and make suggested revisions and reductions. That officer will write down suggestions for budget revisions and forward them to the grants officer (negotiator) who will call you. The negotiator who works with you will rely on notes prepared by the program officer, who may not be familiar with all of the details of your project. Be prepared to defend your budget in order to be able to operate a successful and efficient project. To prepare, you should ask yourself, and then answer, these critical questions.

──**Grant Tip**──
A program officer will discuss the program; a grants and contracts officer will discuss monies.

1. Can I reduce my proposed budget without changing other parts of the proposal? (Probably not, if the proposal was well done in the first place!) If not, there will be choices.

2. Can I reduce personnel and still carry out each objective? If I eliminate a position, will I have to eliminate one or more objectives? Can I still operate the project within the guidelines by eliminating the position and corresponding objectives? Can I reduce a position from full time to part time and still maintain the objectives?

3. If I reduce personnel, should I reduce the number of participants to be served or the services provided for the participants?

4. Can I get by with fewer supplies and materials? Could my department provide some of the supplies and materials or rent-free space to help reduce the budget?

5. Can I reduce or consolidate travel? Are all of the training conferences and other proposed travel absolutely necessary?

6. Is all equipment absolutely necessary? Can I get by with one less typewriter or computer and still perform at an acceptable level? Can I lease or rent rather than buy?

7. Can I modify my evaluation plan and reduce costs, perhaps by using a local evaluator rather than a person from out of state? Could the staff perform some of the evaluation functions, such as collecting and compiling data needed by the evaluator?

8. Will my institution allow me to use all or part of the indirect cost money derived from the grant in the form of supplies, travel, or equipment?

——— Grant Tip ———

The negotiator probably is not familiar with your application. Do not be afraid to defend your budget.

——— Grant Tip ———

If the negotiator requires a budget (cost) reduction, you will need to adjust either or both time and performance to make your proposal work.

By answering these types of questions in advance, you will be better prepared to conduct negotiations. The process of negotiating a new budget may take an hour or more by telephone. Bear in mind as you negotiate that the negotiator from the Department probably is not familiar with your application. The negotiator will be relying on notes provided by your newly assigned program officer. *Do not be afraid to defend your budget.* On one hand, answer the negotiator's questions courteously; explain and clarify points carefully as needed. On the other hand, be prepared to reduce your budget in certain areas. Travel, equipment (especially computers), personnel, and evaluation are often questioned by negotiators. Therefore, either be prepared to reduce your budget in these areas or be prepared to provide a cogent defense.

A well-developed proposal is a tight relationship among *Time, Cost,* and *Performance.* If the negotiator requires a budget (cost) reduction, you will need to adjust either or both of the other variables: *Time* and *Performance.* After you and the negotiator have arrived at a final figure, you will have time to develop a revised *scope of work* and budget estimate. When you send this to the Department, send copies to each person who received the original proposal.

In developing a budget there are several ways to hedge against severe reductions at the time of negotiations. One is to include a *throwaway item* that would enhance your project but is not critical to operating a good, effective project. As an example, one institution submitted an application to fund a project aimed at assisting high school dropouts obtain a GED. The application guidelines said nothing about including an English as a Second Language (ESL) component as part of the project. An unusually large number of Hispanics who were very much in need of ESL resided in the institution's target area. The proposal included a modest but adequate ESL component as one project objective. During negotiations, the ESL component was eliminated. It reduced the budget by a significant amount but did not impair overall project effectiveness. Had the negotiator decided to leave the ESL component intact, it would have enhanced the project's outcomes and provided a needed service to the target population. The writer was able to reduce the budget significantly by *throwing away* the ESL component without seriously jeopardizing the integrity of the project. During the next competition, the writer again included the *throwaway* ESL component, but it was not eliminated by the negotiator, resulting in a major project improvement.

Use caution if you choose to include a *throwaway* item. Do not include items that, if funded, will be impossible to implement or will be so time-consuming and cumbersome as to detract from the effectiveness of your project. *Throwaway* items must be sound, reasonable items or components that clearly are acceptable for inclusion. They should be *self-contained* and have an impact on the budget.

You might include a target area a little larger than what you really expect to serve, both in physical area and also in the number of students or clients to be served. As an example, in proposing to assist high school students in better preparing for college, a logical service area would include schools within 25 miles of the institution. However, by extending the proposed service area to approximately 35 miles, many more schools could receive needed services. The enlarged service area would require more funds for personnel, travel, numbers of participant books and supplies, etc. Although with the increased funds the project could serve the larger area, the project still could provide efficient service in the reduced area for reduced costs.

Sometimes during negotiations, the negotiator insists upon eliminating a line item that you believe is absolutely essential to your project. In such cases be prepared to defend your need for the line item, even if you cannot save the total amount requested. For example, you may submit a budget that includes $1,000 for duplicating services, handouts, classroom materials, exams, etc. Because of severe budget cuts, the negotiator wants to cut the item and have you convince your institution to supply duplicating services. Rather than lose the line

——— **Grant Tip** ———
Estimate on the high but actual cost side. Use tourist air fares to build a budget but hope that you might be able to use super-savers.

completely, negotiate a reduced amount. The purpose is not so much to preserve the amount as it is to preserve the line.

If you preserve the line, at a later date you might submit a budget revision and transfer additional funds into the line. However, if you lose the line completely, it is difficult to receive approval to create a line item through a budget revision. For example, a project director requested funds to continue a newsletter that had been approved in the previous year's budget. Because of a smaller appropriations for the Department, his project officer recommended eliminating the newsletter. Having recognized the importance and the value of the newsletter, the project director was successful in retaining the line item but accepted a reduced amount for it. During the first months of operation, he had savings in other areas and through a budget revision transferred sufficient money into the newsletter line to continue its publication.

After negotiating the budget determine what effects these reductions will have on the objectives and the way you planned to operate the project. Often project directors accept a budget without realizing that severe reductions may render certain objectives impossible to achieve. Such a determination is critical if your project receives points for prior performance (see Chapter 6). Leaving an objective in your document for which the budget has been severely reduced or eliminated may have a negative effect on the number of points you receive in a "prior performance" review later. Before you finalize your negotiations, decide where you will have to modify your objectives. You may need to eliminate an objective or two, or you may need to reduce the number of participants you originally planned to serve. You may decide to keep all of your objectives but to reduce the services each participant will receive. For example, you may have originally proposed to visit each participant a minimum of once each month and to provide each participant with one-on-one weekly tutoring sessions. After negotiation, you might reduce that objective to visit each participant once each quarter and to provide weekly tutoring sessions for groups of six participants rather than following the originally proposed one-on-one format.

You do not have to complete the negotiation process during the first telephone call. If you are in doubt about certain items, tell the negotiator that you must have more time to make the decision or that you must consult with your director, chairman, dean, or other superior. When you have had sufficient time, call the negotiator and complete your negotiations. Chances are good that you will be able to modify your proposal to the point that you can accept the recommended budget. Or perhaps the negotiator will be in a different frame of mind during the second conversation. You are not required to accept passively every budget reduction recommended to you. You must deal with that revised and/or reduced budget for a complete year. In all likelihood you will not be able to increase the recommended amount. Assure that reductions are in areas that you can deal with and still have a project that can produce acceptable results. Remember, the decisions you make during that brief time of negotiations are the decisions you will have to live with for at least a year!

After budget negotiations, you will receive instructions to submit a revised budget reflecting the negotiated changes. Rework your budget while your telephone negotiation conversations are still fresh in your mind. As you rework the budget, also go back through your application and revise and adjust objectives and other items that were affected as a result of negotiations. You will be held responsible for the completion of objectives in their original form unless you provide revisions. You may need to submit a new face page (Form 424) or other required form that bears the signature of an administrative financial officer for your institution. You may want to do a *revised scope of work* after negotiations. This two- to five-page document brings negotiated budget and revised objectives and activities into line.

———**Grant Tip**———
Decisions you make during negotiations are decisions you will have to live with for a year!

The Grant Award Notification

A short time after you have submitted your revised budget, you will receive an official *Grant Award Notification*. A sample Grant Award Notification is reproduced in Figure 8.4. This is your official notification that your application has been accepted and funded. Each item on this document is important.

Block 1 indicates the official name of the award recipient as recorded in the records and files of the Department.

Block 2 indicates the official name of the project. Each time you correspond with Department personnel, be sure to indicate the official name as indicated on this document.

Block 3 contains the names and telephone numbers of persons important to your grant award. These are the people most directly involved in your grant and who will make important decisions as to directions you will take.

Block 4 contains the *PR/Award Number*. This is the control number assigned to your grant. Include it on all correspondence with the Department.

Figure 8.4. Example of a Grant Award Notification

	U.S. DEPARTMENT OF EDUCATION **WASHINGTON, D.C. 20202** **GRANT AWARD NOTIFICATION**	GRANTS AND CONTRACTS SERVICE

1	RECIPIENT NAME UNIVERSITY OF TENNESSEE/KNOXVILLE COLLEGE OF EDUCATION – TAE DEPT. 404 ANDY HOLT TOWER KNOXVILLE, TN 37996	**4**	AWARD INFORMATION PR/AWARD NUMBER P066A10015–92 ACTION NUMBER 02 ACTION TYPE CONTINUATION AWARD TYPE DISCRETIONARY
2	PROJECT TITLE Educational Opportunity Centers	**5**	AWARD PERIODS BUDGET PERIOD 10/01/92 – 09/30/93 PROJECT PERIOD 10/01/91 – 09/30/94

3	PROJECT STAFF
	
	RECIPIENT PROJECT DIRECTOR
	
	  BREWER, ERNEST 615–974–4466
	
	EDUCATION PROGRAM STAFF
	
	  CLINTON BLACK 202–708–8272
	
	EDUCATION GRANTS STAFF
	
	  BARBARA SAUNDERS 202–708–4905
		6	AUTHORIZED FUNDING
			
			  THIS ACTION 263,792
			
			  BUDGET PERIOD 263,792
			  PROJECT PERIOD 515,792
			
			  RECIPIENT COST SHARE 0%

		7	ADMINISTRATIVE INFORMATION
			
			  PAYMENT METHOD ED PMS
			  ENTITY NUMBER 1–626001636–A1
			  REGULATIONS EDGAR, AS APPLICABLE
			                        34 CFR 644
			
			  ATTACHMENTS ABSZJ

8	LEGISLATIVE & FISCAL DATA AUTHORITY: HIGHER EDUCATION ACT OF 1965 P.L. 99–498 AS AMENDED PROGRAM TITLE: EDUCATIONAL OPPORTUNITY CENTERS CFDA 84.066A

APPROPRIATION	FY	CAN	OBJECT CLASS	AMOUNT
91 20201	92	E003033	4115	263,792

9	TERMS AND CONDITIONS OF AWARD
	
	THE FOLLOWING ITEMS ARE INCORPORATED IN THE GRANT AGREEMENT:
	
	  1) THE RECIPIENT'S APPLICATION (BLOCK 2),
	  2) THE APPLICABLE EDUCATION DEPARTMENT REGULATIONS (BLOCK 7).
	
	THIS AWARD SUPPORTS ONLY THE BUDGET PERIOD SHOWN IN BLOCK 5. THE DEPARTMENT OF EDUCATION WILL CONSIDER
	CONTINUED FUNDING OF THE APPLICATION IF 1) FUNDS ARE AVAILABLE, 2) THE DEPARTMENT DETERMINES THAT
	CONTINUING THE PROJECT WOULD BE IN THE BEST INTEREST OF THE GOVERNMENT, 3) THE RECIPIENT SHOWS
	SATISFACTORY PROGRESS TOWARD THE GOALS OF THE PROJECT AND SUBMITS A CONTINUATION APPLICATION.
	
	OTHER INFORMATION AFFECTING THIS ACTION IS PROVIDED IN THE ATTACHMENTS SHOWN IN BLOCK 7.
	
	                                                                                       2 1992
	
	Ver. 2 GRANTS OFFICER DATE

ED - GCS 007 (11/88)

Block 5 indicates the dates for which your project is funded and also approved. This example is the second year of a three-year project. The *budget period* indicates the one-year dates of funding for this particular grant. The *project period* indicates that the proposal was approved for a three-year period. The funding agency may approve a third year of funding on a noncompetitive basis under the conditions specified in *Block 9.*

Block 6 tells the funding level for this funding period. The line entitled Project Period indicates the total amount received for this award up to and including the current year.

Block 7 provides the administrative information. This information will assist the recipient in completing the approved activities and managing the project in accordance with U.S. Department of Education procedures and regulations.

Block 8 gives the name of the authorizing legislation for this grant and the *CFDA* title of the program through which funding is provided.

Block 9 provides the terms and conditions of this grant award. Note some of the terms and conditions in Figure 8.4.

Study the Grant Award Notification document carefully. The reverse side usually contains an item-by-item explanation. If you have questions or you think a mistake has been made, contact your Education Program Staff Officer and/or Education Grants Staff Officer immediately. Their names and phones numbers are provided in *Block 3* of the Grant Award Notification document.

Unsuccessful Applications

Many more proposals are submitted than funded. As a result, many good proposals are not successful in receiving funds. Usually, after all successful applications have been negotiated, the Department notifies the unsuccessful applicants. This may be accomplished by returning the unsuccessful proposals to the submitting institution and notifying the institution by letter that its proposal was not recommended for funding.

If your application was unsuccessful, there are several things presented in Figure 8.5 that you should do. Immediately request in writing that the reviewers' rating sheets and comments be sent to you. In the same letter request that the Department indicate the *cutoff* score and your score as it was calculated by the Department. When you

————**Grant Tip**————

If your application was unsuccessful, request in writing that the reviewers' rating sheets and comments be sent to you. Review and incorporate the pertinent items into your new application.

receive the rating sheets and comments, review them to ensure that an error was not made in calculating your score. Review the comments to determine if they relate to your proposal. Very seldom will a funding agency entertain an *appeal* or a *review* of the scores and comments of the panel that rated your application proposal. If you should find a grave error, such as obvious bias or comments totally unrelated to your document, you may wish to contact the Department and request a review. Experience, however, indicates that such requests seldom result in reversals of Department decisions.

Figure 8.5. Steps to Take With Unsuccessful Applications

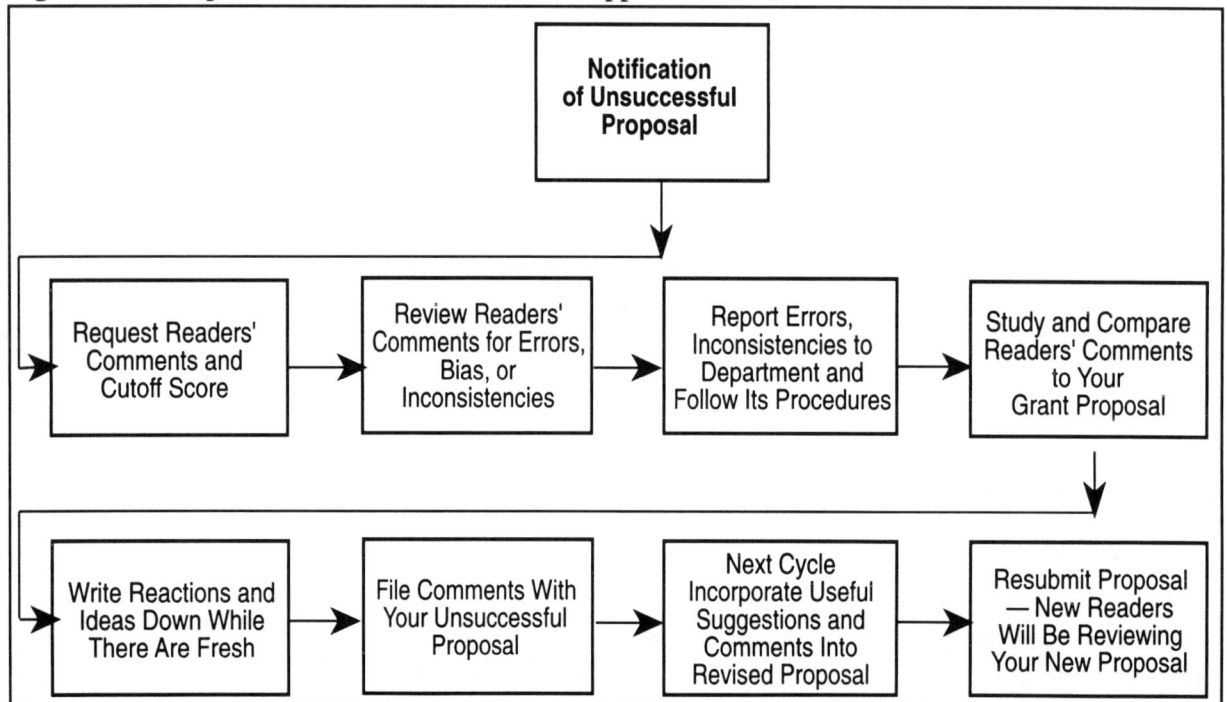

Keep the reviewers' rating sheets and comments in a file. As you prepare your document to submit during the next funding cycle, review the comments and incorporate the pertinent items into your new application. Remember, however, that the next time you submit your application, a different review panel will score it. Therefore, even though you respond to every comment and detail outlined by the first review panel, there is no guarantee that your document will now meet the expectations of the next panel that reviews it.

To help you improve your application the next time, write to the Department and request a copy of the two top-ranked proposals from the previous competition. Once funded, the proposals become part of the public domain, and you have every right to request and review them. These may serve as good models. You may need to pay for duplication of the documents. Remember, top-ranked proposals are only models: Your set of circumstances, needs, and target area will be different. Even though you may glean some good ideas, be sure you address your specific needs, circumstances, and target population.

—— **Grant Tip** ——

To help you improve your application the next time, request a copy of the two top-ranked proposals from the previous competition.

9

The Players and Their Roles in the Process

The Process Starts Long Before You Begin to Write

Before you get your hard-earned grant money, quite a few different groups and people will have been involved. This chapter defines some of those who are involved and sketches out the roles that each is likely to play in your life as a proposal writer. As described in Chapter 1, a proposal is typically an instrument that you use to develop a project that will carry forth the purposes and objectives of a particular program, often a federal program.

A program generally comes into existence in response to a need recognized and championed by some group, often an advocate or influence group that brings the need to public attention. At some point, the group generates enough interest in the need that the need is perceived as a *problem.*[1] Someone in a position of influence may now recognize the political benefits to be gained in responding to the problem. Thus the first players in the (federal or state) grants process are the persons or groups who focus a need into a problem and then promote the problem to prominent, public attention. This social definition of the problem may be quite general and not well-focused.

Political Definition of Need or Problem

The next step is formal political definition of the problem, generally as expressed by a legislative body. The legislature may hold hearings to sample opinion and collect information before developing a bill (legislation) to support attempts to remedy the expressed need. In this way the legislative branch is the first *formal* actor. The

---

[1]Paul Warren (1980) expresses the first levels of "players" in the grants process as those who bring about a social definition, a political and legislative definition, and an agency or administrative definition. We have borrowed his terms here as they seem eminently expressive and sensible. See especially Chapters 1 and 3. Warren's other "definitions" of the problem are the institutional definition (the proposal document) and the operational definition (the way the project actually operates).

---

legislative branch defines the need/problem in a political sense and provides legislation for the program to come into existence. A bill, successfully passed by a legislature and signed by the executive branch, becomes an act, or a Public Law. In federal parlance, public laws are numbered by designating the Congress that passed them and the chronology of the passage. Thus, P.L. 89-10 (the original Elementary and Secondary Education Act, or ESEA) was the tenth act passed by the 89th Congress.

The Key Committees

The federal legislative process works through a committee structure. In both the Senate and the House of Representatives, a major committee works with education and education-related problems, needs, issues, and concerns. In the Senate the major standing committee is the Senate Committee on Labor and Human Relations; the primary subcommittee to work with education is the Subcommittee on Education, Arts and Humanities. In the House of Representatives, the major committee is the House Committee on Education and Labor. Several important subcommittees work on education issues. Figure 9.1 shows the standing committees for education in the Senate and House of Representatives and one example of a subcommittee for each committee. Appropriations committees in both the House and the Senate make important decisions about how much federal support the various programs will receive each year.

---Grant Tip---
The House Postsecondary Education Subcommittee deals with reauthorizing the Higher Education Act (HEA).

The Regulation Process: Agency Definition

After the bill becomes law, representatives of the executive branch take over. Personnel of the agency that will eventually administer the law now develop *regulations.* These regulations go through several steps before they become final. Although it is not our intent to explain in detail the rule-making process in this *handbook*, a brief summary is necessary because during the rule-making process, a prospective proposal writer does have some opportunity to influence the outcome of the rule making. Agency personnel first publish in the *Federal Register* a notice of an Intent to Develop Regulations (see Chapter 3 for details of the *Federal Register*). This notice typically says that the agency is proceeding to develop regulations to govern the implementing of a particular piece of legislation. The notice invites interested people to submit ideas that seem appropriate for imple-

Figure 9.1. Key Congressional Committees That Deal With Education Issues

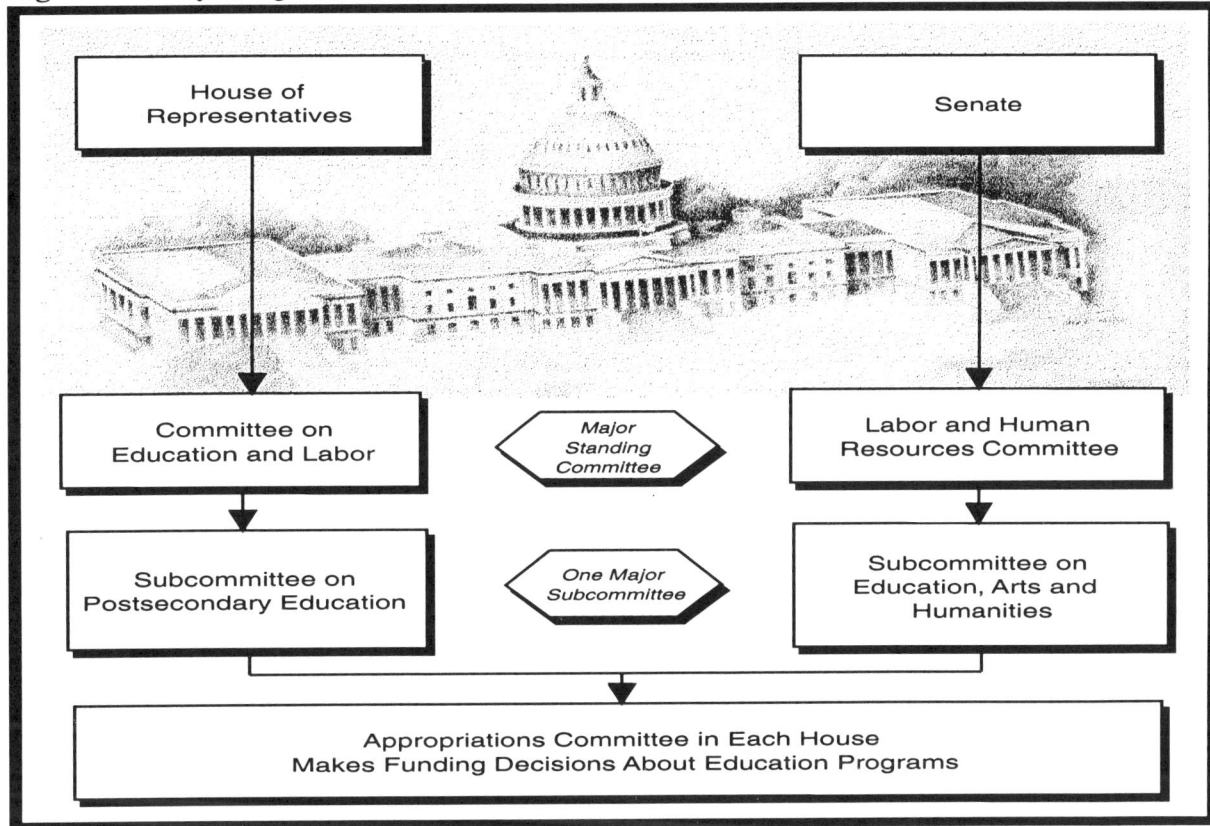

menting the intent of the legislation. The notice will include the name, address, and phone contact of the government agency employee in charge of the rule-making process.

At some later date, usually several months in the future, federal agency personnel will publish in the *Federal Register* a notice of *proposed rules and regulations.* These constitute the agency personnel's initial attempt to translate the intent of the legislation into an operational framework. Accompanying the proposed regulations is information about how an individual or a group can respond to those proposed rules and regulations. At this time individuals, or individuals representing groups or agencies, have an opportunity to comment on the rules and suggest changes. If the regulations are important to many groups, the agency may hold hearings on the proposed regulations at various central points throughout the nation. There is a cutoff date for the comments and suggestions. After that date agency personnel will review the comments and, based upon the intent of the legislation, may make some changes in the rules and regulations or may specify why no changes were made. The agency will publish in the *Federal Register* what are now designated as *Final Regulations*. If the Congress does not take some action to stop the regulations from becoming final, the regulations as published in the *Federal Register* as Final Regulations will become final after 45 days. In reality, the process usually takes much longer. The legislative and administrative branches also have additional prominent roles as major actors in the process at later stages.

Using the Regulation Process

Why is understanding this process important? If you or your organization wish to have some influence on the way a program will be run, you have several opportunities to make your wishes known during the rule-making process. You may write comments to the agency or even appear in person at hearings. (If you appear in person, remember also to provide a written statement for the record.) You may review the comments of others during this comment period. You may encourage your elected officials to comment, or you may work through a professional association to make your points known about the regulations in process.

The proposed rules constitute an agency's best estimate of how agency personnel believe the law should be implemented. The compromise between the proposed rules and final rules can be instructive and may help you develop a stronger grant application. For example, if the proposed rules suggest that stipends for personnel should not be allowed, and if the final rules suggest that stipends can be allowed, you might develop a proposal that has some matching funds for stipends. This would show an intent to meet the agency's best estimate of the way the law should be implemented while still taking advantage of the provision to allow stipends for participants.

Once published in the *Federal Register*, the final regulations have essentially the force of law. They describe the way the agency will implement and administer programs authorized under the legislation. The final regulations become the agency's definition of the need/problem brought to the attention of the legislative branch. Except for legislative oversight and periodic reports from the agency to the legislature, once the rules and regulations have become final, the agency, which is part of the executive branch, will have responsibility for implementing the programs under the legislation. This is

——**Grant Tip**——
Registered lobbyists on Capitol Hill: 36,599; per member of Congress: 68. Average years served in House in 1991: 12.4 years; in Senate in 1991: 11.1 years.

"the bureaucracy." Figure 9-2 shows the general picture of how a social need or problem eventually becomes the program to which you submit a proposal.

Figure 9.2. Process of a Social Need/Problem to a Competitive Grant

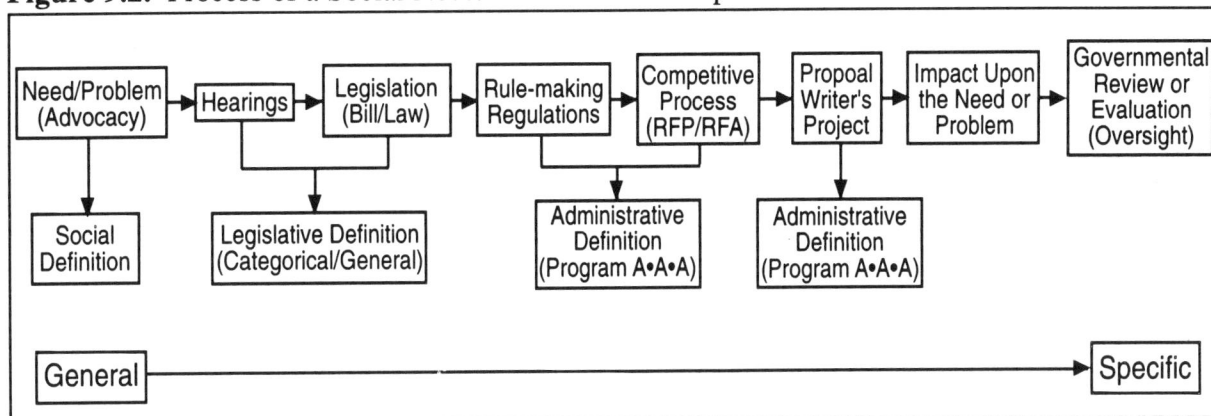

The Federal Budget Process

The federal budget process consists of the following three main phases that you should be aware of as you plan, write, and administer grants: (1) executive formulation and transmittal; (2) congressional action; and (3) budget execution and control. These phases are interrelated with each other.

Executive Formulation—The U.S. federal budget sets forth the President's financial plan and indicates his priorities for the federal government. The primary focus of the budget is on the budget year—the next fiscal year for which Congress needs to make appropriations. The President transmits his budget to Congress early in each calendar year, typically nine months before the next fiscal year begins. The process of formulating the budget is at least 18 months before the fiscal year begins.

Congressional Action—Congressional review of the budget begins shortly after it receives the President's budget proposals. Congress approves, modifies, or disapproves them. It can change funding levels, eliminate programs, or add programs not requested by the President. Congress does not enact a budget as such. It enacts appropriations bills and other legislation. Prior to making appropriations, Congress usually enacts legislation that authorizes an agency to carry out a particular program and, in some cases, includes limits on the amount that can be appropriated for the program. Some programs require annual authorizing legislation.

Budget Execution and Control—As approved or modified through the appropriation process, the President's budget becomes the basis for the financial plan for the operations of each agency during the fiscal year. Under the law, most budget authority and other budgetary resources are made available to the agencies of the executive branch through an apportionment system. The Director of OMB distributes appropriations and other budgetary resources to each agency by time periods and by activities (*The Budget Process,* 1990).

U.S. Department of Education Key Personnel

The U.S. Department of Education's organizational structure consists of some key positions and offices with which you, as an individual interested in responding to a grant, should be familiar. Figure 9.3 is an organizational chart of the U.S. Department of Education, and it is followed by a brief statement of the key positions within that structure (*United States Government Manual,* 1993).

U.S. Secretary of Education—The U.S. Secretary of Education advises the President on education plans, policies, and programs of the federal government. Another major function of the Secretary is directing the Department staff in carrying out the approved programs and activities of the Department and promoting the public understanding of the Department's goals, programs, and objectives.

Under Secretary—The Under Secretary serves as Acting U.S. Department of Education Secretary in the absence of the Secretary and performs on behalf of the Secretary such functions and duties as the Secretary may designate and coordinates federal-state relations.

Deputy Under Secretary for Intergovernmental and Interagency Affairs—This office is responsible for providing overall leadership in coordinating regional and field activities as well as establishing and directing intergovernmental and interagency services for the Department. The office is also responsible for hearings and appeals related to Departmental programs.

Figure 9.3. Organizational Chart of the U.S. Department of Education

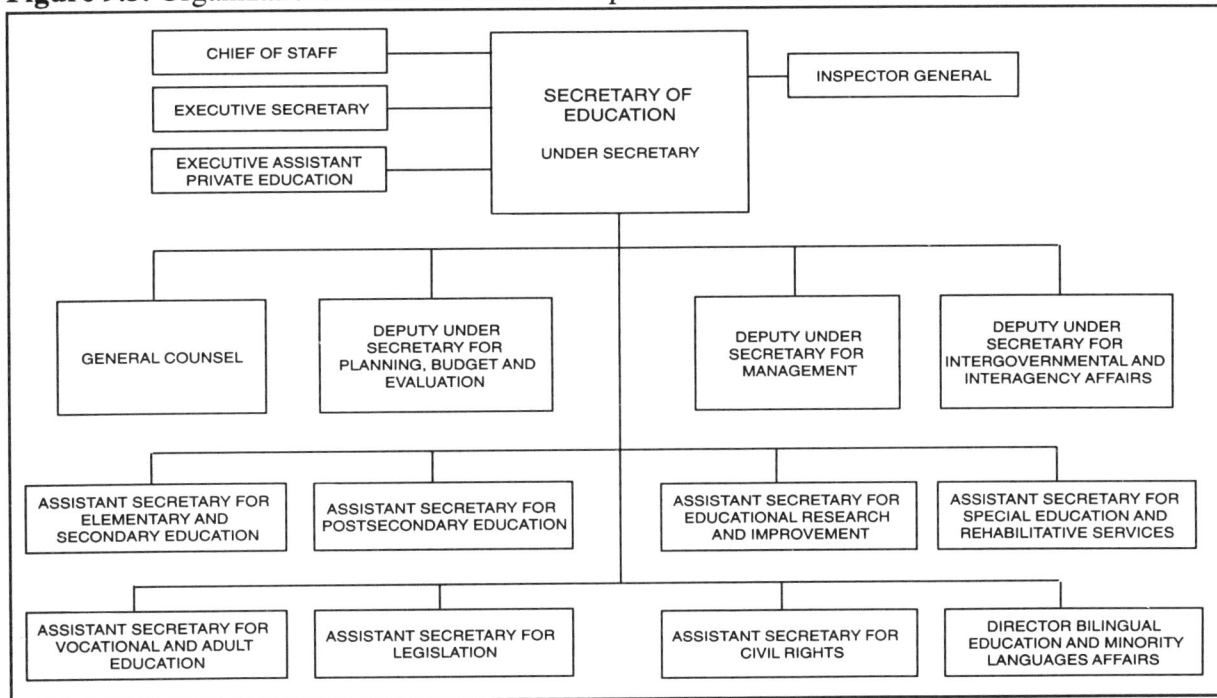

Deputy Under Secretary for Managment—The Management Office provides advice and guidance to the U.S. Secretary of Education on administrative and financial management and provides for the direction and coordination of these activities throughout the Department on a day-to-day basis. These activities include financial management, personnel, training, grants and procurement management, and other supportive services.

Deputy Under Secretary for Planning, Budget, and Evaluation—This office coordinates the Department's activities in the preparation of the Departmental budget, program analysis, and planning activities, and ensures that Department policy and program planning appropriately reflect the results of these activities.

Inspector General—The Inspector General is responsible for conducting and supervising audits and investigations relating to programs and operations of the Department. The office provides leadership, coordination, and policy recommendations to promote economy, efficiency, and effectiveness and to prevent and detect fraud and abuse in the administration of the Department's programs and operations. The Inspector General is also responsible for keeping the Secretary and Congress fully and currently informed about problems and deficiencies relating to the administration of such programs and operations in the Department.

General Counsel—The General Counsel provides legal advice to the U.S. Department of Education Secretary and to the various operations within the Department.

Assistant Secretary for Legislation—The Assistant Secretary serves as the principal adviser to the U.S. Secretary of Education on matters concerning the Department's legislative program and congressional relations.

Assistant Secretary for Civil Rights—The Assistant Secretary is responsible for the administration and enforcement of civil rights laws related to education and the handicapped. In addition, this office monitors compliance in programs and activities receiving federal financial assistance.

Assistant Secretary for Elementary and Secondary Education—This office formulates policy for, directs, and coordinates the activities related to preschool, elementary, and secondary education in the Department. Included are programs of grants to SEAs and LEAs, programs of financial and technical assistance to school districts to meet special needs incident to the elimination of discrimination, and grants for the education of neglected and delinquent students.

Assistant Secretary for Educational Research and Improvement—The OERI administers functions of the Department concerning research, statistics, development, demonstration, dissemination, and assessments. In addition, this office oversees a wide variety of discretionary grant programs to maximize individual program impact on school improvement.

Assistant Secretary for Vocational and Adult Education—The Assistant Secretary of this office is responsible for grants, contracts, and technical assistance for vocational and technical education, education professions development, community schools, and comprehensive employment and training.

Assistant Secretary for Special Education and Rehabilitative Services—This office administers special education programs and services expressly designed to meet the needs and develop the full potential of handicapped children. In addition, this office is responsible for comprehensive rehabilitation service programs specifically designed to reduce human dependency and to fully utilize the productive capabilities of all handicapped persons. Programs under this office include support for training of teachers and other professional personnel, grants for research, and financial aid to help states initiate, expand, and improve their resources.

Assistant Secretary for Postsecondary Education—The Assistant Secretary of this office formulates policy, directs, and coordinates programs for assistance to postsecondary educational institutions and students pursuing a postsecondary education. Programs include assistance for the improvement and expansion of educational resources, grants to improve instruction, and construction assistance for academic facilities. This office oversees the various financial aid programs (Pell Grants, GSLs, etc.).

Director of the Office of Bilingual Education and Minority Languages Affairs—The Director of this office assures access to equal educational opportunity and improves the quality of programs for limited English proficiency and minority languages populations by providing support for programs, activities, and management initiatives meeting the special educational needs of those populations.

Regional Offices—Ten Regional Offices serve as points for the dissemination of information and provide technical assistance to SEAs, LEAs, and other institutions and individuals interested in federal education activities. These Regional Offices are located in Atlanta, Boston, Chicago, Dallas, Denver, Kansas City, New York, Philadelphia, San Francisco, and Seattle.

Program Officers

The agency employs persons to work with the program to assure that its goals and purposes are met and that the program operates according to the regulations. These are *program officers.* They work within the agency, disseminate information about the program, answer questions about the program, and administer the program for the agency. In their role as program administrators, they may well be

——**Grant Tip**——
Program officers hold the grant competition and may also serve on review panels. After the grant competition, they oversee and administer successful projects for the agency.

responsible later for working with the project which the successful proposal writer has developed.

Before proposals are funded, program officers have numerous responsibilities. One responsibility is to hold the grant competition. In this role the program officers prepare application packets, announce the competition, mail out application packets, and check proposals when they come to the federal government. Program officers may also serve on review panels. In this role, the program officer will generally assure that the grant competition is held according to appropriate rules and regulations, that the proposal review process is fair, and that all persons receive the appropriate communications. Program officers may also hold seminars or briefing sessions for persons planning to develop proposals for the program.

After the grant competition successful projects are assigned to program officers who will oversee and administer that project for the agency. The program officer becomes the contact person for the principal investigator or director of the successful project. The program officer generally works with the project for its entire duration and usually gets to know the project and project personnel quite well. The program officer answers questions and is a liaison between your project and the program at the agency. The program officer makes decisions regarding program quality and about the way a program is conducted. The program officer does not make final decisions regarding funding or expenditure of project funds. Funding decisions are the responsibility of the grant and contract officer.

Grant/Contract Officer

———Grant Tip———
After notification that your proposal has been selected for funding, the grant officer assigned to your project negotiates final budget figures with you.

The grant and contract officer is the person who knows thoroughly the federal rules and regulations regarding expenditure of funds for grants and contracts. This person will assist you in any questions about your budget or about appropriate expenditures. After notification that your proposal has been selected for funding, the grant officer assigned to your project will negotiate final budget figures with you for the federal government. This negotiation is based upon discussions with and recommendations from the program officer, but final decisions regarding money matters will rest with the grant and contract officer.

If you plan to make a major deviation from your budget, or if you plan to request a budget change, you will contact the grant and contract officer. (You should, of course, have discussed these changes with your program officer in advance. Indeed, you should send a copy of any correspondence with the grant and contract officer to your program officer, and vice versa.)

Implementation and operation decisions are made by a program officer; the project's fiscal issues are addressed by the grant and contract officer. Each has a particular role in the process. The program officer's responsibility begins long before the grant competition starts. The grant and contract officer's responsibility begins after successful proposals have been funded and the proposal writer has become a project director or a principal investigator.

Some Part-Time Players on the Roster

There is another team of players in the grant process. Members of this team are only part-time players, but they are very important. These are the readers for your proposal. Most grants are awarded after a peer review and scoring or ranking of proposals. In this process a team of readers will review proposals and grade or rate and often rank the proposals. A typical proposal reading team might consist of two persons from outside the federal government and one person from inside the federal government. Agency personnel may mail proposals to reviewers for them to read, or they may invite the readers to Washington and establish a review panel in that manner. (Detail of the review process is provided in Chapter 8, "Understanding How Grants Are Awarded.")

Although the readers will have only a short tenure in working with your proposal, their decisions will have a significant impact on whether or not your proposal receives funds. The peer review process (readers) helps keep politics out of the grant process to some degree and allows the federal government to get outside, expert opinions on the value of various projects proposed to implement the purposes of a program.

Some Early Players Have Dual Roles

The legislative and executive branches have at least one other role in the grant process. When the legislative branch passes a law, one portion of that law will specify how much money is authorized to be expended for each section of the law. This *authorization* is generally a figure considerably higher than that which will eventually be available. In passing a law, the legislature usually intends that the

Grant Tip

The U.S. Department of Education's Application Control Center serves as the point of receiving all grant proposals. The phone number is (202) 708-9495 and it is located in Room 3633, ROB-3, 7th & D Streets, Washington, D.C. 20202-4725.

law will be in effect for several years. By authorizing more funds than are appropriated, the legislative branch maintains continuity and flexibility and can make changes without passing a new law.

If it decides to support activities under a law, the legislature will include the funds in an *appropriations* bill. An appropriations bill designates the amount of funds available to carry forth the purposes of the law. Appropriations are generally for one year, but if the agency is successful in meeting the purposes of a particular program, the legislature is likely to include funds for the agency's program in an appropriations bill in succeeding years, thus ensuring that the program will have some life of its own.

Once monies have been appropriated, the executive branch (through the administering agency) will *allocate* funds to particular program categories. These three steps, authorization, appropriation, and allocation (AAA) are important because they help the proposal writer understand the value of the program to the funding source. This importance can be inferred from the amount of funding authorized and appropriated and the way the appropriated funds are allocated.

The amount authorized is almost always considerably more than the amount appropriated. Cynics suggest that legislators discuss the amount authorized when they speak to groups in favor of particular legislation, but speak only about appropriations or allocations when questioned seriously about their care in watching over public funds.

There are many actors in the grant process. Some important ones are the legislative branch, the executive branch, the program officer, the grants officer, and the proposal readers. Using Warren's (1980) conceptualization, the social definition of a problem is when it becomes evident and is made apparent to the legislature. The legislative definition of a problem is the law passed because of the need. The administrative definition of a problem is the rules and regulations and final allocation of funds for the program.

The Project Director/Principal Investigator (PI)

There is one more extremely important actor. That is the project director or the principal investigator. A project director is the person designated to administer a project. This person is in contact with the program officer and the grant and contract officer in Washington and has the day-to-day responsibility for managing the funded project. The director is responsible to the federal government for meeting timelines and for expending funds in accordance with rules and regulations. The federal government provides rules and regulations to govern the administration of a project, and the director must know those rules and regulations.

Often the project director is the person who wrote the proposal. A cooperative working relationship between the project director and the administrative personnel in Washington will help ensure that a particular project is well-run, well-administered, and successful in meeting its objectives and purposes.

State-Level Reviews

In the federal grants process, there are also state-level roles. Federal Executive Order 12372 requires that you *may* need to review your proposal with a State Single Point of Contact (SPOC). Note that *not all* federal programs are covered under the review requirements of Executive Order 12372. Instructions about this requirement are in the regulations and may also be in the grant application packet.

The SPOC process is designed to see that there is appropriate *coordination* between and among federally supported programs.

Executive Order 12372 notes that persons at SPOC can send comments on the project (proposal) to the federal agency that administers the program. The comments usually have to be at the federal agency at a specific cutoff date, generally 30 days after the proposal's due date. The address for sending SPOC comments to the federal agency is not the same address as that to which you send the proposal. Read these instructions carefully!

The SPOC agency requirements vary from state to state. Some want only copies of a project abstract; some want entire proposals. Learn about your SPOC; *know* the SPOC address, phone number, and preferred process for review.

A grant application may require that you submit your proposals for another state review—for education this may be the State Education Agency (SEA). The application packet or regulations will provide the exact directions you should follow.

Be courteous and communicative. Regardless of the requirements for sending your proposal to agencies or places for review, you should send a copy to appropriate agencies. If you are developing a project to improve pupil reading, be sure to share your proposal with the reading personnel (and possibly the dropout, compensatory education, or other personnel) in the SEA. If your project deals with

—— **Grant Tip** ——
The address for sending SPOC comments to the federal agency is not the same address as that to which you send the proposal. Read these instructions carefully! State Players: Executive Order 12372, Single Point of Contact in States, and State Agency Review or Information.

—— **Grant Tip** ——
Learn about your State Single Point of Contact; Know the SPOC Address, Phone Number and preferred process for review. Appendix B contains a list of SPOC Addresses (1993).

health, send a copy to the state agency that works with health issues in the state.

In sending courtesy and communication copies of your proposal, you need only send the basics — the idea and the plan. You will want to remove excess pages, appendixes, and the budget. Not only is this information usually private, but slimming down the packet will save on duplication and postage, etc. Your purpose is to be informative—to communicate your interest in the problem and in developing projects to work with the problem.

Conclusion

This section provides a summary of the key actors or players in the federal grant process. While omitting some academic and bureaucratic details, we have tried to include ideas and steps to help the grantwriter understand the entrance to the labyrinth and to have a successful start down the twisting path toward competency in the federal grant game. If you move to the major leagues, you'll need a more detailed scorecard!

PART III

Implementing, Operating, and Terminating a Project

In Part III, Chapters 10-13, we examine the implementing, operating, and closing out of a funded project. The Federal guidelines that must be followed *(EDGAR)* while operating a project and the nature of site visits and audits are also discussed. In each chapter, we offer a variety of tips and examples that are helpful to a grant administrator.

10

Implementing a Funded Project

Introduction

Now that you have negotiated your grant and have received your Grant Award Notification, you are ready to implement your project. This phase of your grant can be exciting and fun if you are well prepared and organized. This chapter is designed to help you develop a plan and get you going on the implementation procedures.

Grant Award Notification

Often, the time you have to actually implement your project is very short. It is common to have less than two months between the time you receive your Grant Award Notification and the start up date of your project. You need to be well organized and ready to "hit the road running" the moment you receive the Grant Award Notification. When you negotiated your grant, you were told by the negotiator that the negotiations did not constitute a grant and that you were not to announce your grant or spend any money from it until you received the Grant Award Notification document. Many times it takes between two and five weeks to receive this document.

— Grant Tip —
Be well organized and ready to "hit the road running" the moment you receive the Grant Award Notification.

Pre-Implementation

In the meantime, you can begin to organize your plans for implementation. Some of the areas you need to organize include:

1. Prepare in-depth, comprehensive positions descriptions.
2. Prepare position announcements.
3. Plan the distribution of the announcements.
4. Prepare advertisements for positions for newspapers.
5. Develop interview rating sheets.
6. Select an interviewing committee.
7. Hire personnel.

8. Locate and modify physical space for the project (office, classroom, tutoring, storage, etc.).
9. Set up bookkeeping and accounting procedures.
10. Prepare procedures for participant recruitment and application forms.
11. Outline selection procedures for participant selection.
12. Prepare class schedules, curriculum materials and participant handbook or manual.
13. Outline procedures for gathering evaluation and annual performance report data.
14. Set up files and filing procedures.

Your institution may not provide bookkeeping and accounting services for your project. In such case you will have to have someone on your staff perform this function. It is of extreme importance that you employ a person with experience in working with federal grants. Your business office may provide you with assistance in hiring such a person or you may need to seek the assistance of a private accountant. At any rate, determine this early and make the appropriate arrangements. You will probably expend money from your budget long before you begin to offer services to the target population. Do not delay in having all of the financial procedures in order prior to the expenditure of money from your grant.

—— **Grant Tip** ——

Have all the financial procedures in order prior to the expenditure of money from your grant.

Participant Selection

In the case of grants that serve individuals, another vital part of your project that you can organize while you are waiting for applications to come in and be processed is the recruitment of participants. Take care to make your application form reflect the applicant qualifications as specified in your application. Ask questions that will provide the information needed to make wise selection decisions. No matter how great your personnel may be or how well-organized your project is, if you do not have a good quality of participants according to the guidelines, you will have difficulty in achieving success.

In selecting participants, remember that your project cannot be all things to all participants. You must be selective in choosing those to receive services. You need to devise a rating scale to help you be objective. For example, one project director designed an application form that gathered information in three separate areas. He gave each question in the three areas a numerical value. The scale was from zero to twenty-seven. He and his staff determined that, even though the applicant met the criteria required in the application, if he/she scored above twenty-three points, he/she really did not need the services of the project in order to succeed. On the other hand, if an applicant scored seven or less, the project did not provide the services necessary to help him/her. These applicants were referred to other agencies whose programs were designed for such persons.

This rating scale ensured that the project did not "cream" the applicant pool by choosing only those who would succeed regardless of what the project did, and the other extreme, it protected the project from inadvertently selecting those who could not succeed in spite of the efforts of the project.

Do not underestimate the importance of participant selection. The success or failure of your project in a large measure depends upon wise selection criteria and implementation.

Preparing for the Participants

For those grants that serve program participants, impress your participants by being completely ready for them. As you meet them individually or in an orientation meeting, have their schedules ready, complete with course or project titles, credit hours, classroom numbers, instructors' names, textbooks required, campus map, etc. To do this, you must involve your instructional staff and plan the curriculum well.

Have a packet of materials ready for each participant. Include special items, such as instructions where different services are available, the library, administrative office, health services, bookstore, snack shop, student union or lounge area, tutorial services, directions to the dorms and cafeteria, etc. If your project is to furnish certain materials such as a notebook, pencils, paper, backpack, etc., have them ready for your initial contact. Often it is helpful to put together a participant handbook. Most of the items listed above could be included in an attractive handbook. There are always things that a participant should not do. Often the "do nots" out number the "dos." By putting the other items in the handbook, it does not give it such a negative tone.

A handbook will give all participants an even opportunity to be successful. At the first meeting or contact, they will probably be nervous, surveying the situation to see who their potential friends might be and sizing up the instructors and administrative staff. They may even be fighting back a little homesickness. Having everything written down in a handbook allows them to read it and study it when they are more at ease. It also provides you and your staff with a point of reference in dealing with situations that might arise in the future.

Participants will be impressed by your well-organized and designed initial contact with them. An investment of time in this area will pay dividends.

Record Keeping System

It is very important while setting up your record keeping system that you read and understand the following *Education Department General Administrative Regulation (EDGAR)* that governs federal grants for the U.S. Department of Education. *EDGAR* is described in more detail in Chapter 12. In record keeping, you need to be familiar with 75.730 thru 75.734 regulations that are outlined in Figure 10.1.

Figure 10.1. *EDGAR* Guidelines for Recordkeeping

---

§ 75.730 Records related to grant funds.
A grantee shall keep records that fully show:
(a) The amount of funds under the grant.
(b) How the grantee uses the funds.
(c) The total cost of the project.
(d) The share of that cost provided from other sources.
(e) Other records to facilitate an effective audit.
(Authority: 20 U.S.C. 1232f)

§ 75.731 Records related to compliance.
A grantee shall keep records to show its compliance with program requirements.
(Authority: 20 U.S.C. 1221e-3(a)(1))

§ 75.732 Records related to performance.
(a) A grantee shall keep records of significant project experiences and results.
(b) The grantee shall use the records under paragraph (a) to:
     (1) Determine progress in accomplishing project objectives.
     (2) Revise those objectives, if necessary.
(Authority: 20 U.S.C. 1221e-3(a)(1))
CROSS-REFERENCE. See 34 CFR 74.103 (b) and (c)--Procedures for revising
     objectives.

§ 75.733 [Reserved]

§ 75.734 Record retention period.
Unless a longer period is required under 34 CFR Part 74, a grantee shall retain records for five years after the completion of the activity for which it uses grant funds.

Source: *EDGAR,* 1992, p. 96.

Establish a comprehensive record keeping system that includes at least (1) expenditures records (invoices, transfer vouchers, etc.), (2) personnel records, (3) participant records, if serving participants, and (4) incoming and outgoing correspondence. Often in an audit or a site visit, your visitor will want to review such records. Keep all the information your employees sent you as they were applying for the position. Put their job description in their file. Make sure you have a copy of their signed contract, vacation schedule, and sick leave policy. Place copies of any correspondence you have with them, in addition to commendations, reprimands, etc., in their files.

If you maintain a complete file on each participant, include his/ her application form and related correspondence, a clear reason why he/she was accepted into your project, and what specific needs qualified him/her for participation. Also include your plan for intervention that will assist that participant in successfully completing the project. Place copies of progress sheets, test scores, interest inventory results, etc., in the file. Summarize any counseling or advising sessions you may hold with the participant, along with a report of special action taken as a result of superior performance, disciplinary problems, etc.

When the participant exits your project, take a few minutes and "close" the file by indicating the participant's reasons for exiting (successfully completed the program, became ill, was expelled, had financial problems, etc.), the progress he/she made while in the program, and, if possible, an exit evaluation the participant completed. All of this information will be extremely helpful in maintaining the constant focus of your staff on each participant and being "on top" of any problems or areas of weakness or concern. In addition, in the event of a site visit or in the preparation of your annual performance evaluation, you will have valuable information systematically collected. Financial records are of utmost importance. All program expenditures must be well-documented with receipts, purchase orders, etc. Although the fiscal officer of your institution and/or agency may keep the original copy of the financial invoices, etc., you should maintain a backup copy for your files.

Maintain a complete file of all correspondence, which should include any responses you may receive. Your correspondence becomes important documentation of your performance and organization. It serves as a reference and you will find that, if you systematically keep and file this correspondence, it will be an important source of information.

Annual Performance Report Data Gathering

——**Grant Tip**——
Even before your project begins, determine the types of information you need to gather for an annual performance report.

——**Grant Tip**——
A good rule of thumb is to document and save copies of everything you do.

Almost all federally funded projects must submit an annual performance report of some type. Some departments and offices in the U.S. Department of Education have very detailed outlines and requirements for information that must be submitted annually. Other departments and offices provide almost no guidelines or suggestions. If your particular office or agency provides information, study it carefully. Even before your project begins, determine the types of information you need to gather. Make a list of all the items you need to preserve in order to respond to the annual performance report criteria. Decide now who will be responsible for gathering what information and make sure that these employees are aware of their responsibilities and that they know when the information should be submitted to you.

Select a drawer in a file cabinet that is close to your desk and prepare a file entitled Annual Performance Report Data. A good rule of thumb is to document everything and save copies of everything you do. Put all of this material in your Annual Performance Report Data file.

For example, keep an "official" copy of all the position descriptions you may develop. Buy the newspaper(s) that carry your advertisements of position vacancies and cut the advertisements out. Be sure also to cut out the name of the newspaper and the date. Tape them on a piece of paper and put them in your Annual Performance Report Data file. If you send out position vacancy announcements to sister institutions or agencies, put a copy in your Annual Performance Report Data file.

Save a copy of your employee application rating sheet and the participant selection rating sheet. Compile a complete list of all of your participants, their qualifications and needs, and why you selected them to be in the program. Keep a copy of your participant handbook, forms, information sheets, and accounting and bookkeeping information and put all of it in your Annual Performance Report Data file. Be sure to keep accurate information on those participants who successfully complete your project. Keep newspaper clippings, articles, or other published accounts of your project.

When the time comes for you to compile your Annual Performance Report, you will probably find that you have collected much more information than you need. It is much better to be able to "pick and choose" information from your Annual Performance Report

Data file than it is to have to sit down and have a "creative writing session."

Summary

This chapter has attempted to provide you with suggestions that will help you to implement your project. You will find there are many other things you will need to do, depending on the type of project you have, your institution or agency's policies, and your previous experience. Plan to spend additional time and effort at the start up of your project. It may be difficult, but you will be pleased you did. The smooth operation of a project is impacted heavily by the way you have it organized prior to the actual delivery of services. Give yourself, your staff, your participants, and your institution or agency every advantage of having a successful project by being well prepared.

11

Understanding *EDGAR*

Introduction

*E*DGAR is an acronym that stands for *Education Department General Administrative Regulations*. This handbook of regulations is published by the U.S. Department of Education and is revised often. You can obtain a copy of *EDGAR* by contacting the research office of your institution or by requesting one from your federal program officer. You need your own copy of *EDGAR* so you can mark the important parts that pertain to your project.

Read *EDGAR* before beginning to write your grant application. Usually the grant application or, in the case of a contract, the Request for Proposal (RFP) will refer you to several parts or subparts that relate directly to the proposal you intend to write. Familiarity with EDGAR may save you many hours of revision and possibly legal problems and audits.

The July 1, 1992, revision of *EDGAR* contains eight parts. Figure 11.1 notes the major parts of *EDGAR*.

Figure 11.1. Major Parts of *EDGAR*

Part 74	Administration of Grants to Institutions of Higher Education, Hospitals, and Nonprofit Organizations
Part 75	Direct Grant Programs
Part 76	State-Administered Programs
Part 77	Definitions That Apply to Department Regulations
Part 79	Intergovernmental Review of Department of Education Programs and Activities
Part 80	Uniform Administrative Requirements for Grants and Cooperative Agreements to State and Local Governments
Part 85	Governmentwide Debarment and Suspension (Nonprocurement) and Governmentwide Requirements for Drug-Free Workplace (Grants)
Part 86	Drug-Free Schools and Campuses

This chapter reviews a few highlights of each section of *EDGAR* that will give you a head start on your project. Space does not permit an in-depth discussion of each topic covered in *EDGAR*. You are encouraged, however, to read and study *EDGAR* prior to writing a proposal. Become thoroughly familiar with each part, especially the part or parts that apply to programs of interest to you. After receiving funding for a project, review *EDGAR* again very thoroughly prior to implementing your project. This will help you set up and initiate your project correctly. Part 74 of *EDGAR* relates to the administration of grants.

Part 74: Administration of Grants

Part 74, *Administration of Grants to Institutions of Higher Education, Hospitals, and Nonprofit Organizations.* Each Part, except for Part 77, begins with a comprehensive index that divides the contents into subparts, each bearing the appropriate identifying number. For example, Part 74, Subpart A-General, begins with 74.1, the purpose and scope of the part, 74.2 Scope of the subpart, 74.3 Definitions as used in this subpart, etc. The remainder of this chapter points out important parts and subparts and touches on them briefly.

Subpart D: Retention and Access Requirements for Records

Record keeping is an important aspect of any funded project. Specific instructions tell you how long you must keep records and who shall have the right to review your records. Keep all programmatic and financial records, supporting documents, statistical and other records required by the specific program or in order for you to operate the project efficiently and effectively.

Retention

Records must be kept for a minimum of three (3) years from the starting date of your project. If the project is a *direct grant program* you must retain your records for a minimum of five (5) years [75.730]. If litigation, claim, negotiation, audit, or any other action has been initiated regarding the project prior to the end of the three- (or five-) year period, you must retain all records until such action or litigation has been completed, even though it may extend far beyond the required limit.

If the project is renewed annually or at certain intervals, the three- (or five-) year retention period begins on the date when you submit your expenditure report for that period. In other words, assume your grant was awarded for three years, is not a direct grant, and that your first funding period expires on March 31. You submit your expenditure report to the appropriate office on May 15. The three-year retention requirement for that funding period begins on May 15. If you must submit an expenditure report quarterly, your retention period begins on the day when you submit your report for the last quarter of the fiscal year. If an expenditure report has been waived, retention begins on the day the report would have been due.

This subpart discusses other aspects of retention as it pertains to equipment, income transactions, indirect cost rate proposals, etc. For details, read the subpart carefully.

Access

The Secretary or the Comptroller General or any of their authorized representatives have the right to inspect project books and records. This is true even if you subcontract part of the project to another agency or firm.

This subpart also prohibits you from imposing grant terms that would limit public access to your records and documents. Nevertheless, you are not required to invite public access and inspection of your records. You may refuse public access to certain confidential records and documents if such records would be excepted from disclosure under the *Freedom of Information* regulation. Such a determination must be made by the Department of Education and not the recipient of the grant award.

Subpart J: Monitoring and Reporting of Program Performance

Subpart J provides general timelines and guidelines that apply to the annual performance report. Unless otherwise specified in the particular project, the annual report is due ninety (90) days after the grant year ends. Your grant award document may contain instructions as to the content of the annual report. However, some programs do not have a required outline or form requesting specific information. In such cases, use this section of *EDGAR* as a guide. It requires a comparison of the actual accomplishments to the goals established in your proposal. If goals were not met, it requests reasons for the slippage. It also requests information regarding unexpectedly high costs and, when possible, a cost-per-student or cost-per-unit analysis.

Subpart L: Programmatic Changes and Budget Revisions

Subpart L is very important. During the course of a project, especially one funded for three years or more, it often becomes necessary to make program or budget revisions. Study this subpart if you need to make changes in the project or in the budget.

What constitutes a change? A change has occurred if the project's scope or objectives have changed from those contained in the approved application. A good rule to follow: If your performance does not match the scope and/or objectives of the approved application proposal, submit a request for prior approval for a programmatic revision. You cannot change the scope or objectives without prior approval. Assume, for instance, that one objective states that the project will serve 90 students. For various reasons this becomes impossible, and you can serve only 60. Submit a request for prior approval to reduce the number of students served from 90 to 60. Do not make the reduction until you receive written approval from an authorized Education Department Grants Officer.

In preparing a request for prior approval for a programmatic revision, indicate the modification desired. Include a statement such as:

> Objective A states that the project will assist 90 students to earn graduate degrees in secondary science education. We hereby request approval to amend Objective A as follows:
>
> *Objective A:* The project will assist 60 students to earn a graduate degree in secondary science education.

Provide justification in requesting the modification. Support the request with current facts and figures, letters of support or concurrence, and a good rationale for change.

Other modifications that require prior approval include:

1. Continuing the project during a period of more than three months without a project director.
2. Replacing the project director or principal investigator or other key project people.

——— Grant Tip ———
You cannot change the scope or objectives without prior approval.

——— Grant Tip———
74.102
Prior Approval Procedures
•*When requesting prior approval, make requests to your Grants Specialist— not your Program Officer.*
•*Make sure you include your Grant Number on all requests.*
•*Approvals are not valid unless they are in writing and are signed by the authorized ED Grants Officer.*

3. Reducing the amount of time spent on the project by a key person.
4. Transferring to a third party the actual performance of the substantive programmatic work.
5. Providing medical care to individuals under research grants.

A request for prior approval will stand a chance of approval if it does not require additional money. If a modification results in the need for more funds in a particular budget line or causes excess funds in a line, adjust other budget areas to accommodate the difference.

A budget revision also requires prior approval. According to 74.105, Budget Revisions—Nonconstruction Projects, prior approval to revise the budget is required to

1. Transfer amounts budgeted for indirect costs to absorb increases in direct costs.
2. Transfer amounts previously budgeted for student support (tuition waivers, stipends, and other payments to or for trainees).
3. Increase the total amount of the grant.
4. Transfer funds from one budget line to another if large amounts of funds are involved.

Those selected items of costs in *EDGAR,* Appendix D, Part J, which have the statements such as "except with approval" or "approved in advance by the sponsoring agency," require prior approval. For example, equipment, travel, etc.

Other budget changes may not require prior approval. Try to avoid requesting transfers from student services to other line items such as equipment, travel, and personnel. Such requests often are not approved. Requests that receive a more favorable response request transfers from one "non-student support" item to another "non-student support" item, such as from equipment to travel, or from travel to supplies, etc.

Subpart L is one of the most important subparts of *EDGAR.* Protect yourself, your institution, and your project by adhering closely to its guidelines. In addition, you may want to become familiar with the Office of Management and Budget (OMB; October 3, 1991) Final Revisions to Circular A-21, "Cost Principals for Educational Institutions."

—— Grant Tip ——
74.103 Programmatic Changes Requiring Approval
•*Changes to the scope or to the objectives.*
•*Changes in key people.*
•*Transferring to a third party, by contracting or any other means, the actual performance of the substantive programmatic work.*

Subpart O: Property

Subpart O, *Property,* provides information regarding property, equipment, and supplies. The subsection describes these items and when they are considered part of the grant. It defines several important terms, among them equipment and supplies. *Equipment* is generally defined as "tangible personal property having a useful life of more than one year and an acquisition cost of $300 or more per unit unless your agency uses the Cost Accounting Standards Board (CASB) standard of $500 or more per unit and useful life of two years." This differs from *supplies* defined as "all tangible personal property other than equipment." This section further discusses the use and disposition of equipment acquired for a project.

Appendix D, Part I, *Principles for Determining Costs Applicable to Grants and Contracts with State and Local Governments,* and Part II, *Principles for Determining Costs Applicable to Training and Other Educational Services Under Grants and Contracts with Educational Institutions,* provide long lists of costs allowable in certain kinds of grants. For example, under specific conditions, grant funds can be used for accounting (the cost of establishing and maintaining accounting systems for the management of the grant), advertising for recruitment of personnel, solicitation of bids, disposal of surplus materials, etc. Funds can be included in the proposal for advisory councils; employee morale, health, and welfare costs; maintenance and repair costs for equipment and property; membership, subscriptions, and professional activities; reference materials; meetings and conferences and travel costs for project staff who must travel to discharge their duties.

Appendix D also lists things that are not allowable, such as bad debts, contingency funds, contributions and donations, entertainment costs, fines, and penalties.

Proposal writers should study the appendix carefully prior to preparing project activities and prior to formulating the budget.

Part 75: Direct Grant Programs

Part 75, *Direct Grant Programs,* describes the procedures used by the U.S. Department of Education to award direct grants. The Department of Education may have developed implementing rules and regulations that apply to a specific grant program that falls within the category of Direct Grant Programs. In such cases, the implementing rules and regulations supersede the regulations contained in Part 75. However, if no specific implementing rules and regulations have been established, applicants must use the criteria established in the authorizing statute and the regulations contained in Part 75.

Much information in Part 75 is very similar to the information contained in an RFP or grant application packet. It describes eligible applicants, how to apply for the grant, mailing instructions, deadlines, and the criteria the Department uses for scoring the application and making awards. Part 75 allows the Secretary to distribute an additional 15 points among the criteria as a way of placing more weight in certain areas of the criteria. This procedure often favors applicant institutions or agencies with prior experience in organizing and operating grants of a similar nature. This part describes the process used in dealing with your proposal. This was discussed in detail in Chapter 6, "Writing a Proposal."

Part 75 clarifies the difference in a *project period* and a *budget period.* The project period is the total number of months for which your project is funded. The Department cannot fund a project for more than 60 months. The budget period is usually only one year. The budget for a multi-year project is negotiated each year of the project period.

Instructions for continuing a multi-year project after the first budget period are in this part. Follow the procedure outlined here to receive funding for the subsequent budget periods of the project.

Special or unusual circumstances may make it necessary for you to seek an extension of the project period. Instructions to file for an extension are found in this part. You must submit your request at least 45 days before the end of the project period and follow the remainder of the instructions carefully.

Part 75 also contains the three criteria that you must address in the evaluation section of your proposal. The three areas are as follows:

1. The grantee's progress in achieving the objectives in its approved application.
2. The effectiveness in meeting the purposes of the program.
3. The effect of the project on persons being served by the project, including ethnic minorities, women, handicapped persons, and the elderly.

Part 75 contains instructions for grants containing construction and also instructions in dealing with publications and copyrights, inventions and patents.

Another important part of Part 75 is Subpart F, which describes the general administrative responsibilities you have in relation to your project. This includes fiscal control and fund accounting procedures, obligation of funds, instructions relating to subgrants, a section on reports and records, retention period for direct grants, how to handle the privacy of records, and guidelines on data collection.

Part 75 also provides procedures the Department uses to get compliance, including suspension and termination of projects. This section notes that no official, agent, or employee of the Department of Education may waive any regulation that applies to a Department program, unless the regulation specifically provides that it may be waived. Even if a Department official acts on a certain item, or fails to act, this cannot affect the authority of the Department to enforce regulations.

Part 76: State-Administered Programs

Part 76, *State-Administered Programs,* establishes general requirements that a state must meet in order to apply for a grant from the federal government. A state must have on file with the U.S. Secretary of Education a general application or state plan that meets certain requirements of Section 435 of the General Education Provisions Act. State plans fall into one of 29 different areas, such as compensatory education, migrant children, basic skills, community schools, career education, adult education, math-science programs, etc.

In submitting a state plan a state must include certifications. These include, among others, (1) that the plan is submitted by the state agency eligible to submit the plan, (2) that the agency has the authority under state law to perform the functions of the program, (3) that the state may legally carry out each provision of the plan, (4) that the provisions of the plan are consistent with state law, etc.

The Department of Education, under certain circumstances, may consolidate two or more grants to certain geographic areas called Insular Areas, such as the Virgin Islands, Guam, etc. Consolidation simplifies the application and reporting procedures and provides the area with flexibility in allocating funds to achieve any purposes to be served by the consolidated programs. Consolidation of grants allows the grantee to redistribute the funds as needed. For example, assume that a grantee applied for and received funds under three different programs. The grantee may choose to allocate the funds to all three programs or to allocate the entire sum to one or two of the programs. Instructions are also contained in this section about how consolidated grants are made and how an Insular Area may apply for a consolidated grant.

An interesting difference in how grants are made exists between state-operated grants and direct grants. Once a proposal by an institution or agency for a direct grant is developed and submitted, that organization does not enjoy the right to a hearing before the application is disapproved by the Department of Education. However, if a state submits a state plan, the Department may disapprove the plan only after (1) notifying the state, (2) offering the state a reasonable opportunity for a hearing, and (3) if requested, holding the hearing.

Once a state has obtained a grant to operate certain programs, it may, in turn, provide subgrants to other agencies to carry out the provisions of a project. For example, a state may submit a state plan to carry out a migrant education program. It may then award subgrants to local educational agencies (LEAs) to provide the services of the state plan. Part 76 contains instructions for other agencies to apply to the state for a subgrant. Such agencies also have the right to a hearing at the state level before their applications are disapproved.

The remainder of Part 76 contains instructions to the state and the subgrantee regarding the proper and efficient operation of a project. It discusses items such as evaluation, private school involvement in the projects, the use of public and private school personnel, equipment and supplies, construction, etc. It ends with a discussion of the state administrative responsibilities, which are similar to those previously discussed in other parts, and the procedures the Department of Education uses to get compliance.

Prior to applying for a federal grant to a state or a subgrant from the state to a local education agency, read this part for the important details that will strengthen your proposal and your project.

Part 77: Definitions That Apply to Department Regulations

Part 77 contains a glossary of terms used in *EDGAR*. Often the meaning or definition of the terms is narrowed or modified to fit a specific rule or regulation within *EDGAR*. When used in an RFP or other official document, the term must be defined and interpreted as it appears in this part or in another part. You will enhance your application and increase the confidence the readers will have in you if you use these terms as they are defined. Many of them will appear on the technical review form the readers use. By their use in your proposal, you demonstrate that you have studied them, you are familiar with *EDGAR,* and that your interpretation and the Department's interpretation are the same.

Part 79: Intergovernmental Review

Part 79, *Intergovernmental Review of Department of Education Programs and Activities,* is an attempt to foster intergovernmental partnerships and strengthen federalism by relying on state processes and on state, areawide, regional, and local coordination for review of proposed federal financial assistance. Not all programs are subject to this part of *EDGAR.* Periodically, a list of Department of Education programs under this part is published in the *Federal Register.* Write the Department of Education for an updated list.

If a state adopts a process to review and coordinate federal financial assistance, the Department of Education tries to use this process. It tries to afford the state and local officials an opportunity to express their concerns and to simplify and consolidate existing federally required state plan submissions.

The remainder of this part describes how programs are selected to be under the regulations found in this part, how the Department communicates with the states regarding such programs, how efforts are made to accommodate intergovernmental concerns, the Department's obligations in interstate situation, and how a state may simplify, consolidate, or substitute federally required state plans.

Part 80: Uniform Administration Requirements for Grants and Cooperative Agreements to State and Local Government

Part 80, *Uniform Administrative Requirements for Grants and Cooperative Agreements to State and Local Government,* establishes uniform administrative rules for federal grants and agreements with state, local, and Indian tribal governments. It begins with a lengthy section of definitions of terms followed by an explanation as to which recipients are affected by this part. Among those included in this part are states, institutions of higher education, hospitals, block grant recipients, etc.

Part 80 explains pre-award and post-award requirements. If you are writing a proposal for an agency or entity other than a government hospital or institution of higher education, read this section carefully.

The post-award section provides instructions regarding standards for financial management systems, allowable costs, matching or cost sharing, program income, and audits. It also sets the rules for revisions, equipment, copyrights, and procurement. Much information in this part pertaining to performance and financial reporting, retention of and access to records, is similar to that found in earlier parts.

One section of Part 80 pertains to *after-the-grant requirements.* It describes the process to close out a grant, including the disposition of federally owned property.

Part 80 has a detailed appendix explaining the audit requirements for local and state governments. The appendix gives guidance regarding the Single Audit Act of 1984 (Public Law 98-502). This is an important document for all grant recipients to study, particularly since most fall under the Single Audit Act.

Part 85: Governmentwide Debarment and Suspension

Part 85, *Governmentwide Debarment and Suspension (Non-procurement)* sets out the rules pertaining to persons who have been debarred by the government. Such persons may not participate in financial and nonfinancial assistance and benefits under federal programs and activities. *Debarment,* as defined in this part, is "an action taken by a debarring official in accordance with these regulations to exclude a person from participating in covered transactions. A person so excluded is 'debarred'."

Debarment

Debarment may be imposed for any of these major factors: (1) conviction of the commission of fraud or criminal offense in connection with obtaining or performing a public or private agreement or transaction, (2) violation of federal or state antitrust statutes, (3) commission of embezzlement, theft, forgery, bribery, falsification or destruction of records, making false statements, receiving stolen property, making false claims, or obstruction of justice, and (4) commission of any other offense indicating a lack of business integrity or honesty that seriously and directly affects the present responsibility of a person.

Some offenses for which debarment may be imposed are also included in this part. If one is accused and stands in jeopardy of debarment, this part outlines the options available and the procedure that will be followed.

Suspension

Suspension is defined as "action taken . . . that immediately excludes a person from participating in covered transactions for a temporary period, pending the completing of an investigation" and other legal action. Suspension may be imposed upon adequate evidence of offenses such as those indicated under debarment. Both of these actions are serious legal proceedings. Upon submitting most proposals, the submitting institution or agency must sign and include an assurance regarding debarment and suspension. Failure to adhere to this provision "may result in disallowance of costs, annulment or termination of your award, issuance of a stop work order, debarment, or suspension, or other remedies, as appropriate."

Another section of Part 85 is designed to carry out the Drug-Free Workplace Act of 1988. It requires that a grantee, whether an agency or an individual, certify that, as a condition of the grant, a drug-free workplace will be maintained, that no one connected with the grant will "engage in the unlawful manufacture, distribution, dispensing, possession, or use of a controlled substance in conducting any activity with the grant."

An important list of definitions concerning the drug-free workplace is included; grounds for termination, suspension, and debarment are discussed. This Part ends with a section describing the grantee's responsibilities and emphasizes the need to submit certification to the Department or agency issuing the grant declaring that a drug-free workplace will be maintained.

The appendix to Part 85 includes instructions for certification. Application packages for most grants contain certification forms. Have them properly signed and submitted with your application. Failure to do so will result in a delay in processing your application and may cause your application to be disqualified.

Once you receive funding and organize and implement your grant, remember that you are responsible to ensure that these three areas, debarment, suspension, and a drug-free workplace, are strictly enforced. It would be wise for you to include some questions in your interview process to determine the status of potential employees regarding these issues.

Some Basic Questions and DOs

The following are some basic questions that you may want to ask yourself concerning grantee accountability. The answers to these questions would indicate how effective you are managing your grant and are requirements within *EDGAR*.

- •Are the travel expenditures in conformance with the grant agreement?
- •Did you hire the number of employees as stated in the approved budget?
- •Do the time commitments of each employee agree with the grant agreement?
- •Has equipment been received and is being used as outlined in the approved application?
- •Are proper records maintained by the Project Director?

It is essential to review the Terms and Conditions of your grant that typically comes with the Grant Award Notification (refer to Block 9 on page 190), all applicable program regulations (refer to Block 7), and *EDGAR*. The grant administrator is responsible for managing the grant in accordance with these regulations. If there are questions, the program officer, the grants officer (refer to Block 3), and/or the Regional Grants Representative will be able to assist in answering specific questions. The following *dos* that were provided by a program offical at a workshop may provide some assistance on what to do in relationship to *EDGAR*.

- •Do fulfill all grant Terms and Conditions (e.g., send in a performance report within 90 days after the grant ends) as outlined in program regulations and *EDGAR* (*EDGAR* 75.700).
- •Do a continuation application each year in accordance with the grant Terms and Conditions (*EDGAR* 75.253).
- •Do manage equipment bought with grant funds (*EDGAR* 74.140).
- •Do use the equipment, during and after the project, in accordance with the guidelines (*EDGAR* 74.137).
- •Do develop adequate record keeping systems for financial and programmatic records and keep all records for at least 5 years after the grant expires (*EDGAR* 75.730-734).
- •Do document cost-sharing contribution if it is required for your grant award (*EDGAR* 74.52).
- •Do follow the financial management standards in accordance with the regulations (*EDGAR* 74.60-62).

•Do monitor your project in accordance with the regulations (*EDGAR* 74.81).

•Do inform the program officer of any significant developments (positive or negative) in the project (*EDGAR* 74.84).

•Do seek prior approval in writing from the grants officer for budget revisions (*EDGAR* 74.105 and 74.176).

•Do seek prior approval in writing from the grants officer for programmatic changes, changes in project scope, or changes in key personnel (*EDGAR* 74.103).

•Do administer and supervise the project and keep records in accordance with the regulations (*EDGAR* 75.700-75.732).

•Do notify the grants officer if the project will be without a project director for more than 90 days (*EDGAR* 74.103).

•Do procure supplies, equipment, and other services in accordance with your own procurement policies provided that they are in accordance with the federal regulations (*EDGAR* 74.161-166 and *EDGAR* 75.707).

•Do pay project staff members in accordance with regulations (*EDGAR* 75.519).

•Do coordinate your project with others; however, do not duplicate your project with other activities that serve similar purposes and/or target groups (*EDGAR* 75.590-75.581).

•Do evaluate your project according to the standards established in the regulations (*EDGAR* 75.590).

•Do consult the regulations if you intend to publish and copyright material (*EDGAR* 74.145 and 75.620-75.622).

•Do anticipate a site visit and/or program audits (*EDGAR* 74.85).

In Summary

This chapter reviews important areas of *EDGAR,* the official document that contains the rules and regulations that govern your grant. Become familiar with the entire document. Take time before you begin to write your application to study *EDGAR.* After you receive notification of your grant award, again review especially those parts that pertain to your grant and project. It will be time well-spent and most profitable for your institution and your project.

12

Understanding Site Visits and Audits

Introduction

During the life of a federal grant, project officers or other officials from the sponsoring government agency may conduct site visits or audits. Your project may be selected for attention.

Site visits are generally for the purpose of reviewing the progress of your project and to ensure that you are operating the project according to the terms of your approved application, the authorizing legislation, and the federal regulations. The federal visitor reviews project files and documents, the eligibility guidelines for participants, the procedures for fiscal accountability, etc. He/she will generally interview staff members, an institutional administrator or two, and a representative sample of the project participants and then prepare a narrative describing the findings. Usually this narrative highlights the successes of your project and emphasizes those outstanding elements that may be shared with other similar projects; if deficiencies are found, he/she makes recommendations for improvement. If major deficiencies are discovered, the visitor may request that a formal audit be conducted to provide guidelines to rectify deficiencies and put your project back on track.

Audits are much more formal than site visits and may be conducted by persons more specialized than a project officer. Audits may be conducted as a result of suspected operational deficiencies or questionable expenditure of federal funds. An audit may result in formal requirements being imposed upon the project. These requirements may deal with program compliance, financial requirements, or both. Generally the grant recipient must provide evidence that the requirements are being met.

The remainder of this chapter will help you plan and operate your project in such a way that you will be ready for a site visit or an audit at any given time without having to spend many long hours of preparation.

Site Visits

A site visit to a funded project can be the single most important factor in the funding agency's deliberations regarding the project's worthiness and prospects for future funding. Creating positive images of the project during a site visit depends on several factors, including: (1) progress made in carrying out the specific activities for which funding was granted; (2) effectiveness of planning for the site visit; (3) how the visit is organized and how material is presented; (4) how the visitors are treated; and (5) the general climate established during the visit.

A site visit is a funding agency's review of a funded project, conducted at the location of the project. It may be held for one or more of the following purposes; (1) to review, monitor, and assess project accomplishments; (2) to review and assess project management, in cluding financial systems and controls; (3) to examine and discuss a particular problem that has occurred; (4) to negotiate change(s) in the project's program or budget; (5) to assess the project in terms of decisions to continue and/or refund the project; (6) to provide technical assistance to the project; and (7) to receive and discuss project final reports.

Often a project is selected for a site visit if it is experiencing serious problems. Such problems may be brought to the Department or agency's attention by another department, a project employee, or a participant. Some departments or agencies also give priority for site visits to grantees who have several grants totaling a specific amount, such as $200,000 or more. Other projects are selected because they fall into a "geographic package" that may include other institutions close by with similar grant projects. Length of time since a project was last visited is another factor that may determine when a site visit occurs.

Site visits are designed to assist you, to point out potential problem areas, and to highlight areas of success. When the project looks good, the sponsoring agency looks good. The sponsoring agency does not want to preside over projects that are failures. The site visit is the agency's way of trying to identify problems before they become major. Cooperation with the site visitor and the preparation you put into the site visit will pay dividends in the long run.

Site Visit Activities

You may ask yourself, "What happens on a site visit?" Typically, the first thing that happens is that the agency or department notifies the program by phone and letter to set a convenient date for the visit. Figure 12.1 is an example of a site visit letter that may be sent to your institution or agency. To prepare, the visitor may obtain a copy of your approved proposal, previous site visit reports, and other pertinent information regarding your project. The visit generally begins with an "entrance interview" with appropriate institutional personnel (president, vice-president, dean, etc.) to explain the purpose of the visit.

Figure 12.l. Example of Site Visit Letter

UNITED STATES DEPARTMENT OF EDUCATION
WASHINGTON, D.C. 20202

July 13, 1993

Dr. John Doe, Dean
College of Education
State University of Jonesville
20 Claxton Education Building
Knoxville, Tennessee 37996

Dear Dr. Doe:

This is to confirm the arrangements made by Mrs. Madeline Adams of my staff with Dr. Robert Seaton to review the College Assistance Migrant Program (CAMP) at State University of Jonesville on July 29, 1993. The site monitoring team will consist of Mrs. Lanter and Ms. Lori Jones.

The on-site review will cover the following: (1) the management of the CAMP project; (2) eligibility policies; (3) recruitment policies and procedures; (4) program effectiveness; (5) progress in meeting program objectives; (6) fiscal accountability; and, (7) compliance with existing regulations governing the CAMP projects. It is requested that you have the project records for the past three years available for the review team.

A written report will be forwarded to you within 30 days following the on-site review.

We look forward to continuing to work with your staff in carrying out our mutual responsibilities under these programs.

Sincerely,

Kenton Sweckard, Director
Office of Migrant Education

xc: Dr. Robert Seaton, Project Director

Site visit activities typically follow:

- •Phone Call
- •Formal Letter
- •Entrance Interview
- •Site Visit Activities
- •Exit Interview
- •Formal Written Letter or Report of Findings

The Site Visitors

Site visits may be made by a single person representing the funding agency, or by a team of two or more. It is important for the project staff (including principal investigator, project director, and other key staff) to understand who the site visitors are in terms of their relationship to the funding agency. Visitors may be direct employees of the funding agency, privately contracted consultants, technical experts in the field related to project activities, members of an independent government review panel, corporate or foundation directors/officers, or government auditors. Project managers have the right to inquire as to the identity and qualifications/interests of those chosen for the site visitation team in order to determine how to structure the content of the site visit in appropriate ways. The funding agency program officer who arranges for the site visit can provide specific information on the site visitors.

Roles of Project Staff and Site Visitors

The site visit involves the project staff and the site visitors in a complex set of roles and communication patterns. Site visitors and project staff alike are nervous over the conduct of the site visit. Site visitors are under the pressure of needing to make quick but valid assessments of complicated programs and situations in a very short period of time. Project staff members are under the pressure of making favorable impressions on the site visitors and on their project superiors as well. Primary responsibility for the conduct of a well-planned and managed site visit rests with the principal investigator/project director, with the assistance of the chief project aides.

Entrance Interview

Interviews with the project director and other key personnel may center around the areas of administration, budget, objectives and allowable activities, record keeping, etc. For projects that provide direct services to program participants, the person conducting the site visit will typically interview a representative sample of program participants regarding the program and review the services that they are receiving. On the other hand, if a project was funded to develop curriculum materials, the development process will be discussed and the materials will be reviewed. The visitor will want to spot-check your files, records, and other documents. The reviewer will be particularly interested in determining if your project is carrying out its funded objectives. He/she will also try to become aware of areas in which you may appear to be out of compliance with the rules and regulations.

The visitor may visit with personnel from your business office as well as with several program participants. If you provide services to participants at sites removed from your institution or agency, the reviewer may want to visit these sites and talk to some of the program participants.

Your visitor generally will be willing and pleased to provide technical assistance and suggestions if you ask. Take advantage of this person's expertise, experience, and knowledge while he/she is visiting you.

Primary Areas of Concern

The site visit personnel will generally review and monitor the project in the areas of project administration, fiscal operations, project activities, and procedures used in evaluating the project. Figure 12.2, *Items Typically Reviewed by Site Visitors,* addresses these four major areas.

Exit Interview

At the conclusion of the visit, exit interviews are generally held to provide the project director, key employees, and institutional administrators with a preliminary oral report of the visitor's findings and observations, recommendations, and probable required action. The exit interview also provides the project and institutional administrative personnel the opportunity to respond orally, clarify, and provide important input.

The site visitor will provide a written report of his/her findings, recommendations, and required actions. Because of internal

——Grant Tip——
The site visit personnel will generally review and monitor the project in the areas of project administration, fiscal operations, project activities, and procedures used in evaluating the project.

Figure 12.2. Items Typically Reviewed by Site Visitors

Administration of the Program	**Scope of Work—Program Activities**
Project personnel (staff hired; hiring procedures; etc.) Organizational structure (as proposed and approved) Director (full-time if waiver not approved) Adequate record keeping (personnel, etc.) Adequate space/location Compliance with laws and regulations Institutional commitment Affirmative action procedures Training and staff development Compliance with *EDGAR* guidelines	Documentation of services/activities Achievements to date Time frames—as scheduled, revisions, slippages Are you deviating from approved activities? Are you complying with the laws and regulations that govern your program? Is there duplication of services? Are you serving eligible participants? Are you producing and/or serving those items/ individuals whom you proposed to serve?
Fiscal Procedures and Operation	**Evaluation Procedures**
Documentation of expenditures Cost effectiveness of project Monthly budget reports and current ledger records Time and effort certification Equipment accountability/inventory Sound purchasing procedures Travel limitations Equipment limitations Contracts (formalized; amounts; etc.) Stipends—if any (cannot move monies from participant support without written approval)	Do you have an internal evaluation procedure implemented? Will you have an external evaluation of your project? Do you have internal reporting and management procedures? Can you conduct performance outcomes? Do you evaluate your project staff members on an annual basis? Do you have a monitoring system in place to evaluate progress being made on a monthly basis?

——— **Grant Tip** ———

The key to successful site visits (and audits) begins the day you start to write your application. Defining and documenting are important elements.

procedures, the written report or letter from some departments and agencies may not be available to you for several months, whereas others may have the report to you in a few weeks. Figure 12.3 is an example of a site visit form.

When you receive the report, you must respond in writing as to how you intend to correct any problems found and to implement suggested recommendations for improvement. Most problems identified in a site visit can be rectified by program management. In some instances, however, problems may be serious enough to merit the involvement and assistance of the office of the Inspector General. Such involvement usually constitutes an audit. Audits are discussed later in this chapter.

Defining and Documenting

The key to successful site visits (and audits) begins the day you start to write your application. Defining and documenting are important elements for successful site visits. The previous chapters

Figure 12.3. Example of Site Visit Forms

U.S. Department of Education
Higher Education Programs
Region IV

On-Site Visit Report

Dates of Site Visit:_____
Name of Institution/Agency: _____
Address:_____City:_____State:_____Zip:____

Classification: ___Agency ___Institution: __ 2 year __4 year __public ___ private

Name of President or Chief Administrator: _____Title:_____

Name of Principal Investigator/Project Director: _____

Project Telephone Number: (   )_____Fax Number (   ) _____

Title of Project: _____CFDA #:_____

Type of Project: _____Grant #: _____

Grant Award Cycle :   From ___/___/____ To ___/___/___
Total Number of Years of Participation in Program (years and months): _____

Funding History: Amount of Current Grant: $_____
                    Total Amount of Funds Received Under This Program: $_____

Persons Interviewed:

_____ *Name* _____   _____ *Title* _____   *Phone* _____   _____ *Address.* ____   ____
_____
_____
_____
_____
_____
_____
_____

Site Visit Report Format

Institution/Agency:_____

Program:_____Grant Amount: $_____Dates of Visit:____

I.   **Administration**

  Findings (strengths, weaknesses)

  Recommendations

  Required Actions

II.   **Fiscal Operations**

  Findings (strengths, weaknesses)

  Recommendations

  Required Actions

III.   **Program Activities**

  Findings (strengths, weaknesses)

  Recommendations

  Required Actions

IV.   **Evaluation Procedures**

  Findings (strengths, weaknesses)

  Recommendations

  Required Actions

V.   **Other**

VI.   **Summary**

NOTE: *Each item will typically be addressed in terms of compliance with the laws and regulations that the program is funded under; the degree of success in meeting the funded goals and objectives; the cost effectivness of the project; and the identification of any exemplary practices.*

explained the preparation and documentation necessary to design and implement a project. Your needs assessment documented reasons for which you requested funds. The needs assessment provides a significant portion of the groundwork necessary for a successful site visit. In your assessment you demonstrated that your target population needed the services you proposed to provide. Each need should have been carefully documented and defined. Keep a well-organized file of all the sources you consulted, the individuals who provided you with important information, the surveys you may have conducted or relied upon, and the steps you went through to establish the basis for your project. During a site visit these all constitute important evidence to show that the proper foundation exists for your project.

As you begin to organize your project, take special care to define in writing the procedures you will use. You may wish to compile a

————**Grant Tip**————
*Compile a notebook
with important
"site visit"
information in it.*

notebook with important "site visit" information in it. A section on evidence to show that a proper foundation exists as well as a section detailing the procedures you use would be an excellent way to begin the notebook. Even though these procedures may have been listed in the Plan of Operation section of your application, you need to fill in the details of exactly how you implemented them. For example, as you prepare to hire your staff, ensure that you have well-defined position descriptions that clearly identify the necessary qualifications. Set up reasonable timelines for receiving applications, making sure that you allow sufficient time to reach a large population of potential applicants and that they have enough time to gather the information you request and return it within your time frame. Sometimes seemingly insignificant problems are not properly addressed, and they quickly grow into major problems that may precipitate site visits or even an audit. Items that should be included in a notebook may consist of the following items:

- •Copy of award letter.
- •Copy of approved budget.
- •Copy of approved plan.
- •Organizational chart of project in relationship to the structure of the institution or agency.
- •Inventory of equipment purchased with grant funds.
- •A copy of the project objectives, progress, and performance measures.
- •If serving participants, a list of the participants.
- •Performance reports.
- •External evaluation reports, if any.
- •Copies of recent audits, if any.
- •Documentation of nonfederal matching funds, if required.

As you form a pool of potential project participants, carefully define the eligibility recruitment and application requirements and then ensure that your staff and potential participants are fully aware of these requirements. One project director was careless in defining the requirement for demonstrated academic need of potential participants. He was careful to ensure that each met the citizenship and/or residency requirements, and the age, income, and occupational requirements. He did not document well the academic need requirements. After a year or so of operation, several students who met the requirements, including demonstrated academic need, were rejected for enrollment into the project because there was no room left for them. These students investigated the requirements and discovered that the academic need of several students was not documented. They filed a protest with the sponsoring agency and, as a result, the sponsoring agency conducted a site visit. Even though the major purpose of the site visit was to investigate the protest regarding academic need, the visitors reviewed the entire project and all of the supporting documentation.

In organizing each project component, carefully define the criteria and determine the documentation needed to support them. For example, assume that you are preparing to hire personnel for the position of Educational Specialist and the qualifications you establish require (1) a letter of application, (2) a current résumé, (3) a master's degree in education, (4) three years of experience in similar programs, (5) three letters of recommendation, and (6) because the position requires travel between service delivery sites, a valid driver's license and a reliable vehicle.

In the position announcement explain these specific requirements. Then prepare for the folder of each applicant a check-off list that indicates the documentation you will accept to support each qualification. The check-off sheet may look like the example in Figure 12.4.

Figure 12.4. Example of a Position Announcement Check-Off List

Check-Off List—Educational Specialist

<u>Requirements</u>   <u>Documentation Received</u>
(1) Letter of Application   _____
(2) Current Résumé   _____
(3) MA Degree Transcripts   _____
(4) Experience—Letters   _____
(5) Letters of Recommendation   _____
(6) Copy of Driver's License   _____
(7) Copy of Vehicle Registration   _____

Attach a check-off sheet to each applicant's folder. As the required information is received, date the check-off sheet and file the document inside. This will ensure that each applicant submitted the required documents, each was evaluated on the same criteria, and each had an equal opportunity for the position.

Use a similar check-off sheet for the selection of project participants. List each selection criterion and the documentation needed to support it. Attach this list to each participant's folder. Document all eligibility criteria mandated in the Request for Proposals (RFP) and also for the requirements that your specific project or institution may impose. For example, to satisfy the RFP eligibility criteria, you may need to require documentation of age (birth certificate), citizenship/legal residency status (birth certificate or immigration documents), income status (IRS tax information), and occupational history (check stubs showing current or former employment). Your institution and/or project may require additional criteria, such as residency in your state to determine tuition charges (rent or utility receipts), enrollment or acceptance in your institution (certificate of acceptance for admission), academic need (high school and previous college transcripts), student housing (dormitory deposit or acceptance certificate), financial need (statement of anticipated income and expenses), other financial support (copies of Financial Aid Form, scholarship applications, letters of recommendation, etc.).

Other areas in which you should carefully organize your procedures and staffing patterns are (1) *organizational structure,* including organizational chart and lines of authority for reporting purposes; (2) *staff,* with information such as position descriptions, tenure, academic rank, years with the project, background, affirmative action nondiscriminatory policy, committee assignments, etc.; (3) *institutional involvement,* such as space, equipment, location on campus, in-kind contributions, availability of administrators, monitoring and supervision of grant activities and personnel; (4) *staff training,* who receives and who provides the training, how often, kinds of training, i.e., formal classes, workshops, conferences, in-services, observations, etc.; (5) *records and reporting,* including personnel, participant, budget, and project records, who receives them, what they contain, and what they are used for. Some of these areas are discussed in further detail in the following paragraphs.

Fiscal Accounting Systems

Establish a procedure for expending project funds. This procedure should conform to the institution's approved procedures and federal regulations that may apply. Include documentation required for requisitions, purchase orders, interdepartmental transfers, etc., such as receipts, letters of services rendered, anticipated expenditures, estimates, airline ticket receipts, and so forth. Indicate who is authorized to create requisitions, purchase orders, etc., and who must approve and sign these documents. Set up your ledger sheets that would be in line with your final approved budget breakdown. For example

- Personnel
- Fringe Benefits
- Travel (Professional, Local, and Participant)
- Equipment
- Supplies
- Services
- Postage
- Telephone
- Participant Room and Board, If Needed
- Stipends, If Needed
- Other

Outline a clear description of who receives stipend money, the criteria for receiving a stipend, amounts, when and how paid, and how you document that the participant received the stipend. Establish the route these documents must follow to ensure payment, how they will be filed, and who may have access to the files. Describe the types of financial records that will be kept, official and unofficial, specific responsibility for creating the reports (business office, grants accountant, program director, secretary, etc.), the frequency with which they are created, and who has access to them. Establish the length of time financial documents must be retained for review, conforming to guidelines established in *EDGAR* and by your institution. Write these procedures down and ensure that all project employees have a copy of the procedures, understand them, and follow them. Periodically review them with your staff during staff meetings. Document each time that you review them through minutes of staff meetings or in a log.

Staff Evaluation

Establish staff evaluation guidelines that include the evaluation criteria (general criteria, specific areas such as management techniques, student interaction, peer interaction, instructional effectiveness, etc.), the frequency of evaluation (semi-annually, quarterly, etc.), the results of the evaluation (commendation, recommendations for improvement, dismissal, etc.), appeal and/or rebuttal procedures, and timelines, etc. Document that each employee is aware of the evaluation procedures, by providing each with a copy and by placing a copy in each employee's personnel folder with a signed statement indicating that he/she has received, read, and understands the procedures.

Review each objective and the activities proposed to achieve the objective. Determine the documentation needed to demonstrate successful achievement of each objective. This information is included in the Objective section of the proposal. You may need to expand and refine it. A check-off list of activities for each objective that must be accomplished may include timelines, equipment and supplies needed, person responsible, date completed, and results. Maintain copies of agendas, printed programs, announcements, registration receipts, sign-in lists, etc., that demonstrate the activity was accomplished.

Any time you need to change or modify the procedures for project operation, inform all staff and other related persons (dean, provost, etc.), by circulating a copy to all concerned personnel with a signature sheet that will eventually be returned to you. Figure 12.5 is a sample that you may want to follow.

A Recent Site Visit

Such documentation and paperwork are time-consuming. You may think that it can wait until "things slow down a little." Things seldom slow down, and the time and energy spent on it now are nothing compared to what you will spend if your have to "recreate" this information from memory several months or years in the future. For your own sake, document all that you do.

In a recent site visit a project officer arrived with a large pad of columnar accounting paper. He proceeded to review the proposal to determine the federal and local criteria for virtually every aspect of the project. Under student eligibility criteria, he listed one of the following categories at the top of each column on the accounting pad: age, citizenship/residency, low income, parental college status, academic need, personal need, social need, grade point average, counseling appointments, follow-up. He then randomly selected ten student folders and reviewed each one for the items listed. As he found the documents, he noted if they were complete, current, and contained acceptable documentation.

He then listed the criteria for hiring personnel on another sheet. He randomly selected five employees and reviewed their files for completeness and uniformity. He was complimentary when he found things in order but did not hesitate to note irregularities. On a third

Figure 12.5. Example of a Circulation Copy to all Concerned Personnel

---

STUDENT ACADEMIC EXCELLENCE PROJECT
State University of Jonesville

MEMORANDUM

TO: All Personnel
FROM: Dr. Bob Epley, Project Director
SUBJECT: Change in Employee Evaluation Policy
DATE: May 28, 19XX

The current employee evaluation policy requires that all employees be evaluated on an annual basis. Effective August 15, 19XX all project employees will be evaluated once each semester. The same evaluation form that each of you has in your file will be used. If you have questions regarding this change in policy, please contact me immediately.

Sign this memorandum and forward it to the next person.

Bill Spencer   _____ Date_____
Brenda Belt   _____ Date_____
Eric Johnson   _____ Date_____
Lupe Gonzalez   _____ Date_____
Ed Smith   _____ Date_____
Ben Campbell   _____ Date_____
Ron Brown   _____ Date_____
Greg Petty   _____ Date_____
Michelle Lanter   _____ Date_____

Dr. J. M. Ortiz, Chair_____
Dr. Marta Sanchez, Dean _____
Dr. Margo Smith, Affirmative Action_____

RETURN TO: DR. BOB EPLEY, PROJECT DIRECTOR

---

sheet, he listed the activities and required documentation of two of the project objectives. The last area he reviewed in detail concerned expenditures from the budget. He selected approximately 15 requisitions and interdepartmental transfers and checked each for appropriate approvals, signatures, receipts, invoices, etc.

He repeated this procedure for three federal projects that had been awarded to that particular institution. Two project directors had taken the time on an ongoing basis to ensure that all files and documentation were in order. The visitor's review and subsequent report of these projects were positive and complimentary. The director of the third project had not been so careful in his organization and documentation. Even though the program was running equally as smoothly as the first two, he was unable to demonstrate it. As a result the site visit report imposed many requirements for improvement and remediation and required a follow-up site visit within six months to verify compliance.

The best way to prepare yourself for a site visit is to *define* and *document:* Define your criteria, define what is acceptable documentation, and then gather and organize the documentation.

Review Procedures for Conducting Formal Evaluation

Review and outline your procedures for conducting formal evaluations designed for each individual objective, annual performance reports, external evaluation, in-house evaluations, and project participant evaluations. Place in your notebook copies of the final report of all evaluations that have been completed. If you use any standard evaluation forms, you should also include copies in your notebook.

Another important area requiring attention is samples of exemplary practices or components of your project. Site visitors are always interested in parts of your project that are functioning exceptionally well and that may be shared with other similar projects. Analyze the components of your project that have worked extremely well or that have brought exceptional results. Describe why you feel the component has been so successful, including tips and suggestions that others can incorporate into their projects. Include such exemplary components in your notebook.

Audits

Each sponsoring agency, at its discretion, can request that a given project be audited. Such requests usually are the result of serious alleged problems, unusual reports or information that has reached the department or agency, or a series of smaller events that point to possible major problems or concerns of noncompliance. Audits are not as frequent or as common as site visits. Site visits are usually performed by project officers or others who deal with the project from the implementation perspective. Audits are more formal and often involve persons from the sponsoring agency's audit division.

——**Grant Tip**——
Auditors examine the "financial statements of an organization, reviewing that organization's (i) compliance with applicable laws and regulations, (ii) economy and efficiency of operations, and (iii) effectiveness in achieving program results."

Source: *U.S. Department of Education*

The scope of audits may include areas such as the following:

•Review the reliability and integrity of the project's financial system.
•Review procedures established for complying with policies, plans, laws, and regulations.
•Review how assets are safeguarded and verify the existence of assets acquired through the project.
•Review the effective and efficient use of project resources
•Review project operation to ascertain if it is meeting the established objectives and goals as described in the approved application.
•Review compliance with laws and regulations governing the project.

As with site visits, the best way to prepare for an audit is to document. Become familiar with the laws and regulations that govern your particular project. Most of these are found in *EDGAR* and in the RFP you followed in preparing your application. Ignorance of the laws and regulations regarding your project is not an acceptable excuse for non-compliance. Study thoroughly all laws and regulations that pertain to your project. As you review each law and regulation, compile a detailed list of the specific things you should and should not be doing. Collect documentation to demonstrate that you are doing those items required and that certain practices you are doing do not border on or resemble unacceptable activities. If doubts persists, consult your project officer.

When financial records are audited, you are expected to justify all expenditures through proper supporting paperwork. Auditors look for evidence that you have followed generally accepted accounting practices, such as supplying reliable invoices and receipts for expenditures, complying with required bidding procedures, etc. If documentation is not available, attach an explanation. For example, your institution may require receipts for reimbursement of small expenditures such as meals, supplies, or taxi fare. Some taxicab services do not use standardized receipts. In such cases note the pertinent information on a slip of paper containing, if possible, the driver's signature. Submit this in lieu of a standard receipt. Generally small items of this nature do not arouse suspicion. Nevertheless, you should document even small expenditures including taxi fare, meals, tips, over-the-counter supplies, etc.

If supporting documentation has been misplaced, lost, or destroyed, duplicate copies are generally available from the vendor or

──── **Grant Tip** ────
Become familiar with the laws and regulations that govern your particular project.

supplier. Every effort should be made to obtain such duplicates to support expenditures. Make it a habit of requiring your employees to obtain such documentation. Avoid purchasing supplies, books, registration fees, etc., with your personal funds and then "turning in receipts for reimbursement." The standard procedure is to plan ahead, submit requisitions, and obtain the proper approval prior to expending the funds. This ensures compliance with acceptable procedures and allows for shared responsibility through prior approval of expenditures by a department chair, dean, or the accounting office.

An auditor may look for evidence that each project employee is working the appropriate amount of time. This is particularly important when one employee is employed by two projects. For example, an institution may have two related grants, such as a High School Equivalency Program (HEP) and a College Assistance Migrant Program (CAMP). The recruiter, secretary, and director may share responsibilities in both projects. Assume that the recruiter is contracted for 30% of his time to recruit for the CAMP and 70% for the HEP. Document that he/she not only spent the required amount of time in each project, but that his/her pay is appropriately divided between projects. If you share employees with other projects, ensure that you can account for their time and that each project is being charged accordingly. This is often done through the accounting office on a payroll verification form or other standard document.

This same principle is true when two or more projects share rented equipment, space, and services. If equipment, such as a photocopy machine or a computer, is used by nongrant entities, such as the host organization, have a way to assign appropriate charges to that entity. Equipment purchased by a federal project should be restricted for the use of that project unless provisions are made for other users to share in the cost. Be prepared to demonstrate how those costs are shared.

An audit may also include a review for compliance with the purpose of the project. For example, if your project was to serve low-income, ethnic-diverse participants, the auditor may review your records to ensure that only program participants with those characteristics are being served; if your project was funded to serve a specific number of participants at any given time, the auditor may want to verify that you are serving that number. Therefore, create a student profile that highlights the required characteristics of each participant. Include important information such as the number in the applicant pool and number actually being served, data concerning the geographic distribution of participants, their income levels and academic achievements, and any other important data that will contribute to a successful audit. Prepare for these aspects of an audit as you did for a site visit.

If your auditor finds you out of compliance in any aspect, he/she has various options. For example, he/she may recommend that a percentage of your assistance be withheld until compliance is achieved or that payment for disallowed services or equipment be withheld. He/she may also recommend that you or the institution be required to repay funds if assistance has been misused. A final and drastic recommendation would be that all funds for your project be withdrawn and the project terminated.

Typical Problem Areas Detected By Auditors

According to the U.S. Department of Education's Office of Inspector General, the following are examples of common problem areas.

- Inadequate record keeping for payroll distribution and improper charging.
- Supplanting or replacement of existing support of an activity, position, or program with federal support. For example, an employee continues to perform the same functions as he/she did prior to the receipt of federal funds but is now paid partially or completely with federal funds. Another example would be if funds that are regularly budgeted at your institution or agency for travel, supplies, or equipment are replaced with federal funds.
- Matching requirements have not been met—if required.
- Funds have not been allocated based on counts of eligible program participants and/or funds have not always been used to benefit the intended recipients.
- Poor documentation on eligibility determinations of program participants.
- Not receiving formal approval for changing scope of work.

As with site visits the best way to prepare for an audit is to document. Preparation does *not* begin with the notification that the auditors are coming. Preparation begins when you (1) start to write your proposal; (2) do the needs assessment; (3) receive the Grant Award Document; and (4) when you begin to organize the project. Preparation begins as you set up files, define criteria, and collect documentation. Do this work up front and save many hours of work and headache later.

Summary

This chapter has described how to prepare for a site visit or an audit. Define your criteria and document your actions. Preparation for site visits and audits is an activity carried out throughout all phases of the project. Major problems arise when you procrastinate. It is difficult, if not impossible, to construct a "paper trail" months or years later. The only assurance of a successful site visit or audit review is to prepare for it from the beginning.

Remember, your sponsoring agency, project officer, and others at the federal level want you to be successful. Your success is their success. Rely on them and consult with them for advice and counsel. Read and thoroughly study *EDGAR* and the laws and regulations that pertain to the project. Plan ahead and be consistent in your information gathering and you will be successful in your site visit or audit.

13

Closing Out a Project

Introduction

For a variety of reasons and circumstances, an institution or agency may need to close out or terminate a grant. When this occurs, it is important to ensure that steps are taken expeditiously to complete the proper paperwork, to file the appropriate forms and reports, and to dispose of the assets accumulated by the grant. This chapter addresses some important considerations for properly terminating a grant.[1]

Why Are Grants Terminated?

Grant termination may be initiated by one of three general processes: (1) from the review process, (2) by the host organization, or (3) by the funding source. One of the most common reasons grants are terminated is because the application to continue the project fails to receive sufficient points in the review process. Rarely in such cases does an appeal to the Department result in restoration of the grant.

A host institution may decide to end a project. Some grants are awarded for a determined period of time after which the host institution must fund all or part of the project activity or phase out project efforts. An institution may determine that the need for which the grant was obtained no longer exists and choose to terminate the grant. In some instances a school board or other governing body may decide the grant is too restrictive and either not renew it at the end of a cycle or not submit a continuation proposal for subsequent years; hence the grant ends.

At times grants are ended by Department action. The Department may determine that all applicable administrative actions and

---

[1]Complete details for the administration of a Department of Health and Human Services and most Department of Education Grants—including grant closeout—are in the *CFR* 45, Part 74. A project administrator should have, know, and follow this "bible."

required grant work have been completed by the grantee and the Department, therefore, initiates the process of *grant closeout.*

The Department may determine that grant conditions are not being met and may choose one of several options to deal with the situation. It may implement a *suspension* of the grant, which means a "temporary withdrawal of the grantee's authority to obligate grant funds pending corrective actions by the grantee or a decision to terminate the grant" (*EDGAR* 74.110).

The Department may decide to effect a *termination*, which means "permanent withdrawal of the grantee's authority to obligate previously awarded grant funds before that authority would otherwise expire. It also means the voluntary relinquishment of that authority by the grantee" (*EDGAR* 74.110).

Whatever the reason for ending the project, the host institution or agency is responsible for closing out the grant as promptly as is feasible after expiration or termination and to ensure that the proper closing procedures are implemented and the assets are divested. Upon request, the Department will pay the grantee for any allowable reimbursable cost not covered by previous payments. On the other hand, the grantee must immediately refund or otherwise dispose of, in accordance with instructions from the Department, any unobligated balance of cash that may have been advanced.

Reports

Most federal grants require that annual performance reports be submitted to the granting department or office within 90 days after the end of a project fiscal or performance year. The contents for such reports are generally prescribed in the regulations or in the documents that accompany the grant award. If the grant is terminated or allowed to expire at the end of the program year, the project personnel would complete and submit regularly required reports. These reports include information relating to the accomplishments realized during the reporting period, completion of objectives, evaluation of the project (often in formative and summative terms) in relation to the effect the grant had on the participants, and a complete financial statement.

Year-end reports include a financial report usually due 90 days after the grant is terminated or expires. The financial report discloses the total amount of funds received, the total amount expended by object or category, and the rate of indirect costs and any remaining, unobligated funds. The business or financial office frequently prepares and submits the financial reports but the project director is responsible for reviewing those reports and verifying their accuracy.

Upon receiving a justifiable request, the Department may extend the due date for any report or may waive any report that is not needed. It will do neither, however, unless you request it.

The closeout of a grant does not affect the retention period for, or the federal rights of access to, grant records. Records are to be retained for a minimum of five years after the completion of the activity for which the grantee uses grant funds (*EDGAR* 75.734). If your grant ends and is not renewed in subsequent years, be sure that people remaining at the site understand that the records must be retained for the specified amount of time.

Equipment

If your project has acquired equipment with a high value, the Department will generally indicate the proper disposal, such as transferring it to another federally funded project at your institution or to another institution. Often the "ball park" figure for such transfers is around $1,000. In any case, work closely with the Department to ensure proper disposal of property purchased or lease-purchased with project funds.

Equipment not transferred elsewhere may be used by the recipient or host institution in the project for which it was acquired as long as it is needed even though the project will no longer receive federal support. When it is no longer needed for that project, it may be used in other projects or programs currently or previously sponsored with federal funds at the recipient institution.

In all cases of grant termination, work closely with the appropriate officers in the Department to ensure that the disposition of or continued use of equipment is handled properly and in accordance with the latest Department regulations.

Notification of Grant Termination

Should the Department initiate termination proceedings against your grant, it will only be after both you and representatives of the Department have discussed the reasons and the Department has determined that the situation cannot be remedied satisfactorily. These types of terminations are relatively few and seldom come as a surprise to the grantee.

Often, however, a project that has been successfully operated for one or more funding cycles does not score sufficient points in the reading process to fall within the funding range and, therefore, the Department must close out the grant. The Department generally begins negotiating and funding those programs that are at the top of the funding slate. After all available funds have been awarded, the Department notifies unsuccessful applicants. Generally this is within a few weeks or months of the would-be start up date of your project for the next year's cycle.

If your project is already operating and you have applied for funds to continue for another cycle, timely notification is essential. You may have employees who will need to seek other employment and students who will need to find other means of funding their schooling.

Check and update all employee and student files as soon as you know the project will be ending. Employees will be searching for work elsewhere. You will receive calls and requests from future employers seeking information about your former staff members. You may want to prepare in advance a letter of recommendation with important information to help you respond to such requests and to assist staff members in their search for employment. Most will have little time to find other employment, especially if the grant cycle follows a regular academic year. By the time you know you will not be funded, many jobs in education will have already been filled.

The same is true for any students who may be supported on the project. They will need all the help possible to locate funds (if the project previously supplied tuition and/or stipends) or a new program into which they can transfer. As soon as you receive notification, begin contacting other similar programs in your area. Prepare a fact sheet for your students listing options for them including the names of the programs, start dates, cost, services provided, eligibility requirements, application procedures, etc. This will save time that you use to close out the grant instead of repeating time after time the same information to each student. At the time you receive notification of termination, notify other similar programs in the area. They may send representatives or recruiters to visit with your students to provide choices for them to relocate.

Immediately notify other agencies or institutions with which you work. If you recruit students from or provide services to local school districts, make sure they realize you will no longer be able to receive students into your program nor will you be able to provide services. For example, Educational Talent Search programs, a part of the Federal TRIO Programs, provide extensive academic and financial counseling to large numbers of students in local school districts. Services include assisting students to determine career goals and completing college application and financial aid forms. The loss of the services of an Educational Talent Search program may cause severe hardships on school districts previously served. Counselors, administrators, and others need lead time to prepare alternative services for persons who had been served by the grant.

Future Plans

When you know you are not going to be funded for the next cycle, set up an appointment with your chair, supervisor, dean, and other administrators. Plan for the future. Determine at that time whether you will submit an application at the next cycle to see if you can win a new grant to renew the program, or if the institution has the funds to continue your program even though it may be at a greatly reduced level. What will happen to your employees and physical facilities (office, telephone, office furniture, etc.)? Discuss the academic impact the loss of the grant will cause. Be sure to discuss personnel plans and the need for keeping records for at least five years.

——**Grant Tip**——
Keep all financial and other important records for 5 years— safe and accessible.

For example, if you determine to submit an application the next year, try to negotiate to keep your office space, equipment, furniture, and other things necessary to operate an office even though during the interim others may use the facility or share it with you. It is easier and much less cumbersome to make such arrangements than to start over if you receive a new grant.

If your grant supported an academic program of study, such as an associate, undergraduate, or graduate degree, visit with those involved in academics to assess the impact of project termination on the students' degree plans. Has the academic program been institutionalized, i.e., has it been approved and accepted by the institution and, if appropriate, the State Education Agency? Does it appear in the institution's catalog? Have classes been scheduled for the subsequent semester? What impact will loss of the grant have on the continuation of the degree program? Can individual education plans be created so the student can transfer the majority of classes already taken to a related program? For example, assume that a grant was terminated that supported an undergraduate degree in elementary bilingual education. The project director may be able to negotiate with the chair or the dean to allow students enrolled in the bilingual program to transfer credits to the regular education program or to a related special program.

Summary

Although losing a grant is never a pleasant experience, it is a reality to institutions that seek federal grants. Often the loss of a grant is considered by the institution as a temporary condition inasmuch as a person may submit a new application the very next year. Even so, the necessary steps must be taken to close out the existing grant properly. By working closely with the Department and following the procedures outlined, the chances of obtaining a new grant may even be enhanced.

Become familiar with the close-out procedures from a federal stand-point, and create close-out procedures to meet local needs. Help others understand that what has happened is part of the *competitive* nature of federal grants and that through following the proper procedures and maintaining a good attitude, services may be restored at a future time with another grant. Start planning immediately to seek new funding if such funding is important to you and to the institution.

Preserve as much goodwill within your institution and your service community as you can. In all likelihood, if you stay in the grant business, you will need to call upon them again. Learn from the experience. Going through the processes of closing out a grant will provide valuable insight. Learn from all parts of the grant process. Your actual operation of a grant may be improved to the point that the likelihood of losing another one becomes remote, unless you or your institution choose not to continue.

Just as certainly as there is no such thing as a late proposal, that you can't win a competition without entering it, and that you won't win all competitions, you will also find out that grant-supported projects eventually end. Approach termination with the same zeal you used to seek funding. Do the close-out activities professionally. Learn from the process. Try again!

Bibliography

General

In developing the material we have relied on many federal sources. These are identified throughout the text as appropriate. They include

Catalog of Federal Domestic Assistance (CFDA)
Code of Federal Regulations (CFR)
Education Department General Administrative Regulations (EDGAR)
Federal Management Circulars
Federal Register (FR)
Grant Application Packets
Office of Management and Budget Documents

We have relied upon materials (and quoted as appropriate) from such sources as:

Education Funding Resource Council
The Foundation Directory
The Grantsmanship Center

Specific

A Directory of U.S. Government Depository Libraries (1990). Washington, DC: United States Congress—Joint Committee on Printing.

Achilles, C. M. , et al. (1986). *A grantwriter's manual.* Knoxville, TN: Bureau of Educational Research and Services.

All About ERIC (1990). Washington, DC: U.S. Department of Education.

Brewer, E. W. (in press). New directions for adult and continuing education. In P. Mulcrone (Ed.), *Managing multiple funding sources and writing grant documents.* San Francisco: Jossey-Bass.

Cavin, J. I. (1984). *Understanding the federal proposal review process.* Washington, DC: American Associatoin of State Colleges and Universities.

Fox, R.D., Nanovc, J., & Sowada, E. (1986). *Document drafting handbook.* Washington, DC: National Archives and Records Administration.

Hall, M. S. (1988). *Getting funded: A complete guide to proposal writing* (3rd ed.). Portland, OR: Continuing Education Publications.

Horace Mann Learning Center. (1988). *Reviewing applications for discretionary grants and cooperative agreements: Orientation trainer's manual.* Washington, DC: Government Printing Office.

Krauth, D. (1979). *How to use the* Catalog of Federal Domestic Assistance. Los Angeles: The Grantsmanship Center.

Locke, L.F., Spirduso, W.W., & Silverman, S.J. (1987). *Proposals that work.* Newbury Park, CA: Sage.

Office of Research (1992). *Abstracts of the educational research and development centers.* Washington, DC: Office of Research and Improvement.

Regional Educational Laboratories (1992). *Institional projects funded by OERI.* Washington, DC: Office of Educational Research and Improvement..

Steiner, R. (1987). *Total proposal building.* Albany, NY: Trestletree Publications.

The Budget Process (1990). Washington, DC: Government Printing Office.

United States Government Manual (1993). Washington, DC: Government Printing Office.

Warren, P. (1980). *The dynamics of funding.* Boston: Allyn and Bacon.

Appendix A

Abbreviations

AAAH	American Association for the Advancement of Humanities
AAAS	American Association for the Advancement of Science
AAC	Association for American Colleges
AACD	American Association of Counseling and Development
AACUO	Association for Affiliated College and University Offices
ACC	Application Control Center
ACE	American Council on Education
ACLS	American Council for Learned Societies
ACYF	Administration for Children, Youth and Families
ADAMHA	Administration on Drug Abuse, Mental Health and Alcoholism
AFDC	Aid to Families with Dependent Children
AFOSR	Air Force Office of Scientific Research
AID	Agency for International Development
AOA	Administration on Aging
ARI	Army Research Institute
ARO	Army Reserve Office
ASAP	As Soon As Possible
AVA	American Vocational Association
BIA	Bureau of Indian Affairs
BLS	Bureau of Labor Statistics
CASE	Council for the Advancement and Support of Education
CBD	*Commerce Business Daily*
CFDA	*Catalog of Federal Domestic Assistance*
CFR	*Code of Federal Regulations*
CIES	Council for the International Exchange of Scholars
CPB	Corporation for Public Broadcasting
CURI	College and University Resource Institute
CWS	College Work Study
DEA	Drug Enforcement Administration
(D)HHS	Department of Health and Human Services
DOD	Department of Defense
DOE	Department of Energy
DOT	Department of Transportation
EDGAR	*Educational Department General Administrative Regulations*
EEO	Equal Employment Opportunity
EO	Executive Order
ERIC	Education Resources Information Clearinghouse
ERS	Economic Research Service
ESEA	Elementary and Secondary Education Act

ETA	Employment and Training Administration
FIPSE	Fund for the Improvement of Post Secondary Education
FMC	*Federal Management Circular*
FOIA	Freedom of Information Act
FR	*Federal Register*
FY	Fiscal Year
FYI	For Your Information
GAO	Government Accounting Office
GPO	Government Printing Office
GSA	General Services Administration
GSL	Guaranteed Student Loan
HEA	Higher Education Amendment
HEARS	Higher Education Administrative Resource Service
HED	Higher Education Daily
HENA	Higher Education and National Affairs
HHS	Department of Health and Human Services
IHE	Institution of Higher Education
IREB	International Research and Exchanges Board
LEA	Local Education Agency
NA	Not Applicable
NCES	National Center for Educational Statistics
NCURA	National Council of University Research Administrators
NEA	National Education Association
NEA	National Endowment for the Arts
NEH	National Endowment for the Humanities
NIA	National Institute on Aging
NIAAA	National Institute on Alcohol Abuse and Alcoholism
NIDA	National Institute on Drug Abuse
NIE	National Institute on Education
NIH	National Institutes of Health
NIHR	National Institute for Handicapped Research
NRA	National Rehabilitation Association
NSF	National Science Foundation
OERI	Office of Educational Research and Improvement
OFCC	Office of Federal Contract Compliance
OFR	Office of the Federal Register
OGPS	Office of Grants and Program Systems
OMB	Office of Management and Budget
ORM	Office of Regional Management
OSHA	Occupational Safety and Health Administration
OTA	Office of Technology Assessment
PHS	Public Health Service
PIC	Private Industry Council
RFP	Request for Proposal
RSPA	Research and Special Programs Administration
SBA	Small Business Administration
SEA	State Education Agency
SRA	Society of Research Administrators

Appendix B

State Points of Contact

ALABAMA

Ms. Moncell Thornell, SPOC
Alabama Dept. of Econ. & Comm.
State Clearinghouse
401 Adams Ave.
P.O. Box 5690
Montgomery, Alabama 36103-5690
Telephone: (205) 245-5491

ARIZONA

Ms. Janice Dunn
Arizona State Clearinghouse
3800 North Central Avenue
14th Floor
Phoenix, Arizona 85012
Telephone: (602) 280-1315

ARKANSAS

Mr. Joseph Gillespie
Manager, State Clearinghouse
Office of Intergovernmental Service
Dept. of Finance & Administration
P.O. Box 3278
Little Rock, Arkansas 72203
Telephone: (501) 371-1074

CALIFORNIA

Glenn Staber
Grants Coordinator
Office of Planning & Research
1400 Tenth Street
Sacramento, California 95814
Telephone: (916) 323-7480

COLORADO

State Single Point of Contact
State Clearinghouse
Division of Local Government
1313 Sherman Street, Room 520
Denver, Colorado 80203
Telephone: (303) 866-2156

CONNECTICUT

Assistant Director, SPOC
State of Connecticut
Office of Policy and Management
Policy Development & Planning
Division
80 Washington Street
Hartford, Connecticut 06106-4459
Telephone: (203) 566-4057

DELAWARE

Ms. Francine Booth, SPOC
Executive Department
Thomas Collins Building
Dover, Delaware 19903
Telephone: (302) 739-3326

DISTRICT OF COLUMBIA

Ms. Lovetta Davis, SPOC
Office of Intergovernmental Rel.
Room 416, District Building
1350 Pennsylvania Avenue, N.W.
Washington, D.C. 20004
Telephone: (202) 727-9111

FLORIDA

Ms. Janice L. Alcott
Director, Florida State Clearing-
house
Office of Planning & Budgeting
The Capitol
Tallahassee, Florida 32399-
0001
Telephone: (904) 488-8114

GEORGIA

Mr. Charles H. Badger
Administrator
Georgia State Clearinghouse
270 Washington Street, S.W.
Atlanta, Georgia 30334
Telephone: (404) 656-3855

HAWAII

Ms. Mary Lou Kobayashi
Office of the Governor
P.O. Box 3540
Honolulu, Hawaii 96811
Telephone: (808) 587-2802
FAX: (808) 548-8172

ILLINOIS

Tom Berkshire
State Single Point of Contact
Office of the Governor
State of Illinois
Springfield, Illinois 62706
Telephone: (217) 782-8639

INDIANA

Mr. Frank Sullivan
Budget Director
State Budget Agency
212 State House
Indianapolis, Indiana 46204
Telephone: (317) 232-5610

IOWA

Mr. Steven R. McCann
Division for Community Progress
Iowa Dept. of Economic Dev.
200 East Grand Avenue
Des Moines, Iowa 50309
Telephone: (515) 281-3725

KENTUCKY

Mr. Ronald W. Cook
Department of Local
Government
1024 Capitol Center Drive
Frankfort, Kentucky 40601
Telephone: (502) 564-2382

MAINE

State Single Point of Contact
Attn: Joyce Benson
State Planning Office
State House Station #38
Augusta, Maine 04333
Telephone: (207) 289-3261

MARYLAND

Ms. Mary Abrams, Chief
Maryland State Clearinghouse
Department of State Planning
301 West Preston Street
Baltimore, Maryland 21201
Telephone: (301) 225-4490

MASSACHUSETTS

State Single Point of Contact
Attn: Ms. Beverly Boy
Exec. Office of Communities &
Development
100 Cambridge Str., Rm 1803
Boston, Massachusetts 02202
Telephone: (617) 727-7001

MICHIGAN

Milton Waters
Michigan Dept of Commerce
P.O. Box 30242
Lansing, Michigan 48909
Telephone: (517) 373-6223

MISSISSIPPI

Ms. Cathy Mallette
Clearinghouse Officer
Office of Policy Development
455 N. Lamar Street
Suite 120
Jackson, Mississippi 39202
Telephone: (601) 359-6765

MISSOURI

Ms. Lois Pohl
Federal Assistance Clearinghouse
Office of Administration
P.O. Box 809
Room 430, Truman Building
Jefferson City, Missouri 65102
Telephone: (314) 751-4834

MONTANA

Ms. Deborah Staton, SPOC
Intergvtal Review Clearinghouse
c/o Off. of Budgt & Prog. Planning
Capitol Station
Room 202 - State Capitol
Helena, Montana 59620
Telephone: (406) 444-5522

NEVADA

Department of Administration
State Clearinghouse
Capitol Complex
Carson City, Nevada 89710
Attn: Dana G. Strum
Telephone: (702) 687-4065

NEW HAMPSHIRE

Mr. Jeffery H. Taylor
Attn: Intergovtal Review
        Process/James E. Bieber
2 1/2 Beacon Street
Concord, New Hampshire 03301
Telephone: (603) 271-2155

NEW JERSEY

Richard J. Porth
Attn: Andrew Jaskolka
State Review Process
Division of Community Resources
CN 814, Room 609
Trenton, New Jersey 08625-0814
Telephone: (609) 292-9025

NEW MEXICO

George Ellicott
State Budget Division
Rm 190, Bataan Memorial
Building
Santa Fe, New Mexico 87503
Telephone: (505) 827-3640
FAX: (505) 827-3640

NEW YORK

New York State Clearinghouse
Division of the Budget
State Capitol
Albany, New York 12224
Telephone: (518) 474-1605

NORTH CAROLINA

Mrs. Chrys Baggett, Director
Intergovernmental Relations
North Carolina Dept. of Adminst.
116 West Jones Street
Raleigh, North Carolina 27611
Telephone: (919) 733-0499

NORTH DAKOTA

North Dakota State Single
Office of Management & Budget
600 East Boulevard
Bismarck, N. Dakota 58505-0170
Telephone: (701) 224-2094

OHIO

Mr. Larry Weaver, SPOC
State/Federal Funds Coordinator
State Clearinghouse
Office of Budget and Management
30 East Broad Street, 34th Floor
Columbus, Ohio 43266-0411
Telephone: (614) 466-0698

OKLAHOMA

Mr. Don Strain, SPOC
Oklahoma Dept of Commerce
Office of Federal Assistance Mgt.
6601 Broadway Extension
Oklahoma City, Oklahoma 73116
Telephone: (405) 843-9770

RHODE ISLAND

Daniel W. Varin
Statewide Planning Program
Division of Planning
265 Melrose Street
Providence, Rhode Island 02907
Telephone: (401) 277-2093

SOUTH CAROLINA

State Single Point of Contact
Grant Services
Office of the Governor Room 477
1205 Pendleton Street
Columbia, South Carolina 29201
Telephone: (803) 734-0494

SOUTH DAKOTA

Ms. Susan Comer
State Clearinghouse Coordinator
Office of the Governor
500 East Capitol
Pierre, South Dakota 57501
Telephone: (605) 773-3212

TENNESSEE

Mr. Charles Brown
State Single Point of Contact
State Planning Office
500 Charlotte Avenue
309 John Sevier Building
Nashville, Tennessee 37219
Telephone: (615) 741-1676

TEXAS

Mr. Tom Adams
Goverment's Office of
Budget & Planning
P.O. Box 12428
Austin, Texas 78711
Telephone: (512) 463-1778

UTAH

Utah State Clearinghouse
Office of Planning & Budget
Attn: Ms. Carolyn Wright
Room 116, State Capitol
Salt Lake City, Utah 84114
Telephone: (801) 538-1535

VERMONT

Mr. Bernard D. Johnson
Assistant Director
Office of Policy Research & Coord.
Pavilion Office Building
109 State Street
Montpelier, Vermont 05602
Telephone: (802) 828-3326

WASHINGTON

Ms. Marilyn Dawson
Washington Intergovernmental
Review Process
Dept. of Community Development
9th and Columbia Building
Mail Stop GH-51
Olympia, Washington 98504 4151
Telephone: (206) 753-4978

WEST VIRGINIA

Mr. Fred Cutlip
Community Development Division
Gov.'s Off. of Community &
Indust. Development
Building #6, Room 553
Charleston, West Virginia 25305
Telephone: (304) 348-4010

WISCONSIN

Mr. William C. Carey
Federal/State Relations
Wisconsin Dept of Administration
101 South Webster Street
P.O. Box 7864
Madison, Wisconsin 53707
Telephone: (608) 266-0267

WYOMING

Ann Redman, SPOC
Wyoming State Clearinghouse
State Planning Coordinator's
Office
Capitol Building
Cheyenne, Wyoming 82002
Telephone: (307) 777-7574

TERRITORIES:

GUAM

Mr. Michael J. Reidy
Bureau of Bdgt and Mgt Research
Office of the Governor
P.O. Box 2950
Agana, Guam 96910
Telephone: (671) 472-2285

**NORTHERN MARIANA IS-
LANDS**

State Single Point of Contact
Planning & Budget Office
Office of the Governor
Saipan, CM
Northern Mariana Islands 96950

PUERTO PICO

Patria Custodio/Israel Soto Marrero
Puerto Pico Planning Board
Minillas Government Center
P.O. Box 41119
San Juan, Puerto Rico 00940-9985
Telephone: (809) 727-4444

VIRGIN ISLANDS

Director
Office of Management & Budget
Number 32 & 33 Kongens Gade
Charlotte Amalie, V.I. 00802
Telephone: (809) 774-0750